*I would like to dedicate this book to all the people who were nice to us as we traveled throughout this great country, America—God Bless you all.*

*Thank you*

# 4 Strokes West

## AN AMAZING
## AMERICAN ADVENTURE

Mark DerMugrditchian

4 Strokes West

An Amazing American Adventure

Mark DerMugrditchian

ISBN (Print Edition): 978-1-09837-389-4

ISBN (eBook Edition): 978-1-09837-390-0

# TABLE OF CONTENTS

# CHAPTER ONE

# The Bachelor's Three

I had an idea, which then became a dream. The dream became a fixation, which became a reality, and the reality would swell to include Muhammad Ali, national television, Mexican bandits, a gorilla in a tree in Louisiana, an ill-tempered Hell's angel, a narcotics drop, a canine conspiracy involving a backpack of mine, and an (allegedly) stolen diamond ring.

But at first, it was just the idea of an adventure, and it's not an adventure if you know where you're going to wind up. When Indiana Jones ran away from that boulder at the beginning of *Raiders of the Lost Ark*, he never could have guessed that he would eventually be watching the opening of the Ark of the Covenant.

Whenever Steve, Tom, and I gathered in the small apartment we shared, the stakes weren't as high as opening that forbidden Ark—none of our faces had melted and we hadn't put the world in jeopardy—but we weren't ever quite sure where things were headed.

Our personalities were a recipe for unpredictability. Get a Virgo, an Aries, and another Aries in one room, and that's what happens. Show me a person who always knows what comes next, and I'll show you a person who may not know the exhilaration of uncertainty.

I had met Tom fourteen years earlier when we were both in our town's competitive marching band. Even at that age, we were both, if I may toot my own horn, accomplished musicians on several instruments, including the clarinet, sax, sousaphone, and bongos. Between band and our feverish love of sports, our friendship was off to a rip-roaring start.

Tom was quiet—still is. Common sense is tragically rare, and in my more reflective moments, I wonder if that might be because Tom got more than his share of calm and wisdom. He was considerate as well. But, lest you get the impression that he was some sort of stoic, quiet, Vulcan-like Spock, I'll also say that if you ever got Tom talking about one of his passions, you were in for a monologue that might still be going at sundown. When he got excited about something, you could watch everyone else in the room get excited as well.

By the time we were sharing that bachelor pad where the adventure would take shape, Tom was twenty-four years old, weighed 180 pounds, had dirty-blond hair, and was built like an athletic fire hydrant.

Steve was the opposite of Tom—the Aries to his Virgo. Loud, aggressive, arrogant, ambitious without being a schemer, and putting the feelings of others first was not always his top priority. He was a brown-haired, athletic, twenty-five-year-old fireball. When Steve got rolling on something, when he was trapped in a moment or a thought, sometimes it was hard for him to make room for other people. But he wasn't a jerk. Steve was as nice as anyone I knew. But he wasn't nice all the time, and he enjoyed having a head of steam up about something. Some people are more combustible than others and they can't ever pass up a chance to get riled.

I met Steve at the University of Massachusetts where we were both physical education majors. He walked into the gym one day to find an unfamiliar guy in double-knit slacks and an endless last name setting up an obstacle course. Mark DerMugrditchian—that's me. The name is Armenian, and if you can get it right at the local spelling bee, don't let anyone tell you you're not a genius. And rumor has it that if you look in the mirror and say my name backwards three times, I'll appear and tell you a story.

I was somewhere in the middle of my two friends. I'm also an Aries and same age as Steve. I liked to lead, I liked to be heard, and I felt like a modern-day pioneer, even on days when I couldn't have expressed it in quite those terms. Of the three of us, I was the most given to dreaming, thinking big, and exploring, and was pretty good at dragging them into my plans. But the three of us were pretty interchangeable as far as our ages, weights, builds, and aspirations. We were all good athletes, strong and fast, and Tom and I were also musicians. Despite our differences in personalities, our interests were like those of most young men across the ages: sports, women, beer, and fun.

We'd all been living together for about a year when I got the itch. No, that's not quite right. It's when I got the itch *again*. I'd been feeling it in one way or another since I was sixteen years old.

Here is the idea: I wanted to take a trip. Coast to coast, all the way across the country, and I wanted to do it on a motorcycle. The timing had never been quite right. For that matter, I'd never had two friends who would have been quite right for the trip. You can learn a lot about someone when you travel, and a lot of the time you learn that you have no business traveling together, especially when the stress of the trip turns you both into beasts.

But I thought the three of us could do it. If there had ever been a trio who could enjoy a trip like this, I knew it was us.

I thought about it for a while before mentioning it to Steve.

"I . . . don't know . . ." he said at first. "Huh. I don't know."

Okay. He didn't know. But he didn't say *no*, and I knew I could bring him around, little by little. Steve wasn't sure about quitting his job, or leaving his family and friends for a while. *Quite* a while. There's really no such thing as a quick trip across the country. And then there was the part about camping out, and lots of it. No matter how fun the trip was, he knew it would mean some inconvenient nights. And this wasn't in the days of cell phones and apps that would plan every mile of your route for you and help you find addresses and directions. We were going to be on our own.

But "We're going to be on our own" wasn't a great selling point, so I tried to keep that out of his head as I talked up the excitement of seeing so many new things, new places, new sunrises and sunsets, new girls, new food, new most everything. Peopled are wired to respond to novelty, and a trip like this would would be nothing but the unknown. That was the whole point.

I wasn't sure if I could coax Tom on my own. He liked to take his time and think things over. And over. And then some more. To less patient people, his contemplative nature could feel like madness and tedium.

"But I can talk him into it with your help," I said to Steve. Together we'd wear him down.

It was a Wednesday night in the middle of April 1976. Steve and I plotted, strategized, evaluated, and role-played the conversation, laying the snare that would get the three of us out onto the open road for nearly ten thousand miles. Tom wasn't going to know what hit him.

It was ten thirty when he got home. He'd just come from a business administration class, tired and bedraggled. I'd never seen someone who looked like he needed an adventure so desperately.

"Hey Tom, come in here," I said in what I hoped was my most casual voice.

Tom came slowly around the corner and assessed the situation. He could tell we were conspiring in dark corners, because he immediately said, "What are you two instigators up to? I can tell. What is it?"

"Tom, pull up a chair," said Steve. "We've got a super idea."

I watched Tom's eyes. Nowhere behind them was it registering "Steve and Mark have a super idea, and I can't wait to hear it!" He didn't move. One of Tom's favorite hobbies was being suspicious of us. Skepticism can be a valuable asset, but it wasn't going to do much for getting the show on the road. "Super . . . huh?" he said slowly. "You don't say. Come on. Tell me. What are you two trying to get me into?"

I gave him quite a speech, which Steve added to whenever he thought of something to say. Trying to be objective, I went into so many pros and cons that I felt like an attorney making his case in a courtroom, laying out exhibits, evidence, potential outcomes, and reasonable doubt. There was nothing easy about what I was proposing. I wanted to do the trip, but I wasn't romanticizing it in any naive way that I could see. I knew we'd have to quit our jobs, lose our income, and leave our friends and family behind for who knew how long. We could plan out a strategy that would have made General Patton proud, and there would still be unoforeseen challenges. The sun had nearly risen when I asked Tom if he had anything to add.

Of course he did. Of course.

He wasn't nearly as excited about it as we were, to put it lightly. If we thought the plan was a pie with ice cream, he thought it was a dry saltine cracker that we were trying to force-feed him.

But in the face of the united front put up by Steve and I, he gave in over the next two weeks. It was really going to happen. These were two of the best friends I would ever have, and we were supposed to do it together. I wanted to burst into song when he finally said he was all in.

Then it was time to get down to the less glamorous business of planning the trip. We decided to head south towards warmer weather first before heading west. We planned on picking our roads as we went. There wouldn't be any shortage of scenic highways, and most of them weren't going to be too busy. The logistics involved in a cross-country trip on motorcycles are dizzying. Sometimes, nightmarish. There were so many things to consider that I often had the feeling that there were questions I needed to ask that weren't even occurring to me. And again, there were no smartphones. No technology more advanced than a paper map was going to bail us out.

A year earlier, we had each bought a Honda CB360 T. They were light, compact, sleek, and mostly reliable bikes. They weren't ever going to set the world on fire, but they'd do the job.

In the planning phase, a year after buying the bikes, after Tom had already agreed, some naysayer sowed a bit of doubt in Steve's head. "Oh, those things are way too small," he said when he came home one night, studying the bike with the critical eye of a sudden worrywart. "They'll never make it all that way."

"They will, Steve," I must have said a thousand times. "You've got to trust me, not someone who wants to rain on our parade and pretend to be the grand Poobah of motorcycle know-how. It's going to work."

"I don't know, Mark."

"Well, I do."

Over the next few summer months, life continued as usual while we fleshed out the plan. There were beach parties, softball games, trips to the mountains, and the occasional run-in with weirdos. It was a typical summer for us.

Tom was invaluable at this stage. He would have made a great air traffic controller. He was a model of punctuality, elevating the concept of being on time, crossing the t's and dotting is the i's, and executing due diligence to something like a religious duty. Sometimes this could be obnoxious, but given that Steve and I treated waiting until the last minute as an equally solemn duty, we were lucky to have Tom's insistent tunnel vision when it came to the details. "You're not going to make it unless you get this done." "You're not going to be ready unless you have these things." "You're not going to know what's going on unless you think about . . ." He repeated it all over and over like a monk's chant, drilling it into our heads.

We all had jobs that summer, but we had to make time to take care of the basics of planning the trip so that we didn't court any unnecessary disasters for ourselves once we were traveling. Tom was the right taskmaster. I was the Boy Scout in our group, so I picked out the camping gear, including the tent, sleeping bags, alcohol stove, pocket knives, mess kit, etc.

Finally the summer ended, and it was time. It was Cross-country-motorcyle-trip Eve, and I was way more excited than I'd ever been the night before Christmas. The whole unseen country stretched out before me in my head, inviting, beckoning, pleading for me to come to it, to make it my own and learn its lessons. The night before we were supposed to set out, Steve set himself an important task: "Tom, Mark, there's no point in packing all the booze, right? Let's finish off all these open bottles."

"Sounds good!" I said. Nothing could possibly go wrong when three guys who are humming with excitement decide to drink with purpose.

Moments later, Steve was running up the stairs in his socks, a glass of Johnnie Walker Black in each hand. And so the night began to spiral out of hand. We were all loaded by nine. Me, perhaps, most of all; no, definitely. Before long, I was running around, destroying the place, breaking furniture, spilling food and booze, generally acting like a whirlwind to the point where they thought they had an obligation to stop me, not that I was completely aware of any of this. I know this thanks to them recounting the night in vivid detail the next morning. They chased me around the place, and I evaded them with ease, determined not to let them lay a hand on me. Finally, I gave them an opening when I fell over a chair and then tried to scramble to my feet while they pounced.

"Get him while he's down!" Steve yelled. Once they jumped on me, I went into shock, fighting like hell, unsure of who these maniacs were who were trying to muscle me around. "Grab his feet so he can't get up!" Tom tried to obey, and I kicked him in the jaw for his efforts. He was determined, though, and didn't let go of my feet. Or maybe he was just pissed off that my foot had made serious contact with his face and wasn't about to let me go without some payback. Steve was trying to get me into a headlock while I thrashed and twisted. Eventually I went unconscious, and they dragged me up the stairs to Tom's room because it had air conditioning and they didn't want the heat killing me in my drunken stupor.

They went back downstairs to clean up the blast zone I had created. Five minutes later, they were prompted to come right back up at a run because they'd heard an enormous crash coming from the room in which they had left their inebriated pal. I was apparently rolled up in the sheets on the floor, not snug as a bug in a rug, but fighting whatever ghost or monster or evil bedsheet had me in its clutches. Sometimes, after a few drinks—or a dozen—there's this thing that looks like me, and it just wants to fight the whole world.

"That's it! You're not staying in my room!" said Tom, picturing the destruction I could cause if a fight started in there. "Steve, let's drag him back downstairs."

They manhandled me down the stairs with admirable effort, but I was getting a second—or maybe it was a third—wind. Roaring like a bull, I threw Steve right through the dining room set. I wish I could say that it was none the worse for wear, but it was obliterated. Then, not satisfied with my work, I tossed Tom into the wall and left a massive dent in the plaster.

"Grab him before he kills us!" Steve was screaming. "Or himself!" Once again, they wrestled me to the floor, where I started to run out of gas.

Tom was trying to catch his breath. I had given his lungs and willpower an incredibly annoying test. "I've got him, Steve. Go turn on the cold shower."

Steve went and turned on the shower, and then returned to help Tom drag my loose, limp, drooping, drunken body to the bathroom.

Obstacles arose. "He can't stand up," said Tom. "Come on, get in. We have to hold him up."

And so it was that the three of us wound up in the shower. That's when I started screaming. "Help! Help! I'll drown! Get me out!"

But they hung on until my wits returned. I would admire their commitment, if I could remember any of it. Finally, I was saying, "Okay. Okay. I'm alright. Man, that booze hit me hard."

"You're not kidding," said Tom, holding his sore and swollen jaw.

I apologized for the whole mess, although it wasn't all my fault. I wasn't the one who demanded that we finish all the booze. We exhausted warriors then retired to our rooms and sacked out.

In the morning I felt like I had been run over by a train, which isn't what you want when you're about to get on a motorcycle for dozens of days. I got up and looked into a full-length mirror. Holy moly. With all the bumps and bruises, it looked like I had been in a gang war.

Mark DerMugrditchian, gang of one.

I went downstairs and stumbled into what looked like the aftermath of World War III. It was an inauspicious beginning to our adventure, to say the least. After making coffee, I went onto the porch and licked my wounds.

"Hey," said Tom, coming outside. "I always wanted a fat lip. Thanks for that."

"I'm really sorry," I said. " I didn't know what I was doing."

"It hit you pretty hard. It's okay."

"Look at this place." Steve was walking through the debris. "What a wreck," he muttered. "Broken table. Broken chairs. Popcorn and pans all over the kitchen. The couch is turned upside down. Boy, do we have some cleaning to do. But first, tea."

He made his tea and came out to sit by us. "Man, I can hardly move my left arm. You really took a bite out of it. Look at those teeth marks!"

Dutifully, morosely, regretfully, I looked. Yes sir, those were teeth marks. My teeth. I ran my tongue over my incisors, wondering if there might be a piece of Steve's arm in there somewhere.

"Tom and I were trying all night to calm you down so you wouldn't hurt yourself."

They explained the whole sordid scene to me. We all shook hands, agreed that mixing liquors was a bad idea, and set about the monumental task of cleaning the place. Of all the potential delays I had imagined taking place on the trip, my transformation into a drunken loon of destruction hadn't been among them.

But it's not like this was a bad omen or anything. Nothing else could possibly go wrong. We cleaned up our apartment, repaired anything that was broken and moved out back to our parents homes to get ready to leave for our big trip.

# CHAPTER TWO

# Blastoff

Wednesday, September 8, 1976. I got up at seven and packed my bike for the longest journey I would ever take. Everything was familiar and easy in that room. No matter where I looked, I knew what I'd see. It didn't quite feel real that by nightfall I'd be in another city, sleeping in a place we hadn't even found yet. And the day after that, and after that, with the other side of the country so far away. The morning was warm, sunny, full of promise. It was one of those days when you feel like you can't make any wrong choices, which is the right feeling to have when you're about to embark on something crazy.

After puttering around on last-minute things, I waited for Tom and Steve to come to my parents' house in Hudson, Massachusetts, so we could say goodbye to my parents and get out of town.

Tom was right on schedule, which was no surprise. His bike was loaded up and he had a mischievous look on his face. You could have put him on the cover of *US Troublemaker* and know you had nailed it.

"Are you all set to go?" he said, looking over my gear.

"No, I have a few more things to pack. Hey, what did you do, buy a sissy bar for your bike?" A sissy bar is a passenger backrest for your bike. I wasn't sure if anyone was going to be getting on the back of Tom's bike in the days ahead, but he mainly wanted it so he could hang supplies like his backpack off of it.

Since Tom was nosy enough to inspect all of my stuff, I returned the favor. Maybe another set of eyes would make sure that we weren't forgetting anything.

"Yeah, I bought it for sixteen bucks when I was in Long Island last week visiting my girl."

"Well," I said, "I'll see how it works the way I have it now, and maybe if we go through Long Island for sightseeing I'll buy one and put it on there, because it does look better than my pack just laying across my seat."

Steve was half an hour late, which was also not a surprise. When he rolled into the driveway at eight thirty, Tom and I got to our feet. "Okay, I'm here. Let's go," said Steve, like he'd been waiting on us instead of holding us up.

You should have seen his bike. Things were strapped and tied and hooked and dangled every which way. It was as close as I'd ever come to seeing the car from *The Beverley Hillbillies* in real life. The whole thing looked so wobbly and awkward and precarious that I couldn't even imagine him keeping his bike balanced.

"Look at that mess!" said Tom. "You can't ride like that. You'll lose something for sure."

He was right. It was like Steve had woken up that morning and thought, *Hmm . . . how can I guarantee that I'll create some sort of disaster with my packing skills? I'll just throw this on here, tie this, close my eyes, shove something else in between these, and hope for a miracle.*

Believe it or not, all we had for clothes were two pairs of jeans—one we wore and one was packed—two flannel shirts, two T-shirts, two pairs of underwear, and two pairs of socks—one we wore and one was packed. We wore construction work boots and packed our tennis shoes, gym shorts, and tennis rackets. We only had one mountain jacket and one down vest. That's it. We each had $1000, and knew we would have to get jobs as we traveled. This was not just a trip straight west to California; this was an adventure to be experienced throughout our great United States of America!

While we rearranged Steve's gear into something less cataclysmic, Tom's parents arrived. It hit me: we were saying goodbye because we were *going*. It was really happening.

After some quick chit-chat, we got Steve's gear squared away, and then my mom shooed everyone inside for some French toast. I wondered how long it would be before I might sit at that table again. I had so many comforts at home, and was about to let go of them all.

Then I didn't have time to wonder about sitting at the table in the future, because the moment had come. *Start your engines, gentlemen.* My mom started crying like I was riding away to Judgment Day and not just heading out on an ambitious lark. Not to be outdone, Tom's mother started crying, too.

"Hurry home!" they kept saying. They reminded me of sniffling ladies waving handkerchiefs at a boat as it left for war.

"Have a good time. Be careful," said my dad, which was exactly what I would have expected him to say. I wondered if he was envious at all.

Tom's dad echoed mine: simple, short, fast, and efficient.

The neighbors started emerging to see what the fuss was about. There were well-wishes and hugs and it was all nice, but it was almost making me so impatient that I was itching. We put our helmets on and got on our bikes. Everyone who had a camera snapped pictures, and we posed and hammed it up. Finally we got out of there and headed to Steve's house in Milford, a half hour away,where we would say what I hoped would be our final goodbye of the day.

Steve's mom acted just like ours had. It was like they'd all been trying to land a spot on the Olympic Crying Squad. His dad did what he could to comfort her, but he couldn't do much besides just be there for her. Steve was her only son, her only son was now a man, and she was just going to feel whatever she was going to feel.

Then, finally, finally, *finally*, we were headed south onto I-495. At eleven in the morning, in the middle of the week, the traffic wasn't busy, but I felt like we were caught up in something so exhilarating that I wanted to shout.

It was like we were at the starting line of a high-stakes race around the world. In that moment, I pitied everyone who wasn't us.

About ten minutes later, a disembodied voice interrupted my reverie and cut through the background hum of tires on asphalt.

"You boys on motorcycles, two hands on the handle bars."

We looked around in bewilderment. Where in the world was this voice coming from? Maybe my mom had been right and we were riding to Judgment Day after all, and here was God, offering a wise bit of advice to three young men who thought they were invincible.

It wasn't anything so grand or divine. A police cruiser passed us on the left. As if we hadn't heard his squawking, the officer blurted out the warning again through the loudspeaker he had mounted on the outside of his car. Ever the gracious diplomats, we sniffed and snickered as he passed, grateful for his wisdom. And as soon as he was out of sight, we resumed the more casual handlebar stances he'd warned us about.

We spent the morning cruising down to Long Island. When we got there, we went to a Honda dealer. "Is this where you got your sissy bar, Tom?" I asked.

"Yeah, they're less expensive here."

Steve and I each bought a bar and went back outside. After unlocking our gear and taking most of it off, we installed the new bars and started reassembling everything like a jigsaw puzzle. I was the mechanically inclined guy amongst us. It was like installing a luggage rack. It all fit like a dream, and now there was plenty of room, or as much room as you can create on a motorcycle.

Once it was getting on towards evening, we headed south on I-95 to the New Jersey shoreline, rolling through the warm September night. Everything sensory was heightened, from the feel of the wind on my hands, to the colors of the trees, to the soft fluffiness of the massive clouds. We hit the New Jersey border at 11:00 PM but kept driving until we made it to the

Sandy Hook Recreation Area, where we went down to the beach and cut the motors. After that day of revving and rumbling, it was soothing to listen to the Atlantic ocean pounding against the shore. Every wave seemed to whisper, "You were right, Mark. You were right. This is perfect. You were right."

"This is great, isn't it?" said Tom. "Let's just pitch the tent right here on the beach."

No one argued. It was a clear night with a full moon, a perfect situation for bedding down for that first night on the road.

We slept deeply, but in the morning the sun woke us up a little earlier than we might have liked. After breaking down the tent and packing it up, we saw that Steve's rear tire was flat. It didn't take much investigation for me to find the culprit. A hellacious six-inch spike had gone all the way through the tire and was sticking out both sides. There are so many things about motorcycle maintenance that can go wrong, especially if you're careless, but this was just one of those things you can't control. It's not like we had ignored a sign that said, "HERE THERE BE SPIKES."

"Well," I said, "I guess we'll just have to spend another day here." By the time we unpacked Steve's gear again, fixed that flat, and repacked, it would be getting into the early afternoon, too late to resume the trip for a long stretch.

"It's only the second day of the trip and we have to fix a flat already," said Steve, irritated. "And of course it had to be *my* bike." But there was nothing to do but fix it, and we were lucky that we knew how. This would turn out to be one of my favorite things about being on our own: you had to sort out your own problems and couldn't count on anyone to show up to rescue you.

Once we were done with the tire, we decided to do some body surfing. After changing into gym shorts, we messed around in the water and enjoyed the sun. Before long, Old Man Hunger came calling for us. What is it about the water that makes you feel as if you haven't eaten in a year?

"Let's get Italian tonight at Regina's," said Tom. Regina's was a little pizzeria in the center of town. There were no complaints from me and Steve. After a night of stuffing ourselves like hogs in the dimly lit restaurant, we went back to the beach to sleep. All things considered, we could have had a way worse day than we had, especially for day one.

Friday morning settled in with drizzling and coolness. Rolling out of a tent and seeing a storm bearing down on you when you have to get on a motorcycle right away is a very different experience than seeing it come from behind the safety of your bedroom window. We got the tent packed in a hurry. If we didn't get out on the road ahead of the coming storm, we were going to have a situation. If you've never been on a motorcycle, take my word for it: they don't offer much in the way of protection from the elements, not to mention that you can slip on a wet road and lay the bike down before you even know anything is wrong. But it wasn't time to think about that yet.

"Let's get breakfast," I said, prioritizing hunger over safety.

"No, we've got to wait until we're on the road," said Steve, barking like a drill sergeant. "That weather doesn't look very good."

His rationality trumped my growling stomach. Off we went, after agreeing that we'd stay on the road for at least an hour before stopping. But before long, I was signaling to Steve and Tom to pull off the road. A light rain had started and our margin for error was shrinking to almost nothing.

The clouds were downright menacing all of a sudden, like they'd decided to spring a trap on us. "We better find some cover," I said.

We made it to the outskirts of a town and pulled under the canopy of a store called R & S Auto Supply, the worsening rain chasing us at every step. It was the kind of rain that made me think of someone up there overturning buckets on us.

"Might as well get comfortable," said Tom. "We're not going anywhere for a while."

I remembered that I needed some chain lube and a can of compressed air. "Let's go in and see if we can find anything we might need," I said. "It'll be a good way to kill some time, at least."

It was a pretty small store and we didn't kill much time—such a phrase—in there, but I got what I needed. It was still raining furiously when we emerged, so we sat on the cement next to our bikes and played a ferociously competitive game of cribbage. We all loved to win *and* hated to lose, and we slapped the cards down and moved the pegs like our lives depended on it.

Around eleven, Steve noticed that the rain was letting up. "Hey guys, let's just put on our rain gear and get out of here during this lull. Maybe we can outrun it."

If you're bored enough, there's only so much time you can kill before you're willing to risk getting killed yourself. We put the cards away and donned our orange plastic rain suits, looking like workers in hazmat suits. Back on I-95 South, we headed for Baltimore. Driving a motorcycle with the rain blurring your visor, and feeling clammy and damp all over, and seeing the miles tick by ever so slowly, isn't exactly high living, but there was no stopping until we got through it. Was it Churchill who said, "If you're going through hell, keep going"? This wasn't hell, but we were going to be relieved to be on the other side of it.

The rain had stopped by five that evening, but we wanted to keep going, particularly since we'd lost some time.

"We're in Baltimore!" I yelled when we crossed the state line, like I was Columbus entering the New World. The sun gave way to another clear night. The sky was a riot of stars, so we decided to sack out without the tent on a school playground.

"Feels funny sleeping in center field, doesn't it?" said Tom. I was too drowsy to answer. Steve was already asleep.

Tom was the first one packed in the morning, up and ready to go like a rooster. He drove down the path that led out onto the field while waiting for us to finish getting ready.

A patrolman appeared and stopped him. "What are you doing here, son?"

"Oh, we were just leaving," said Tom. "We slept over there by the fence last night."

"Oh yeah? Well, why don't you undo your gear so I can have a look?"

Tom was angry. He didn't like the guy's tone, he didn't like being told what to do, and we hadn't done anything wrong. But he did what he was told while we watched from the other end of the field.

Once the patrolman was satisfied, or once he figured he had hassled us enough, he said, "Okay, you and your friends may leave, but you make sure that place is clean." He got in his car and drove away. There are people who can get notions of grandeur with even a little bit of power. There was no doubt that that guy was going to spend the rest of his day flexing on innocent people while telling himself he was ridding the world of evil.

Tom waved us over, giving the all clear.

"What did he want?" asked Steve.

"I don't know. He just wanted to check our gear," said Tom.

"We better go before another cop sees us," I said. "I don't want to have to unpack all my stuff; it's too hard to get it all back on the same way." The luggage shuffle would get easier with practice, but in those early days of the trip, it felt like I had to do it for the first time, every time.

We hit a donut shop for breakfast and then headed towards DC, entering that teeming hub of American democracy around noon. It was funny driving through those city streets on bikes that had obviously been packed for hard travel on country roads. We didn't quite fit in, and that was fine. Part of being a pioneer is *not* fitting in.

"Hey, let's check out the White House," said Steve.

"You guys can," said Tom. "I've already seen it. But go ahead and I'll stay with the bikes in the parking lot." It seemed strange doing a walking tour of the White House dressed in blue jeans and a flannel shirt. The facility was very impressive and packed full of history.

After the tour, we got back to where Tom was waiting. "We might as well go," I said. "We've already seen all of the other monuments."

Back on I-95, we rolled along at an easy fifty-five miles per hour. We were weary by dusk, and it was a relief to pull into a safari campground in northern Virginia. The owners were a pleasant Armenian couple from California. I could have listened to them for days and never come to the end of their stories, which were all about food, family, and tradition, all punctuated with blasts of laughter. After a quick meal, we made camp before it got dark and were asleep in no time. The day had gone by so fast.

The next morning, on Sunday, I broke character, decided to be a hero, and got up first. After gathering some firewood, I started making breakfast. Even when I was almost done, my sluggardly comrades still weren't up so I took my turn barking out orders. "Come on, you guys, get out of the sack. I've got breakfast." Maybe that cop had been on to something. Giving orders in the early morning suited me just fine.

Tom rolled out of the tent, rubbing his eyes and yawning, but he came over to pitch in. "Is Steve still sleeping?" he asked. "Does he expect us to do all the work?"

Steve managed to appear at the last moment, just before we were getting ready to put breakfast away.

"Nice of you to get up, Steve," I said. "Since you didn't help make breakfast, you can clean up after it."

Steve mumbled a few words—the dialect of the early morning—that no one could understand. Then he sat down and ate his share of the scrambled eggs. When he was done, he took the dishes and wandered away to parts unknown so he could wash them.

While I was taking care of a few final items before leaving, Tom left to go mail some cards. Fifteen minutes later, he was walking down the road on the way to the camp office when he saw Steve washing our dishes. He put on his inspector hat and went over to see if Steve was skimping on the details. Steve had seemed so sleepy that it wouldn't have surprised Tom to find him trying to wash the dishes with mud. But it turned out to be worse than that.

"Hey!" yelled Tom. "What the hell are you doing?"

"I'm washing the dishes," said Steve. "What does it look like I'm doing?"

Tom grabbed his own head in both hands. "Don't you know what this place is for?"

"Yeah," said Steve. "The sign says disposal station. So it's a disposal station. Isn't that hose for washing dishes?"

"It's a sewage dumping station for trailers! Not a water station, you dummy!" Our dishes weren't state-of-the-art or museum-worthy, but they deserved better than to be washed right next to a sewage station.

"Well, I've never been to a campground before!" said Steve. "And besides, it was close to our camp. Look at the sign." Tom looked. "It says dumping station," said Steve. "And I thought it meant to dump your garbage here." He sighed as if the world were too mysterious for words.

Tom had to laugh. "Okay, but don't wash our dishes here anymore."

Our Sunday plan would always include washing and waxing the bikes, as well as checking them over for loose or damaged parts. If you're a rider, or you ever want to be one, having a light maintenance routine is the best thing you can ever do for yourself and your bike's longevity. And after a couple of weeks, those Sunday mornings took on the comforting feel of a ritual.

We broke camp on Monday morning and hit the road at nine. After making a last-minute inspection of the bikes, we said goodbye to the owners and were on our way. Other than Steve's flat tire, so far the bikes had been running like a dream, averaging forty-eight miles to the gallon. This stuff matters when you have to be careful with money and have an entire country to explore. "Not bad with all the added weight we're carrying," said Steve, always thinking like a bookkeeper. I had an image of Steve wearing a green accountant's visor while riding his motorcycle, and had to stifle a laugh.

We kept going on I-95 until we hit Fredericksburg, Virginia, where we turned onto I-17 and headed all the way down to Virginia Beach. Virginia is a gorgeous state, an incredible mixture of green pastures and mixed hardwood forests full of old trees that may outlive us all. The whole thing must be a dream come true for people who know how to paint.

Virginia Beach was winding down from the summer and getting ready for the fall and winter months ahead. The bright sand was a brilliant contrast to the blue water, and the sound of the waves crashing onto the shore was a hypnotic lullaby. Even though it wasn't the peak of the season and the weather wasn't ideal, there were still plenty of travelers touring the country. Up and down the boardwalk, there were young people like us, seeing it all for the first time, and retired seniors, the elder statesmen of the road, who would leave and then ride until sunset.

That night, we were sitting around a fire at a campground when one of the old-timers joined us. He'd been traveling for a year at that point and would put into words some of the ideas that I had suspected and thought on since leaving home. In *Walden,* Thoreau writes, after living alone in the woods, "I learned this, at least, by my experiment: that if one advances confidently in the direction of his dreams, and endeavors to live the life which he has imagined, he will meet with a success unexpected in common hours."

The man across the campfire from me had advanced confidently in the direction of his dreams, as had I, and this was surely a success at an uncommon hour.

"Boys," he said, "traveling is the surest way of really understanding and learning about people and yourself. Traveling teaches you about life in a real sense. It gives you an opportunity to broaden your perspectives and speeds up what you are going to learn." My goodness, he seemed wise. It was like auditing a class at Campground University. He wasn't highly educated with an array of college degrees, but that didn't mean he hadn't spent his life learning. He had worked hard for all of his years, and his education had been hard-won by experience. Traveling had refined his worldview and given him a new set of questions to ask about the world. When someone is excited about something, it's hard for me not to get excited as well, and his words could have been my own, even though I hadn't traveled as many miles or years as he had. I thought about all the people we had yet to meet on this trip, and part of me was thrilled at the lessons we would continue to learn.

But not all of our concerns were so profound. The next day we hit the beach, and it wasn't long before Steve sprang into action. A beautiful girl wearing a see-through blouse and no brassiere had noticed us noticing her. Who knows what she thought about the three lookalikes who had suddenly appeared on the beach.

Steve moved first, seeing what he must have taken as an invitation in her eyes. He got up and jogged by her slowly, testing the waters. Then he went further, down to the actual water, and dipped his toe in. On the way back to tell us about how perfect the water was, he saw that she was waving him over.

"Hi, I'm Cindy," she said. "I saw you all ride in on your bikes. Where are you guys from?"

"I'm Steve," he said. "I'm from Massachusetts and am heading for California." He sat next to her in the sand.

"Are you three brothers? Two of you look like you could be twins."

"No, but it's not the first time we've heard it." Nor would it be the last. "Lots of people notice, but we're not even related."

"You both look very Italian," she said. "Are you?"

"Yes, I am, but Mark is a full-blooded Armenian and Tom's a Portuguese thoroughbred."

Cindy was twenty-six, divorced, and was traveling with a guy and a girl named Carl and Nancy. Nancy was twenty-four, also divorced, and had a twenty-seven-month-old baby boy. Carl was a driver and Nancy's friend. They were delivering a camper to a private owner living in Florida, and they had come all the way from Anchorage, Alaska—what a trip! Short of driving across the ocean to Hawaii, that was about as much of a comprehensive tour of America as you could get. As part of the deal, they were able to use the camper, but they had to pay for their own gas, oil, any tolls they ran into, and food and trailer parks along the way. It still looked like a pretty perfect opportunity to see the country.

"Only six or seven years ago they used to have to pay you to drive a vehicle anywhere in the US," said Cindy.

"That sounds like a better deal to me," said Steve.

"Hey, where are you guys staying?" she said.

"We're at the Holiday Inn campground off Atlantic Avenue, two miles from here."

"That's great!" she said. "We're camping there tonight." A car horn honked from the parking lot. Cindy's friends were waving her in for lunch. "I have to go," she said. "I'll watch for your bikes later this evening, though. I'll bring Nancy, too. She likes to have a good time." Cindy jumped up and started folding her blanket. "I'm so glad we met." As she walked away, she yelled back over her shoulder, "I'll be looking for you guys! Say about 8:00 PM!"

When Steve came back, we were pretending we hadn't noticed his new female friend.

"Hey, did you guys see that girl?" he said breathlessly. "She was beautiful. Eager, too." He flashed a Jimmy Carter smile.

"She wasn't bad," said Tom in the most bored voice that he could muster, turning over onto his stomach.

"She's twenty-six and divorced and her girlfriend is twenty-four and *she's* divorced, too. They're going to drop over by the campsite tonight after dinner, if you guys think you'll be up for some good, old-time fun and frolics. These girls sound like eager beavers to me. Prepare to get your doors blown off, because she's the kind of girl who can do it." Steve was acting like he had studied Cindy for years and had become the ultimate authority on her habits, moods, likes, dislikes, and so on.

"Okay, Steve, we'll see," I said, sitting up. "But now let's actually go for a swim."

We swam and then ate dinner, by which I mean I ate so much dinner that I started regretting it about halfway through but pushed on and on, bite after bite, until I was a portrait of bloated suffering. Tom looked over at me and smirked. "You know, 'all you can eat' doesn't mean you have to eat until you get sick."

Before I could retort, Cindy walked in off the dark road with Nancy.

"Hi guys!" she said. "I'm Cindy and this is Nancy."

Steve lit the fire with a big I-told-you-so smile on his face. He quickly introduced us all. "Pull up a log and join us!"

Tom and I helped the girls get situated around the campfire. After an hour, a thin middle-aged man suddenly trotted into the firelight. It was Carl, their driver. It was pretty obvious that the girls didn't want him around, especially Nancy. They both turned away from him slightly. Every aspect of their body language said, "Not interested."

"He thinks he's got something going with her and he really doesn't," Cindy whispered to Steve while everyone else was talking.

Nancy forced herself to introduce Carl to us. He sat on the edge of the picnic table, mostly glum and quiet, giving one-word answers to questions we didn't even want to ask him. He was just a pure lump of awkward, invasive discomfort, only there to get Nancy to come back to the trailer with him. Eventually she got up and said she had to go check on her son. It was obvious that she was just making an excuse to get Carl away from us and spare us the dubious pleasures of his oppressive company.

Cindy stayed behind with us.

In the morning, we crawled out of the tent under a cloudy sky. Cindy was still in the tent, yawning. When she stuck her head out, she looked at the three of us in our jocky shorts. "I can't believe I met three good-looking guys all at the same time, and I like all three of you equally as well."

Unlikely or not, it was an improbability that we were thrilled with.

The water was calling us again, or two of us, at least. Steve and I were both strong swimmers, water safety instructors, and completely at home in the surf. Steve had seven years' experience teaching swimming, and I had two, on top of our lifeguarding experience. We both felt the pull of the ocean.

Tom wasn't into swimming, so he stayed behind to write some letters. I invited Cindy to come with us, but she wanted to go check on her friends to see if they'd be moving on today. "Besides, that water's too rough for me," she said. "But Carl doesn't like traveling in a storm, so if it keeps looking like rain, we'll probably be staying another night. See you later."

"Let's do some body surfing," said Steve. Storms always bring in big waves, and those waves belonged to us. Steve jumped into his gym shorts and then onto his bike. The rain tried to change our minds, but we tore down to the beach. We could see the huge waves breaking before we got there. And then, the heavens conspired, literally raining on our parade and forcing us to look for shelter in a hurry. I saw a closed restaurant nearby. We parked our bikes between a couple of its tables and hid under another canopy, listening to the downpour.

When it let up a bit, we charged out onto the beach, leaving deep foot-prints in the sand. Few things inspire awe like the sight of a churning ocean. Anyone who gets a grandiose sense of their own importance only needs to see the ocean in its wrath to be reminded of their fragility and insignificance. Six- to seven-foot rollers were everywhere, and we weren't the only two crazy enough to challenge the omnipotent sea. Surfers were taking advantage of the storm's magic, which was producing waves of a size that they'd never see outside of a tempest.

We spent some time being tossed around by the water like rag dolls. "These waves are knocking the hell out of me," I said when I surfaced after going under briefly. I closed my mouth fast before a wave could rush down my throat.

"They're strong!" yelled Steve, nodding and trying to catch his breath.

Before we came on the trip, I'd spent some time thinking about how many memories we were going to make, but also how many experiences we might forget. I wanted to document whatever I could, whenever I could remember to do so. A few minutes later, I jogged to the bikes and got the camera so I could get some film of us on the waves. Steve was ready for action when I returned.

"Okay, you go first," I said. "I'll capture you high on a wave struggling to get free. Make it dramatic." After a few shots, I put the camera down, Steve took a few shots of me, and we rushed back out to push our luck again.

Two hours later, we called it quits for the day and laid back on the beach, tapped out. After a while, I raised up on one elbow and watched a surfer who was trying to tame a particularly formidable wave. "That just gives you a super feeling," I said with a sigh. I didn't know the guy and I didn't know his story, but we had an obvious shared interest in crazy behavior and I felt an instant bond with him. I looked away for a moment.

"Hey, look!" Steve was suddenly screaming and pointing out into the water. "That surfer just got *crushed* by that wave. Brutal! How do you even survive something like that?" I jumped to my feet, adrenaline immediately surging through me. We watched anxiously, waiting for the wave to roll itself back out. Finally we saw the surfer's black wetsuit. "He looks like he's in trouble," said Steve.

We automatically sprang into action. Steve ran for the surfer's board that had just washed ashore. Then we waded out into the furious water. The guy was hurt. He wasn't more than ten feet away from shore, but fighting the relentless waves made it seem like he was miles distant. The waves threw us back, so we'd throw ourselves forward. We made slow progress. What felt like forever as we tried to reach him were only a few minutes. Finally we were able to push the now-unconscious guy onto his surfboard and swim for the shore. With one arm each we held him on the board and paddled with the other arm, trying to keep our balance amid the turbulence.

Once we reached the shore, I unzipped his wetsuit to check for a heartbeat and also to relieve the pressure on his chest. No heartbeat. No breathing. By the time a rescue squad arrived—a man who had been sitting in his parked car had called them when he saw us go into the water—Steve was giving him CPR and mouth-to-mouth. We were about to pass out ourselves when the paramedics took over and hooked him up to a resuscitator. They quickly put a respirator on him, trying to replace the oxygen he had lost.

A medic kept checking for a heartbeat, and then gave him a hypo shot. Another medic had prepared the defibrillator and was ready to go. After placing the paddles on each side of the boy's chest, he gave him two volts for just a second. *Thwap.* The boy's body twitched and jerked as the current raced through him. Steve and I both watched. I said a silent prayer.

Finally the medic said that his heart was beating again. "Guys, you did a super job. You saved his life." Before jumping into the ambulance, he shook our hands. Slowly, our heartbeats returned to something like normalcy.

"Steve," I said after they were gone, "before you know it, that guy's going to be running around again. But I bet he'll never forget the day when he almost died. Let's go see what Tom's doing. He'll never believe this." It was an acute reminder of how vulnerable we all are. Everything that guy's life was leading to, all the things he would ever do, all the days he would ever have lived, had almost been taken away in that endless water.

Off we went, the rain still pouring down. We were exhausted from our two hours of swimming, the rescue—CPR is surprisingly demanding, physically—and had to take it slowly. "It feels like pins shooting into my skin!" Steve yelled. I could barely hear him over the rain. Finally we caught sight of the camp entrance. Steve ran to our tent to grab some dry clothes, soap, and towels.

There was a note on one of the sleeping bags, written on a postcard. Steve picked it up, not knowing what it was, and took it to the showers. When we were drying off, I saw the postcard. "What's this?"

"I don't know. Could be from Cindy or Tom," said Steve, drying his hair. "Not sure."

I read the message, which was from Cindy, out loud. "A very enjoyable meeting," I read.

"I can vouch for that," said Steve. "Come on, what does she say?"

I kept reading. "She hopes that our paths cross again and she wants us to write occasionally. Then she says 'I'll miss you. Sounds strange to say that after so short a time, but you made my heart smile. Thanks! Love, Cindy.' And she left us an address."

"Gee, Mark," said Steve, "that girl really ended up liking us."

"Everyone likes us, Steve," I said. "And why wouldn't they? We're always up for some good fun." Then we dashed out into the rain and headed back to the camp, wondering if there was a single dry spot left on earth.

Tom was reading in the camp office lounge when he noticed us scrambling for dry ground. He hustled over to us, and we went to the camp grocery store. "How do you guys like the rain?" he asked after closing the door behind us.

We didn't want to talk about the rain because we had a story to tell. Steve and I took turns and watched Tom's eyes get wider and wider. "Well," he said when we finished, "there's never a dull moment wherever you two guys are."

I had said that everyone liked us, and it was mostly true. And Tom was right as well: things were rarely dull when Steve and I were together. The two truths felt like blessings. Never bored, mostly beloved—that was us.

The rain wasn't done yet. It came down harder, and harder, and harder, to the point that I expected houses to start floating by. We weren't going to be able to leave for dinner, so Steve suggested that we just buy sandwich meat and eat it there in the store.

By the time we got back in our tent, we knew that its strength would be tested that night. "It's been raining since ten thirty this morning," I said, "and it's eight thirty now." Ten hours of this nonsense!

"Let's just hope it keeps us dry tonight," said Tom.

Well, yeah. What else could we hope for?

I opened a book, while Tom and Steve played cribbage. Soon, Steve noticed some water seeping from the floor of the tent. There was no escape. Whenever we changed positions to get comfortable, there seemed to be more of it. It was ridiculous, but the endless storm was starting to feel personal. I knew we had signed up for whatever might happen to us on this trip, but the night was quickly turning intolerable.

"Hey," said Steve, "I thought this tent was supposed to be waterproof! Why's the water coming through the floor?" You can call a tent waterproof, but if you toss it in the middle of a pond, it's not going to keep you dry. Steve tried to drag his sleeping bag out of the way. The water followed him.

"Tom, what time is it?" I asked.

"Ten."

Just then we heard a voice yelling and the flashing of a light from outside. "Hello in there! You guys better move your tent to higher ground or you'll be washed away. The river's overflowing behind you!"

Oh, wonderful. When I unzipped the tent and looked out, I couldn't believe my eyes. We were sitting in water three inches deep. The road in front of us was flooded, and the guy was right—the river was overflowing its banks, headed straight for us. Our bikes were sinking in the mud. Mine looked like it would tip over at any second. I pictured it going beneath the surface of the mud for the last time, leaving behind one insolent bubble as it descended towards the center of the earth.

In a rush, we put our clothes and sleeping bags and gear into big garbage bags, tying off the tops to hopefully keep it all dry. Then we flew out of the tent one by one like we were jumping out of a plane.

The entire world had become a swamp. Wearing only the Jockey shorts that Cindy had admired, we moved our tent and gear to higher ground on the other side of the road. "Okay," I said, "it should be safe here." Safe, but not dry.

"Quick, let's get the bikes over here," said Steve, rain dripping down his face.

Once we got the bikes, Tom yelled, "Let's run to the showers to get warm!"

Once again we dashed to the showers. It was starting to feel like I'd always be running and I'd always be wet, and I'd never get to sit still or be dry again.

After showering, we looked for an open building where we could sleep for the night. We found a laundry room where we were greeted by two girls who were waiting for their sleeping bags to finish drying. They were obviously surprised, and maybe a little embarrassed, to see us, the nearly-naked trio, walk in.

"You can never tell what lurks out in a rainy night, can you?" said one of them.

"Hi," said Steve. "I'm naked, so is Tom and so is Mark."

One of them said nothing. The other laughed her head off and managed to say hello when she regained her composure.

"We were washed out of our tent and are now searching for a dry place to spend the rest of this drab night," said Steve. "We can't afford to get our clothes wet, because we're traveling cross-country and, you know, don't have unlimited clothes."

Steve's explanation made them relax.

I thought about all we had done that day, all that had happened. But no matter how I might have said it, what popped out of my mouth, somewhere between a sigh and a howl of giddy disbelief, was, "Oh man, what a hell of a day!"

# CHAPTER THREE

# True Grit

On Thursday, September 16, we got up at eight thirty and went to a local diner for some bacon and eggs. On the way back to the campground, we picked up some oil for the bikes.

"Let's go to the rear of the camp so we don't make a mess of the place," I said. Changing the oil on a motorcycle can leave you looking like you just swam through an oil slick if things go wrong. We were done by eleven thirty. It's a sensitivity that only comes with enough time on a bike, but when you have clean, fresh oil hitting the moving parts of your engine, you can feel the difference.

Our tent had finally dried out enough in the sun so that we could pack it. Every day we learned a new trick for folding the tent or an easier way to pack and load the equipment. It sounds like a small thing, until you've ridden a motorcycle across the country. Each time we learned how to save ourselves a few seconds was a few seconds more we could spend on the road.

"I guess experience is really the best teacher," I said when we were ready to go, realizing that I sounded both wise and clichéd. But hey, clichés stick around for a reason. There's always some truth in them.

After leaving camp, we drove through the center of town and stopped at a small sub shop on the outskirts. By the time we finished eating and gassing up the bikes, it was four in the afternoon.

"Man, it's taken us a long time to get rolling today," said Steve. "We'll be driving late if we want to get to Harrisonburg tonight." There was nothing to do but get to it.

In no time, we had driven 120 miles, and then we drove off Route 64 into Richmond, the capital of Virginia. It was starting to get dark even though it was only six thirty.

"Since we're here," I said, "we might as well spend some time looking around." There are people who travel in such a rush, who stick to their itineraries so rigidly, that they forget what got them out the door in the first place: seeing new things. That had been my philosophy for the whole trip, right from the beginning. If we didn't take our time and see everything that looked even remotely interesting, we were shortchanging ourselves. I didn't want to rush from place to place like a tourist. Every gift shop looks the same after you've seen two of them. I wanted to spend some real time in any place that looked intriguing, and to get to know the people and the land on which they lived. That, to me, was travel. It was more than just moving from point A to point B and saying, "Well, that's that. I traveled."

Luckily, Tom agreed, because he would usually agree with whatever Steve and I decided to do. But Steve was different as far as this went. I'm not saying it was contrarianism, but like clockwork, he would always disagree and want to move on from what we were doing unless it was something he was dying to see. And you never had to wonder what he thought or wanted because he wasn't one to suffer in silence.

At a Burger King, while I was waiting for my buddies to join me at the table, I drummed up a conversation with the young couple across from me. When they found out we were heading to California, they gave us an address and all but begged us to drop in if we were ever in their area. Life on the road created a sort of kinship. You might not strike up a conversation with a stranger in your own city if they sat down next to you on a bench or subway, but it felt natural to talk about travel with other travelers.

Surprise, surprise, it started pouring as soon as we got back on the bikes. In a show of ever great efficiency, we stopped, put on our rain slickers (unfortunately they were cheap plastic suits), and covered the gear.

"It was your idea to hang around Richmond. Now look at us," said Steve. "Now we have to ride in the rain at night and we are getting soaked."

As if we hadn't noticed that it was raining and we were getting soaked, good grief.

"You can't tell when it is going to rain," I said. It's not like we were prognosticators divining the signs of the weather from the flight path of birds and the patterns of insects. "And besides, we shouldn't run away from a place we haven't seen just because of the rain. We should be able to handle a change in the weather without fussing like this."

An angry Steve drove away from the gas station where we had stopped to put on our rain suits, and we followed him, riding through the backdraft of his palpable exasperation.

At the next stoplight, Tom, forever the mediator, said, "We've got to find somewhere to bed down for the night." We were getting so wet that I could almost hear my thoughts sloshing. Between the rain, darkness, and the fact that we were in a city, it was hard to find a free place to bed down. Eventually Tom got so tired of riding in the rain that he pulled into a gas station and asked the attendant where we could find a motel. The guy gave him directions. The directions turned out to be wrong, of course, which compounded our agony and irritation. Some people are too proud to rely on other people for help. But it's also true that some people aren't reliable enough to offer help that's useful in any way.

When we finally found a hotel, we walked into the office, still wearing our dripping helmets, like three frogmen newly emerged from the depths of the ocean. I asked the middle-aged gentleman behind the desk how much a single room would cost.

"You'll have to rent a double room because there are three of you. That'll run you $24.92 for the night." It was obvious there wasn't going to be any wiggle room.

As soon as I looked at Steve and Tom, I knew the answer, but Tom said, "Let's go talk it over outside," before I could say anything. So we went out, leaving three little lakes on the office floor behind us.

"I want to do it," said Tom. "I'm too tired."

"No, it's too expensive here," said Steve. "If we didn't spend so much time in Richmond, we wouldn't have to be spending our money now." He said this to both of us but was obviously directing it at me. I kept it together and didn't say anything, but I was steaming. However, rather than waste more time arguing, we rode on in the rain on Route 64 North, destination Harrisonburg. Steve kept complaining and complaining, and when I thought he was done, it turned out he was just taking a deep breath so he could complain some more. Finally, enough was enough. I raced ahead and left them behind. Maybe the anger that was heating my scalp would dry me out and warm me up.

They were smart enough not to keep up with me, given the hazardous conditions of the weather and my temper.

Once I lost sight of them in my rearview mirrors, I slowed back down to sixty miles per hour. Forty miles later, I decided to pull off the road and hide so I could follow them when they passed by. But after forty-five minutes, I started to worry about them. I couldn't have gotten *that* far ahead. The rain had stopped so I took off my rain suit in the dark and packed it away. Still no bikes in sight. The highway was desolate, an open road with thick forests on both sides. A solitary deer occasionally scampered across the highway, and every once in a while a car passed. But where were Tom and Steve? I was starting to regret my decision to zoom off into the night.

Finally Steve and Tom rode right by without a clue that I was lurking nearby like a troll. I gave them a little head start before setting out in pursuit.

By twelve thirty in the morning, it looked like they had managed to get even more tired, because they took the Charlottesville exit. I followed them to the police station where they got off their bikes and went inside. I hid around the corner, incredibly pleased with myself and my stealth operation. Five minutes later, they came out, got back on their bikes, and drove to a park just up the road.

The park wasn't much to speak of: just a little patch of grass on the top of a hill, right in the middle of Charlottesville. After Tom and Steve put up the tent, I decided to end the suspense and let them know I was alright. So I drove up the steep grassy hill and parked my bike next to theirs like it had been the most normal evening in history. I walked over to the tent with my sleeping bag under my arm. "Hi guys, you sure picked a funny place to set up camp."

No answer. It was like I was talking to statues. Figuring that they were mad, but unwilling to beg them to relax, I just rolled out my bag in the tent and gave in to sleep, content that my friends were drying out and safe. Even though they wouldn't say anything, I knew they were happy to see me.

The sound of big city buses and people walking every which way woke us up around seven thirty the next morning. In our tired, bleary-eyed, road-weary, frayed-synapses desperation, we had pitched our tent right in the city park. That tent looked just as out of place in the hustle and bustle of the morning rush hour as a giraffe would have.

Without much discussion, the tent was taken down once more, the bikes packed up, and we were off for a small breakfast at a local diner. We made friends with the cook, and found out he had owned his little business for fifty years. At seventy-six, he was still going strong. We should all be so fortunate. As soon as we finished breakfast, we thanked the man for his fine service and headed for yet another in the endless sequence of gas stations.

At the station, our various anxieties boiled over. Apparently we weren't going to get away with ignoring the previous night.

"You shouldn't have left the group the way you did, Mark," said Tom. "We didn't know where you were or if anything happened to you."

I wasn't above snapping back when snapped at. "I couldn't take Steve's selfishness and complaining anymore. I just needed to be alone for a while."

"Well, you were the one who said we should never split up while we're on the road," said Tom.

"I know I was wrong, but I can only take so much of that bull," I said. When I'm calm, I've never had a problem admitting my mistakes.

Steve was quiet. Maybe he was contemplating his follies, or maybe he was just wishing we would shut our yaps so we could get on with it.

With the bikes gassed up and ready to go, we headed northwest on Route 64 until we reached the Shenandoah Skyline Drive where we turned due north. It cost $2 to get into the park, but it was worth it. The scenery was beautiful from the road on the crest of the Shenandoah Mountains. It was a sight and a stillness that would make you weep: big green valleys and mountains covered with hardwoods and hemlocks where once mountain men used to live and trap furs. I was reminded once again of the reverence that nature seems to force on people. The woods are like a church that everyone can step into and respect out of pure instinct.

"Hey guys," I yelled, pointing to the forest. "Why don't we do some backpacking for the weekend? It looks great out there."

"Sounds good," said Steve. "Let's check into this ranger station and get a permit. Then we can stock up on some food." I was glad to hear him talking again, but I could tell that he was holding something in. There was no sense trying to pry it out of him with a crowbar. He'd talk or not, and we'd be there to listen when he couldn't keep it to himself anymore.

After getting the permit and food, we took everything off the bikes and chained (we each carried a three-foot length of a 3/8 chain and a big pad lock) them together in a parking lot, which meant we had to strap anything we wanted to take with us to our backs. We studied the trail map, and I figured out how far we would have to go to reach our first campsite. I oriented my compass and checked the time: two thirty. "We have about three hours to hike to our first available site, which is six miles away," I said.

"Let's get moving then," says Tom. After one final equipment check, I volunteered to carry the tent first. After swinging it onto my back, in addition to everything else loaded on my packs, I was carrying close to sixty pounds. It doesn't sound like too much, but if you're not used to that much extra weight on your back, fatigue can catch up with you fast.

What a gorgeous day it was. The sun was shining but not blazing, there was a cool northerly breeze, and the height of the season was over so the trails were not crowded. The only sign of potential unrest was at the head of the trail, where a fading sign told us, "BEWARE of the BEARS."

Our first leg of the Appalachian trail was downhill most of the way. Six miles later, we were at the basin looking for a place to set up camp.

"Well," I said, "the rules of the park are, you can't camp within sight of the trail, or within sight of other campers. Also, you must be a 150 feet from a stream and can't have an open fire."

It seemed impossible to guarantee that we could be completely out of sight of other campers. What were we supposed to do? Yell "Don't look at us!" if anyone else appeared in our field of vision? We found a level spot that looked like it had been used for camping before, so we figured it was okay. The tent was out of its bag and set up in seven minutes. I filled the gas mountain stove and got the cooksets ready for dinner. Steve and Tom were preparing a hanging bag to keep the food in at night, safe from the bears and other wild animals.

"I'll climb that tree and throw the line over that branch over there on that other tree," said Tom. "It should be high enough, shouldn't it?"

"Yup," said Steve, "but we need more line to hoist the food bag up with."

"Hey Mark," said Tom, "get the roll of nylon line out of my left pack pocket and throw it up here, will you?"

"Okay, but hurry up. Dinner will be ready soon," I said. I didn't want bear trouble any more than they did, but the food I wanted in my stomach in that moment almost seemed more important than the food a curious bear might want later that night.

Steve tied one end of the nylon line to the bag and threw the other end over the line that Tom just hung between the two tall alder trees.

While Tom was trying to get down from the tree, I grabbed my camera and got a picture of him. "Hold it . . . Okay, I got it. You can come down now if you can." Tom made it out of the tree in one piece, and then we ate.

It didn't get really dark until after seven. "Boy, that freeze-dried beef stew was good," said Tom. I wondered if those words had ever been spoken aloud before, not that he was wrong.

We were all still trying to pay back a massive sleep debt, so we turned in early.

After breakfast the next morning, on Saturday, we each took our share of the dishes down to the stream for washing. The water was crystal clear and cold. It was all lovely, the kind of stream you'd see on a calendar or a screensaver on a computer. Using the fine sand from the stream bed, I cleaned the egg from the frying pan, while Steve and Tom did the dishes and cups farther upstream. When we were done, the ritual of packing and stowing gear played itself out again.

"Okay," I said, "how about hiking the Big Run Trail? It's only six miles long, and if we leave now, we'll make it back by three thirty. That's including an hour for lunch and a reading break somewhere at the top of the mountain."

With a quick check of the trail map, the compass, and the position of the sun, we left for a day's hike in the Shenandoah Mountains. The sun shone through the yellow alder tree leaves, and a crisp breeze was in the air.

After no more than five minutes on the trail, Steve decided he had to take care of some business. He was already unbuckling his belt when Tom said, "Steve, you know what the rules say. You have to be twenty-five yards from any trail, so get your ass over there."

By that time, Steve was already squatting with his pants down. He looked up with a disgusted expression. "Can't even take a shit in peace," he muttered, as if we had barged into his private palace bathroom.

While he wandered off, we kept walking up the trail and yelled that we'd meet him at the top of the knoll. Once Steve caught up with us, feeling invulnerable and adventurous, I told them that I was sure I could blaze a shortcut using my compass for the way back.

"No thanks," they said, almost in unison, "we'll stick to the trail."

"Hey," I said, "I was a Boy Scout for years, and in case you forgot, I majored in forestry for a year at college." Surely, this would convince them of my authority, beyond question.

But no. They still wanted to hike the trail like children being led about by a governess, so I said I'd meet them back at the camp. I checked my compass, and then headed off the trail for parts unknown. Every ten minutes, I'd stop and listen to hear where my two doubting Thomas's were. I got back on the trail well ahead of Steve and Tom, and started leaving signs along the path. Just before getting to the camp, I hid just off the trail, waiting like a snare.

Sitting down in the light of the sun, with my back to a hemlock tree, I took a short nap. When their voices and footsteps thumped down the trail, waking me, I got ready to surprise them. I exploded out of the underbrush, roaring like a bear. Once their heartbeats settled down, Steve and Tom admitted that they were surprised I'd found my way back to the camp. Oh, ye of little faith.

That night after supper, we were sitting in front of the tent on our foam ground pads. Steve and Tom were playing cards by candle light. "Good game, Tom," said Tom, as if he were auditioning for the role of a sarcastic, ungracious winner in a TV pilot. "Too bad you lost. Okay, Mark, ready for a turn in the loser's circle?"

I refused to play, which he didn't like but couldn't do anything about. If your style of winning means that no one ever wants to play a game with you, you've lost, and it doesn't matter what the scorecards say.

Again, we settled in for another early night in the sack. The last flashlight was shut off at eight thirty, and we enjoyed the buzzes and rustlings of the night.

Sunday morning was sunny and warm, and seeing the rays of the sun shining through the trees and bouncing off the stream below was an enviable vision. I was up first, so I started getting breakfast ready. As soon as they smelled food, Steve and Tom scampered out of the tent to help.

Then Tom froze. "Don't move or say anything. Just slowly look to your left."

There were two small does, twenty feet away, feeding on fresh alder leaves. We sat very still for ten minutes and watched them. Then, to our astonishment, they wandered right into the campsite like they'd received a formal invitation.

"Look, this doe is coming for my food," whispered Steve. He slowly held out a piece of sharp cheddar cheese, and the doe nibbled it out of his hand and then walked back into the forest. She'd taken it with such confidence that I couldn't help but wonder how many times she'd been fed by people on the trail. For all I knew she was eating better than we were.

That was our last day in the park, so we broke camp and got ready to hike out. Before we finished packing, a park ranger on foot patrol stopped by, in the mood to reprimand us for camping near a trail.

"We didn't know that fire road is considered a trail."

The ranger was a short little guy with a mustache. He wore black glasses with plastic rims and a wide-brimmed hat like the one Smokey the Bear has.

He was very pleasant and patient while he explained the camping rules to us. Then he said he was going to issue us a ticket, but if we cleaned up the site so he couldn't tell anyone camped here, he would just give us a warning.

We couldn't argue with that. We cleaned up the campsite so well that it looked like no human being had ever set foot on it. When the ranger came back, he left us zero citations and one cordial "Have a nice day." We just stood there bewildered, never having received a written warning for camping in the wrong spot before. Even though I was sure that some of the rangers probably overdid it, it was better that they were trying to preserve the park than letting people mash it into ruins.

"Who's going to carry the tent?" I asked. "I already had my turn."

"I'll take it. Bring it over here," said Steve.

Just after ten, Steve, energetic and rested, took the lead and headed out on a fire road leading to the Patterson Ridge Trail. He set a fast pace, but I was right behind. Tom went slower because he knew the trail ahead would be uphill most of the way.

Eventually, Steve's pace dropped off, and I took the lead. Two hours later, we were still climbing. I maintained the pace, but Steve was looking ragged. Tom's slow pace had paid off and he was fine. We took frequent breaks. The trail dipped occasionally, but it was always a tease, starting to climb right away.

Three-quarters of the way up the trail, Steve collapsed. We took his gear off and tried to help him relax. He was only semi-conscious. As he came to, we were right at his side.

"Here, drink some water," I said. We asked him how he felt, over and over. Seeing someone as strong and vital as Steve lose the ability to operate under his own power was a frightening signal that something had gone very wrong.

"Weak, I feel weak all over," Steve said. "I don't think I can make it."

"Hey, don't say that. We don't want to hear that kind of talk," I said. I took out my share of the beef jerky and offered it to him. "Here, eat this. It'll give you more energy." I forgot the little feud Steve and I had going. There's nothing like a potential disaster to give you perspective. I took the tent off his pack and put it on my own.

"Let's get him on his feet," said Tom when he looked a little better.

We helped Steve up and put his pack on his back.

"Do you guys want me to use my compass and try to cut out some of the extra hiking?" I asked. "I think it would be a good idea. Just have a little faith in me and we'll make it out of here."

They agreed. I led the way, picking the easiest path through and over the rough terrain. Fifteen minutes later, Steve collapsed again. Tom shouted for me to come back; I was up ahead making sure we were going in the right direction. I hurried back to see Steve sitting down, leaning against a tree, still wearing his pack.

"What's wrong?" I asked.

"He feels weak again," said Tom.

"Well, we'll just have to sit here for a while," I said, crouching down beside Steve.

Tom offered Steve some salt packets and water. But after that, we were starting to get low on water and were completely out of food. The sun was setting fast on the east side of the mountain where we were sitting.

"How much farther do we have to go?" asked Steve, now eating plain ketchup from a packet he got from Burger King.

"I'm not sure," I said. "I'm looking out for familiar trail signs, so I can tell how much of the marked foot trail we bypassed. But I think we should get going soon because we can't get stuck up here on the mountain without food or water. Think of this as a test of survival, Steve. You know you don't want to lose, so come on; get tough and we'll all make it."

I led the way, whistling what I hoped was a cheery, inspiring tune, trying not to think about how serious our situation could turn if Steve got worse. His head drooped and his breath was ragged right behind me. Tom brought up the rear to keep an eye on Steve and make sure he wouldn't collapse without us knowing.

After hiking through a marshy, gloomy area, I finally saw the trail again. "Hey!" I yelled. "We're okay. Here's the trail and we only have about a half hour to go."

By now my legs were starting to feel heavy and the muscles in my back were in full revolt against the extra weight of Steve's pack. No amount of inspirational speeches would change that. But finding the trail gave me a boost and acted like a temporary anesthetic, numbing my hurts as I just kept placing one foot in front of the other. We were relieved that we were so close. Steve even smiled a little.

When we finally got back to the ranger station, we were starved and tired. We hadn't gotten to the point where we might have started considering cannibalism, but we were ravenous and desperate. We dumped our packs outside the canteen and went in to chow down anything in sight. It was now 3:00 PM, and we were sitting down eating and thinking back to that morning and the workout we just went through.

"Wow, we just hiked eight miles in five hours with sixty pounds worth of gear with the trail being mostly uphill and I made it!" said Steve. "We all made it!" He looked at Tom. "Mark has the strength and endurance of five men."

I took a bow and tried to accept the compliment graciously, but I was too tired to do more than that.

Then we saw our reflections in a mirror. It was wild to see the difference three days in the woods could make. Our incoming beards were really filling in and starting to look good; at least the itching was gone.

After showering and putting on clean clothes, we packed all the gear back onto the bikes. "I'm glad my bike is carrying this junk and not me," said Steve.

## CHAPTER FOUR:
# The Good Deed

Three days of hard hiking makes getting back on a motorcycle feel like a picnic. Later that afternoon when we rode down the mountainside into the Shenandoah Valley, it was like we were riding on air ... relaxed and fully enjoying the twenty miles down the valley into Harrisonburg.

We pulled into Harrisonburg early that evening. We had a mission for the night. Two summers earlier, Steve had been hired as a waterfront director for a summary YMCA resident camp in New Hampshire. It took about five seconds before he'd hit it off with a classic beauty named Debbie, who had been so lovely that it looked like she had stepped off a sculpture pedestal in a museum. I'd gone back to school, Madison College, with Steve a year after that, and had done just as well with a gorgeous girl named Patty. Now we figured it was time to swing back by Madison College to check on them. But first, as always, would be eating. After a few pounds of Chinese food, we drove to the school to surprise the girls. Not for the first, or the last, time on this trip, we were the surprised ones. One of the girls had graduated, and the other had dropped out of school. It let the air out of us like we were balloons.

"That's great," said Steve, stalking around and fuming. "We come all this way and they're not there." I let him stomp around for a few minutes before reminding him that there were more than two girls in the world, a fact he seemed to be in danger of forgetting.

But we'd gotten our hopes up and the hustle was on for the night. We didn't have a place to stay yet, and when it came to options, the thought of being taken in by three happy, stunning females beat anything else, so we had to try.

But there's a reason why dating manuals don't say things like, "To win her affection, spend three days on the road, smell like it, look like it, and act like you're borderline desperate for a place to stay." We could play Romeos when we needed and wanted to, but even Romeo might have struck out in our sorry state that night. We literally smelled as desperate as we looked. So we came off empty-handed, again.

"Okay, what do we do now?" Steve asked in a lifeless voice. "I'm so tired, I could sleep standing up." But Tom already had the same idea, and had fallen asleep against the nearest tree.

"Let's go down to the police station and let 'em know we just got here," I said. "If we tell them we're tired and need a place to roll out our bags for the night, they might let us. Think positive."

Steve was too tired to argue, so we woke Tom up before the bark of the tree could make deeper marks in his face and we took off again and headed to the police station. When your options are few, there's not much to lose, but we stood to gain about six hours of sleep if we could get some help from the cops.

The police station was near Main Street downtown. We locked our front forks and marched through the front doors and right up to the office desk like weary soldiers coming home from a tough battle. Honestly, I was so tired I would have settled for a jail cell if they'd offered one. I took a deep breath and told our story to the officer. He called the sergeant on patrol to come in and handle it, since he was the only person who could authorize us sacking out behind the station. I must have told the story well, because when the sergeant heard me out, he saw that, under the grime and fatigue, we were bonafide, well-mannered travelers.

"You boys can put your bed rolls down in this grassy section of land right behind the station," he said in classic, Southern hospitality style. "If you want to wash, you have my permission to use the restroom in the station. No one will bother you here."

After thanking him, I turned to Steve and Tom. "I like how hospitable these people in Virginia are. I don't think the Massachusetts police would have been so friendly. I doubt they would have offered us their backyard for the night."

We had a place to sleep, but it was a cold night under the stars. After rolling out the insulated foam pads on the soft grass, we unfurled our sleeping bags and crawled in. We pulled their cords tightly to keep the cold air out, and were all snuggled up warm inside our fiber-filled mountain bags within a couple of minutes.

"Hey," I said through my bag, "can you believe that we're sleeping behind a police station in Virginia?" It hadn't been the easiest day, but if we hadn't come on the trip, I would have been in my bed at home after a day of work that would have probably been less than thrilling. It would have been just like any other summer for the three of us.

There was no reply, so I turned over and closed my eyes, beneath that massive Virginia sky.

I was the first one up at seven the next morning. My bike and sleeping bag were both covered in a bright sheen of dew that was just starting to evaporate in the early sunlight. Once the guys were awake, we washed up and brushed our teeth. Then we were rearing to go.

"I wonder what is in store for us today?" asked Steve.

We really *could* have done anything that day. There was *no* routine. What a gift. Some of this I'd see only in hindsight, but we were free out there in a way that many people never give themselves the chance to experience.

"First, I think we should check the National Chimney State Park," said Steve. " It's about fifteen miles from here if we head south on Route 42."

"Isn't that the campground the sergeant told us about last night?" Tom said.

It was.

"Once we have a place to go back to for the night, we can relax and do what we want all day without worrying," Tom said, strapping on his gear. "Let's go take care of that first." Hell, he had a point. There was nothing wrong with being sensible once in a while, although I doubted we'd ever make a habit of it.

After setting up camp at the state park, we took what we needed for the day and drove into Harrisonburg. We wanted to go play tennis and work out at Madison College, but first came the less glamorous business of laundry. After we'd washed our clothes and given ourselves a better shot at smelling human the next time we put them on, we washed and waxed our bikes before heading to a Honda dealer, hoping he could fix a small problem for me. After I explained to the service manager what was wrong, he had one of the mechanics clean off my spark plugs. The mechanic then told me I was burning a bad tank of gas. So far on the trip, you couldn't throw a rock without hitting a helpful, generous expert. The mechanic was even nice enough to tighten a loose bolt on Steve's front clamp exhaust pipe. It was a huge relief that there were no major problems with my bike, and an even greater pleasure to find that people here seemed to be as kind as they were in Virginia.

Finally, errands and hassles at an end, we drove to Madison College to play a few sets of tennis. Like most things in my life, I've never seen the point of playing if I'm not going to play hard, which meant that after we were done, I was dripping with sweat and desperate for a hot shower. Tom and Steve needed it just as bad.

But of course, everything had to be a riddle. "How are we going to get into the gym to take showers?" asked Tom. "You need a college ID to get in the front door and there is always a checker sitting at the desk."

It was true. The checker guarded that desk and door like a Roman sentry pacing the watchtower, looking for barbarians.

"Don't worry, Tom. Mark and I learned this trick when we were here last year," said Steve. Walking around to a side door, Steve took out his Swiss Army knife and pulled out the square-ended can opener attachment. He had the door open in seconds.

"Not bad," said Tom.

"Leave it to the pro," Steve said with a grin. It was a minor caper, but we were pleased enough with ourselves that we might as well have pulled off a big jewel heist.

After showering and eating dinner, Tom wanted to watch the intramural basketball game in the gym. Steve and I walked to the college library to do a little reading and writing and discuss the goals of the trip. As is frequently the case in college libraries, we didn't get much reading or writing accomplished, but when we were done talking, we both had a clearer definition of our vision for the journey. It basically boiled down to this: I didn't want to hurry, or to ever feel like I had to rush, and I didn't want Tom or Steve to feel that way either. If someone wanted to go somewhere, we would go. Everyone had to be satisfied. Fair was fair, the air had been cleared, and I felt better than ever. It was like we'd knocked some future obstacles out of our path before they even had a chance to appear.

"Hey, it's eleven," said Steve, looking at his watch twice in quick succession. "I told Tom we'd meet him back at the bikes." I gathered my stuff, put on my jacket, and said softly to Steve, "I'm not looking forward to the cold fifteen miles back to camp." It was as cold and as long as I had anticipated, but we got it done, like always.

In the morning, Steve poked his nose out of the tent and was greeted by the brilliant morning sunshine, surrounded by blue sky. "Hey, you guys, it's super out. Come take a look."

Super or not, his voice cut through my sleeping bag and I had to see it for myself. He was right. It was an exquisite sight. I was gaining an appreciation for mornings that I hadn't had in the same way back home. Every morning was now the start of something new. Things were going to happen that day, and every day on the trip, that we couldn't anticipate.

"Hey," I said, after we ate and packed, "let's take a tour and go check out the National Chimney."

Walking through the entrance gate, we were greeted by a beautiful garden of every imaginable flower you could think of. Towering above us were four different sized columns of rock—the Chimneys—connected at one place or another, standing strong and proud throughout the ages, now looking down at the three small bodies gazing up, awestruck. As we walked, we stopped at each station that had a diagram of the chimneys, accompanied with a tape that explained how the chimneys were created. Off to the left of the towering columns was a field where jousting events were held, according to the recording.

"How do you like that?" I said. Every third week in August, year after year, they had jousting tournaments on that field, like King Arthur and all of his knights showing up in the Shenandoah Valley. "That must be a thing to see."

"We didn't miss it by much," said Steve, staring into the field, dreaming of the clash of armor and sparks flying from the clash of metal on metal.

Tom interrupted our Medieval reverie by yelling, "Hey, do you guys realize that it's almost noon?" He pointed at his watch. "It must be ninety degrees out in the sun. Let's ride into Harrisonburg and play some tennis at Madison College."

Another morning, another day, another ride, another trip to the college, and more tennis. After two hours' whacking the balls back and forth at each other, Steve jerryrigged the door into the showers again. The perfect crime! While dressing, we decided to relax and read for a while at the library before going to dinner. This time, we *really* intended to read, and we managed it. Just before leaving for dinner, with our minds dwelling happily on whatever we were about to stuff our faces with, Steve reminded us that every night the most pressing question was always, "Where are we going to sleep?"

He wasn't wrong, but no one was in the mood for practicality.

"Don't worry, Steve," I said. "The night is young, and if worse comes to worse, we can always go back to the state park."

This satisfied Steve, and we headed out to the bikes. After kicking over his motor, Tom noticed his trip odometer. It was time to refuel. "We should get gas before going to dinner," he said.

"Let's hit that Exxon station across from the college entrance," I said.

After waiting for the traffic to go by, we revved our engines to 4000 RPM and raced across the four-lane roadway to the Exxon station. I was still sitting on my bike and reaching for the pump when the station attendant walked out to help.

"Can you tell us where there's a good Italian restaurant?" asked Steve. To our profound dismay, apparently there were no Italian restaurants in Harrisonburg. The attendant looked as sorry about it as we all felt.

A tall, heavyset, well-built man stepped out from the garage. "If you boys are looking for a good dish of spaghetti, then you want to eat at The Famous Dinner Restaurant. Where you boys traveling from?"

"Massachusetts," said Tom, leaning back on his bike while Steve finished filling his tank. While I paid the attendant, I asked the man who'd overheard us if he knew of a place or anyone that would let us lay out our bed rolls for the night.

"Well, I don't know," he said. "Do you think they would let these boys sack out on the intramural field over at Madison College?" he asked the attendant.

The attendant suggested they call Bill, head of security at Madison College, to find out. I tried to insist that they didn't need to go through all the trouble on our account, but they were determined. "No bother, boys. It will only take a second to find out!" yelled the attendant.

While the man who had suggested the restaurant walked into the station to call Bill, Steve leaned over to the attendant and asked in a low tone, "Who's our helpful friend?" He said the man's name was Pete. He was a retired Virginia State Trooper, always liked to help people out, and was thought of far and wide as "Good Old Pete." The name fit, lucky for us. It occurred to me that, if you've done enough good in your life so that people referred to you as "Good old" you, you'd be doing something worth aspiring to.

Soon, a white Madison College cruiser pulled into the station. Pete walked over to greet his friend and asked him if we could sack out for the night in the college's empty intramural field. After discussing it, Pete and the security officer walked over. "There's a private college beer party taking place out there tonight, otherwise I wouldn't mind," he said.

It would have been much better if he had finished that sentence with, "And that college beer party is desperately in need of your drinking abilities," but it was not to be.

"But there's a campground out off of Three called Gerundo, and it's only seven miles from here," he continued.

"Thanks for the help," I said. "We appreciate what you've both done." I returned their smiles, which made them smile bigger, which made me smile bigger yet. "And we'll try that Famous Dinner Restaurant for their spaghetti. If we see you again, Pete, we'll let you know if you gave us good advice about Italian food."

And so we raced into the night in hot pursuit of an Italian dinner.

It was eight by the time we sat down to order, but the place was empty and the wait would be short. "This is a pretty big place with a lot of seats, but not sitters," said Steve in his best Groucho Marx impression. "Maybe it's the chef's birthday and everyone is eating the birthday cake in the kitchen." He pointed at Tom. "Follow me Harpo. Chico, you stay here and guard the door and don't let anyone in unless they know the password," he said to me.

"What's the password?" I said.

"Swordfish! Swordfish!" Steve answered, still talking like Groucho.

Just as we turned to check out the kitchen, a pretty waitress pushed open the swinging door from the kitchen. "Ah," said Steve with a smile. "Here comes our party hostess now, coming to invite us in for coffee and cake."

The waitress walked up and asked Steve how many were out front. "Three for dinner." Steve turned around to look at us, and then back to the waitress. "Actually, my dear, what is your name?"

"Lynnie," she said, covering her mouth with her hand and giggling. You couldn't have broken Steve out of character with a hammer, and now it was time for his grand finale. "Lynnie, we have a bus load and I came in here to see if there's enough room to sit everyone down to eat, and by the looks of things, there seems to be plenty of room." Lynnie started giggling again. "How's the food here? If you give me your number, I will let you sit with us." Now she was cracking up. Charm isn't everything, but whenever I watched Steve do his thing, it was obvious that it was *something*.

"You guys are crazy, but I'll get you three menus." She walked away, still laughing. We took off our jackets and sat down at a table.

When Lynnie returned with the menus, she explained that Tuesday nights were slow. I looked into her pretty blue eyes and ordered three spaghetti dinners. "We're *really* hungry," I said, pouring it on, hinting at our bottomless appetites, hoping that she'd get the message to the chef and urge him to go heavy and hard with the food.

I watched Lynnie walk into the kitchen—it was hard not to. Then I put a spoon in my hand and pretended it was a cigar. "I could sit on her lap all day if she didn't stand up." The Groucho competition was on.

After dinner, I couldn't resist mentioning to Lynnie that we needed a place to spend the night. With great reluctance, she said she'd made other plans for the evening and wouldn't be at her apartment, which was only ten miles away. But she did give us her phone number. "I'll tell you what, call me tomorrow. I'll call a few of my party-time friends over and we'll have a party and you guys are invited to spend the night. Now, make sure you call. It will be a good time," she said. "I wish I didn't have this date tonight. You guys are a lot of fun," she said with a smile.

I got up to pay the bill while Tom and Steve buttoned up for the cold ride to Gerundo Campground. Returning with a piece of paper, Lynnie handed me the directions to her place. "Sorry I couldn't help you guys out tonight, but please call me tomorrow sometime." She gave us all the seductive eye, and we felt its pull like the best sort of black magic.

"Thanks, we'll do that," said Steve. "We love to party and have a good time." That was the understatement of the century. Then we waved goodbye and hit the cold road.

Seven miles down Route 33, Tom spotted a Gerundo Campground sign lit up on the left. We were trailing behind, so he flicked on his left blinker to warn us that it was just up ahead. We rode through looking for a spot. Once Tom found a place, it only took five minutes to lay out the sleeping bags and crawl in like bumblebees wriggling into their hives.

"Hey guys, do you remember seeing that girl playing tennis today?" I said. "Wasn't she as big as a cow?" I'd no sooner finished talking when out of the darkness came the loudest "moooo" from a cow in a nearby pasture. Everybody immediately burst into laughter.

"Great timing," said Steve from the depths of his mummy bag. "You two would make a great comedy team at Caesar's Palace in Vegas."

I pictured myself standing next to a cow on the Vegas strip, telling jokes while the cow mooed. Who could say? Maybe it would be a huge hit. "Goodnight, Tom," I said. Tom didn't reply.

"The sandman has Tom in dreamland," Steve said, turning over for a comfortable position, soon to be washed away in the sands of his own sleep.

The next morning, Tom got out of his sleeping bag and checked his watch with his eyes half open, squinting against the glare of the bright morning sun. "It's ten o'clock already!" He muttered it loudly enough for me and Steve to hear. We began stretching, and then crawled slowly from our cocoons, ready to tackle another day.

"Boy, that was the best night's sleep I have had in a long time," said Tom.

I had slept well, too, but there was something irking me. "With this country being as big as it is and rich as it is, why do we have to pay if we're only using the ground to sleep on? I could see it if we used the showers and laundry room facilities, but if we come in late at night like we did, and leave right away in the morning, like we are, then we shouldn't have to pay. I'll tell them at the office. Maybe since we didn't use anything and it's off season, they won't charge us."

"Sounds reasonable," said Tom as he rolled up his bag.

At the office, Steve looked in the window. There wasn't anyone around. "Mark, we could ride right out of here and no one would know the difference," he said as he returned to his bike and checked out the straps.

"Let's give Mark a chance with his speech," said Tom.

I was glad he said that. Despite my sense of injustice, I wouldn't have felt good about just leaving. Finally, a lady walked out from her house to the office, unlocked the door, and invited us inside. She was pleasant, in her fifties, and all business when she said, "Okay, boys, that will be $4.84 for the three of you."

I gave her the speech while she listened intently. She heard me out, but then she said, "Those are the rates for everyone, boys."

Well, I tried. "You wouldn't happen to know of anyone needing three hard workers now, would you?" I said, handing her the three dollars.

"Well, it just so happens I do. I saw it in the paper only the other day and it's a good job picking apples out at Singers Glen. It's the Ruttles Apple Orchards. Tell Mr. Wrenn that Floyd Gerundo sent you."

After giving us directions to Singers Glen, we thanked her and walked to our bikes. While warming up the motors, we put on our gloves and zipped up our jackets to get ready for another cold fifteen miles. Lo and behold, here came Mrs. Gerundo again, coming out of the office. She walked over to Steve and stuck the three dollars back into his pocket.

"Hey, what's this?" said Steve.

"I didn't open the register yet," she said, walking away and waving good-bye. "You need it more than I do," she said over her shoulder. "Good luck."

It pays to be nice. It was a lesson I never got sick of learning. No matter what happens, it's always a comfort to be reminded of how many good people there are, and Virginia seemed to have a disproportionate amount of kindly souls. When you turn on the news, it's easy to get the impression that everything's going to hell and people are nothing but monsters, but that's just because no one tunes in to hear about all the good things that are happening in the world alongside the bad.

The ride to Singers Glen was a beautiful jaunt with miles and miles of grassy land and rolling hills. There was country farmland everywhere you looked. The smell of lye was strong in the air, and it was a great reminder that you can see forever when there's no smog mucking up the sky. There was such pleasure in having clean, fresh air to breathe. There were so many parts of the trip where I felt like I was remembering things I already knew, but had forgotten from time to time. Like, say, that there were still vast swaths of country that were clean, well-kept, and relatively unpolluted.

After we got to the orchard, we looked around for a while before finally spotting Mr. Wrenn. He was driving a tan truck down towards us when we flagged him down. "I hear you boys have been looking for me," he yelled, sitting in his truck with his engine still running.

"Yes, sir, we have," said Steve. "Could you use three more hard workers? We could use the money."

"Sure I could. Pays $2.50 an hour and we have a good mother of hard work ahead. You can start tomorrow morning at seven thirty and we work till four thirty. How'd you find out about the job?"

"We spent the night at Floyd Gerundo's campground and asked her if she knew anyone looking for help. She told us about your ad in the paper and told us to tell you she sent us here," said Steve.

"Good old Floyd," he said. "Nice lady. Okay, boys, see you in the morning."

"Thanks, Mr. Wrenn," we said while waving goodbye. We'd met "Good Old Pete" the night before, but it was getting easy to picture everyone in Virginia being called "Good old somebody" by everyone else. Steve looked at me with a grin, and I knew what he was thinking—we were going to have some extra money in our pockets and it made us feel invincible. "Lay five on me," said Steve, and he slapped his hand down on ours. "Alright, we got a job! Now let's go play some tennis and eat lunch."

"Right, and I'll call Lynnie and tonight we'll really celebrate," I said.

Tom clocked the orchard to be only an enjoyable thirteen-mile ride from the Madison College tennis courts and the college girls.

After tennis and lunch, I went to call Lynnie while Steve and Tom walked to the college library to relax, read, and write in the daily journals they'd started on September 8. I was all smiles when I came back.

"It's all set and better than we figured," I said. "She's cooking a big spaghetti dinner for us and I spoke with her two gorgeous-sounding friends on the phone. They're helping her cook and are as psyched up as we are about tonight." It all felt unbelievable. We were living in good country air, we had a temporary job that was going to be a lot cleaner that most of the other things we might have found, we were near a college with plenty of girls, the weather was right, and we were going to party all night with a free dinner. "I must be dreaming! Pinch me!" I yelled.

Steve reached out to pinch me, and I slapped his hand away.

"What time did they say to come over?" said Tom.

"About six thirty," I said. "It's four o'clock now, so we'll leave here by six. That'll give us time to spare."

With that, I put my feet up and read for a while. As the hour of six drew nigh, I finished a page and closed the book. "Finish up what you are doing so we can be at the bikes and ready to go by six." We were on the road within minutes, cruising to three gorgeous girls who were preparing dinner, our heads whirling with dreams of snuggling up to beautiful women in front of a nice warm fireplace, and sipping wine after dinner. Every mile brought us closer to the fantasy.

When we finally arrived, Tom and Steve started to calculate some probabilities about Lynnie's two friends, whom they hadn't seen yet.

"Steve," said Tom, "since Lynnie is pretty, her two friends have to be good-looking, don't they?"

Steve nodded. "Yeah," he said, treating the idea that one pretty girl must necessarily only have pretty friends is something as simple as arithmetic. Steve kept chewing his gum and watching the house, looking for signs of life, signs of beauty, or both. And honestly, there's not much difference between beauty and life.

"And Mark said they were gorgeous-sounding on the phone," said Steve.

"Well, yeah," I said. "But you know . . . that's not a promise; it's just a *sound*. But look, quit worrying about it. You'll find out one way or another. Let's go. That's Lynnie's car parked in the garage."

An outside porch light flicked on, lighting the way to the back entrance. I took the lead and strolled out into the light, helmet in hand. Tom and Steve follow closely behind. Lynnie popped out and greeted me before I could knock on the door. "Come in, guys. Dinner's almost ready. Let me take your coats; you can leave your helmets here or bring them in with you."

I looked into Lynnie's blue eyes and handed her my coat. I'm rarely at a loss for words, but she was a stunner and I could only manage to say, "Okay."

"Hey, you guys look cold," she said.

All three of us started laughing, and then Tom explained what it was like to ride a motorcycle in fifty-degree weather, speeding here at sixty miles per hour. "The speed produces a wind chill factor and lowers the riding temperature ten degrees further. After twelve miles of that, the cold starts to seep into your bones," he said, handing his jacket to Lynnie. "We're lucky we survived at all, but that's how desperate we were to get here," he said with a wink. "We're very courageous."

"I heard the weather report for tonight and it's supposed to go down in the thirties," I said. "That means frost on the ground in the morning. Tom's right. We're very, very brave."

Lynnie laughed. "Well, I'm glad to have such devoted heroes at my beck and call. We have the fireplace going in the living room to keep us warm," she said with a flirty smile. "Now come meet my friends."

Lynnie led us into the living room. We felt the delicious warmth from the roaring fire at the doorway as we entered. "Girls," said Lynnie, "I would like to present to you, the Marx Brothers, Groucho, Chico, and Harpo. These guys are too much." She turned to us, "Guys, meet Diana and Jackie."

After Lynnie's introductions, we took a step closer to the fire, and reintroduced ourselves.

"It's a splendid fire, girls," said Tom. "Well done."

"Thanks," said Diana. "You either learn how to make a fire or you freeze. The fireplaces are the only way to heat this old house."

"It certainly makes things cozier," I said. It wasn't a subtle hint, but so far there wasn't much reason to think that subtlety would be necessary.

But Tom and Steve weren't in the mood for things to get cozier as they studied their dates for the night. It wasn't so much that they weren't as pretty as Lynnie, but next to her, their appearances and demeanor were way more boyish. Lynnie and I couldn't have hit it off better, though. She was spunky and full of laughs. And since I never seemed to run out of things to say or jokes to crack, she was eating it up.

For Tom and Steve, however, the evening ended up as a wrestling match and a toss-up. It wasn't long before they both conceded that romance was not in the offing. But to salvage the evening, Tom and Steve gave in to the two girls' demands and armwrestled them for some imaginary championship.

I knew they were trying to put a good face on things, but while they spent a romantic night armwrestling with two tomboys, I knew how jealous they were of me and Lynnie as we snuggled and gazed into the fire.

Before going to bed, Steve looked around to make sure no one else was listening, and said, "So much for your theory on good-looking girls hanging out together, Tom." Tom rolled over without answering.

I don't know what they were thinking about as they tried to go to sleep, but I had apples on my mind. Our new, temporary profession would start bright and early in the morning.

Late to bed but early to rise into the freezing cold temperatures, Steve and I awoke at six thirty. "Man, it's freezing up here," said Steve. We hurried downstairs to try and warm up by the stove.

Tom was still asleep on the downstairs couch. "Hey, get up," we yelled. "Time to get up!"

Tom slowly got out of his bag to face the cold morning air. Lynnie and Diana were making coffee. Not having much time, we drank the hot coffee as quickly as we could handle and said our goodbyes. Our bikes had frost on them and our breath floated before us all the way to the orchard, although the bikes warmed up fast. The ride to Ruttles was freezing. Our gloves, insulated vests, long johns, jackets, and the bandanas over our mouths helped a little, but it almost felt like we might as well have been riding naked. The roads were barren, so it didn't take long to go the twenty miles to the orchard.

We pulled in at seven thirty and parked our bikes in a row of trees that had already been picked. "I'll go find Mr. Wrenn," Steve said, walking towards a group of men in the distance. Before he got there, an old gray-haired man wearing a baseball hat, blue jeans, and a gray work shirt stepped in front of him.

"Are you boys starting work today?"

"Yes, we are," said Steve.

In a voice nearly as deep as Darth Vader's, he said, "Well, come on then, I'll get you boys a picking sack. We can't have them apples setting on the trees for the birds to eat."

This was Bill Deavers, the foreman of the picking crew. He was sixty-four years old and as wild and wooly as they come, like a good-natured ruffian straight out of a Steinbeck novel. We'd see in the days ahead that there was no stopping Bill when he set his mind to doing a good hard day's work. You could pitch in and try to keep up, or you could get run over by him.

I had a hard time putting on the picking sack. It was similar to when Don Quixote was trying to put on his creaky old armor and couldn't figure it out at first. For some reason, I couldn't get the straps that hold the sack on to cross correctly across my back. Finally, a worker saw me struggling and came over to help bring the comedy of errors to its conclusion. With the sack on correctly, I grabbed a picking ladder and walked over to a tree. Then, there was nothing to do but start picking. Simple, but not easy—big difference.

Despite the freezing morning ride, the day was perfect for picking apples: sunny and cool. It took us about an hour to get the hang of the job. It was monotonous and tough, but satisfying. The apples were on the tree, then they weren't, and you could see the difference you'd made. I was determined to make the most of the opportunity, and was aware the entire morning of how few young men our age were doing something like this, voluntarily. We were already deep into the day's adventure before many people even opened their eyes! Dreamers learn that you have to get out there and take risks, even if it occasionally turns the dream into a nightmare. When you put yourself in interesting spots, doors tend to open for you, and they're often doors that you didn't even know existed.

At noon, the workers left their sacks and ladders by the trees and went home for lunch. We stayed in the orchard, ate a few golden delicious apples, and then slept in the sun.

After lunch, Mr. Wrenn came to the orchard to work. When he saw that his three new workers hadn't left to eat, he offered us lunch at the little all-in-one post office, diner, and general store at the end of the road, on him. We thanked him for his offer but said that we couldn't take advantage of his generosity.

"I insist," Mr. Wrenn said, so we had a good lunch from that day on, every day that we worked. No matter what your intentions might be, when people like Mr. Wrenn start insisting on things, you find yourself persuaded. The man was a force of nature.

"You did a great job today," said Mr. Wrenn when our shift ended at four thirty. That was music to our ears, newcomers that we were. Bill walked over and joined us. Steve explained our trip to him and laid out some of the particulars—and particular challenges—before asking if we could pitch our tent in the orchard that night.

"Why don't you boys come on over to my house?" said Bill. He said it quickly, almost as if he'd be getting more out of it than we would. "I don't have much, but it's better than sleeping in a tent. You can do your cooking there too."

While we mulled the offer, he started walking away. "Well, you let me know, boys; I can't sit around all day. Got chores to do."

When Bill was out of earshot, Mr. Wrenn waved us over. "Listen, boys. Bill's wife passed away not too long ago, and between us, he could use some company out there on his farm."

Well, that was enough for me. "I think we should go live with Bill for a while and do the cooking and cleaning or whatever he needs to be done," I said to Tom and Steve. "After all the nice things the people have done for us on this trip, it's our turn to do a good deed."

Steve liked the idea, but Tom wasn't sold. "That's really going to restrict us," he said. "Do you want to play tennis and socialize and do whatever we want, or this?" I didn't think he was wrong, exactly, but it *was* the wrong way for him to look at it. Sometimes the best thing you can do is forget about yourself, and there's no better way to do that than to help someone out.

"There's no downside to service," I said. It might not have been the most convenient thing, but I knew I was right and there was no way around it. Tom still wasn't convinced. "Well," I said, "we're going to Bill's for supper. You can do what you like, and we'll meet you here in the morning." Tom deliberated as Steve and I got ready for the ride, fighting some private, low-stakes war inside himself, and then agreed to come with us.

Bill's farm was only a mile from the apple orchard. It was a simple place. There was a small white four-room house in the middle of his land. There was a barn in front, with a collection of junked tractor parts scattered around the front of the house. Chickens, dogs, cats, and roosters ran loose in the yard and there were cattle a ways off to the left. It was a regular menagerie, rustic and quirky and full of charm.

Given what I'd seen of Bill, it was no surprise that the inside of the house was furnished with life's bare essentials. There were potbelly wood stoves in the bedroom and the living room, which were always burning to combat the chill. Back home when we got cold, all we had to do was turn on the thermostat. Out here, splitting wood was a necessity just to stay warm, and it would be part of our daily duties while we were with Bill. It's never a bad thing to be reminded that not everyone has it easy. Hell, Bill had only had an indoor toilet for the past two years. Otherwise, we'd have been running to the outhouse every time nature called.

That night, we cooked and then sat down to a good steak dinner. Bill was happy to see that we could cook so well. My entire life, I've never gotten tired of feeling useful. That night, realizing it again felt like another of those things that I felt like I was remembering, rather than learning for the first time. We were really doing this. We could cook, travel, take care of ourselves, find jobs, and didn't have to depend on anyone but ourselves. It was an intoxicating freedom. After dinner, Bill went into the living room to read while we cleaned up the kitchen.

"I guess he was used to his wife doing all the work," I said, bemused.

"What do you mean?" said Steve.

"Well, he just got up and left the table to go read without pitching in to help. Oh well, that's what we're here for."

After cleaning up the dishes, we three cooks went into the living room to chat with Bill. "Hey, Bill, how many heads of cattle do you have?" I said.

"Only about six or seven. I used to have a lot more when I was younger." Then he got to talking about the old days and how he had a bigger farm and still did a day's work for Mr. Wrenn. Bill could really turn a phrase and tell a folksy story. "Years ago, people used to eat in and shit out; now all they want to do is eat out and shit in." It was a hoot to hear someone rhapsodize nostalgically about the outhouse days. When we were talked out, everyone grabbed a piece of the newspaper and sat back for a relaxing evening of reading.

At nine, Bill got up with a groan. "Well, boys, time to go to bed. We got to get up early in the morning. There are a lot of apples still to be picked."

"Well, we're going to stay up for a while and read, if that's okay," said Tom.

"Sure, sure, but don't stay up too late. Everyone has to be up at five thirty," Bill said.

"Why five thirty in the morning? Isn't that kind of early?" I said in a voice that probably had some panic in it. I wasn't backing out of my desire to do a good deed, but it's hard to feel like a good Samaritan at five thirty in the morning! We were tripping all over ourselves trying to get an explanation for rising at such an unholy hour.

"We have to feed the animals, eat breakfast, and be to work by seven, so we can be ready to work at seven thirty," he said.

Shell-shocked, I said, "Okay, we'll be up. Good night, Bill."

Just before calling it quits for the night, I said, "I've been sitting here for an hour and only counted two cars go by. This is a beautiful, peaceful place."

There are things you can only see in hindsight. When I look around today, so many people have lost the ability to sit in solitude. They can't handle being alone. And the beautiful stillness of Bill's land would have felt like isolation to them, particularly if deprived of their smartphones. Something gets lost when we can't simply sit and be content with our own company.

To bed, then.

The night went by at an unfairly rapid pace. "Okay, up and at 'em!" shouted Bill when the gruesome hour arrived. Grumbling, we rolled out of our sleeping bags, which we'd slept in on the big double bed in the room next to Bill's. Steve had slept in his bag on the couch in the living room.

Our eyes were barely even open, but we started getting dressed to go out and feed the animals with Bill. Our poor muscles were so sore and stiff from their first day's work on the apple farm. We'd been up to the challenge, but it didn't mean our bodies were used to it yet. They protested and creaked and rebelled as we tried to get moving and start feeling human again.

Once the animals were fed, we came in for breakfast and got ready to leave for work. Bill was nearly out the door. "You boys lock up the house and leave the key under the pail over by the well. I'll see you at work. Don't be late. We got a lot of picking to do."

As if we could forget. But I wasn't dreading it, and I knew that I'd have some energy once we got to the orchard.

It was another good day for picking apples—clear and brisk—and this time, once we were warmed up, the job didn't seem as hard. "Hey, guys, look. I got this picking sack on all by myself at the first try. Not bad, huh?" I said, like a kid asking his teacher for a gold star.

"Yeah, that's super," said Tom. "Just grab a ladder and start picking." His mood was a bit darker than my own, the tone of his voice saying, "Beware of the man who woke up at five thirty to feed animals against his will."

"Okay, okay, grouch," I said, as I took a ladder over to the base of a tree.

One hour into the day's work and all of a sudden, a loud bellowing scream made everyone look down to the last tree in the row. The bellower was me, because there I was, sliding down my ladder, ass first, from the top of the tree. *Crash!* I hit the ground hard enough to rattle my teeth. Apples spilled out of my sack, and the ladder fell to the ground.

Everyone rushed over to check on me. "Are you alright?" asked Bill.

"Yeah, yeah, I'm okay. That branch up there let go on me," I said, more embarrassed than hurt. I looked at the ladder. Frankly, I'm not sure how I *didn't* get hurt.

"Okay, everyone get back to work. Didn't you ever see anyone fall out of a tree before?" shouted Bill. Of course, many people probably *hadn't* seen someone fall out of a tree, but most people had never picked in an orchard, either. Tom and Steve waited until everyone else left, and then asked me if I was actually okay. I was. "Nothing wounded but my pride," I said.

At noon, we drove down to the little store for lunch. The lady behind the counter took our orders and cooked them right away, knowing we had to hurry to get back to the job. She helped Virginia keep its streak of everyone being completely warm and friendly at 100 percent.

The afternoon shift seemed to go by slowly, so every now and then, we'd take a short break to munch on an apple. But that was no problem because Mr. Wrenn was one of the best bosses in history. You had to work hard, but he wasn't a whipcracker. You weren't ever going to look up and catch him glaring at you with murder in his eyes just because you'd taken five seconds to wipe your brow. He was always smiling, forever soft-spoken.

Later, we were all carefully working the same tree, when Mr. Acrobatics did his thing again. With a sudden crack, the branch that my ladder was leaning against let go. Down I went, again, "*Ohooo*," right through the center of the tree. One worker tried to grab me as I fell, but he missed. Just before I hit the ground, I caught a branch with my right arm and held on. With a little help from my friends, I was out of trouble and out of the tree. "Man, it happened so fast, I almost couldn't react," I said.

"What are you trying to do, kill yourself today?" Steve said.

"No, it must not be my day."

Steve raised an eyebrow, apparently unconvinced that I wasn't trying to commit suicide by apple tree.

I looked up. "Man, those branches look perfectly safe and then, bang, they let go and let go fast. There's no cracking sound to warn me that the branch can't hold the weight," I said, rubbing my arm. "It's fine and then . . . it's not."

But we got right back at it. I thought more than once that day that there were people who didn't get to make excuses, people who did their jobs because to leave them undone meant to go without food, or shelter, for themselves and their family. I got back into the tree after falling twice, while fully aware that there were people who wouldn't even be able to complete a day's work of apple picking even *without* falling. Bill and Mr. Wrenn had done this for so long, and that's just the way it was. No one gave them anything; they just did what had to be done. And it inspired me.

When our work was over for the day, we followed Bill to a small store. It was two miles west of the farm and looked like an old one-room shack with a few cars parked in front on the dirt driveway. Inside, the first thing we saw was a big old potbelly stove right in the middle of the room. To the left were a few men sitting on a bench, talking to pass the time. Behind the counter was a little gray-haired lady. The store had probably been there for many years and served the few people who lived in the area. These small country stores carried a little of everything. It didn't take long before I called Steve and Tom over. "Look at this box of vanilla wafers," I whispered. "You have to scrape off the dust just to read the name."

"Just buy what we need and no more," said Tom. "Things probably don't move too fast in this store." We bought what we needed and thanked the lady. Bill said bye to everyone, and we left for the farm.

Again, we cooked supper and then sat and told jokes and relaxed after a hard day's work. It was a grueling business, but it felt good to know we were capable of it, just like Bill and Mr. Wrenn. The line between inspiration and intimidation can be a fine one, but when I looked at Bill and thought, *I can work as hard as you and I'm proving it*, it just made me want to do better and better.

Saturday, September 25, was only a half day at work. We took the spare time to go to a laundromat in Harrisonburg. No matter how great the adventure was, life was also still made of small chores and practical necessities, like having clean clothes and not smelling like a pigsty. Bill probably wouldn't have complained about our smell, but we had to maintain a *little* self-respect when it came to our hygiene.

That evening, after dinner, Tom and I stayed in the Student Center at Madison College reading, writing letters, and watching some TV. Steve was watching TV in a girls' dorm near the center of the school. After a while I wandered around the lobby and saw a notice on the school bulletin board. I called Tom over. "There's a party on Route 42, a mile from the school," I said. "Only two bucks for all the beer you can drink. Sounds pretty good."

"Okay, let's check with Steve to see if he wants to come." We walked over to Hoffman, the girls' dorm where Steve was sprawled out on the couch watching Kojak.

"Hey Steve, we're going to a party. Want to come?" asked Tom.

"Where's the party?"

"On Route 42 South, a mile from here."

"Nah, I think I'll stay here with Cathy," he said, pointing to a girl on the recliner chair nearby. "She needs some company."

We got the idea. "Well," I said, "we'll see you in the morning. Nice meeting you, Cathy."

We drove to the party and parked our bikes in the vacant lot of a hamburger joint. There were girls and guys everywhere. Outside, inside, upstairs, downstairs, wherever you looked, there were people, packed in like sardines looking for a good time. We walked around and socialized but, most importantly, made sure we got our two dollars worth of beer. I was walking through a doorway when someone recognized me.

"Hey, Mr. Racquetball!" called out a voice.

I looked around, and then recognized a friend I'd met at Madison College two years ago. We had, indeed, played a few games together. "Hi John, how have you been? Are you still playing racquetball?"

"Sure am. What are you doing down here?" he said.

"My friends and I came down to visit a couple of girls we knew here, but we found out they had graduated."

"Well, I have to catch up with my girl. Take care, Mark," smiled John as he ran off.

"Okay, nice seeing you," I said, waving at his back. It wasn't the most stimulating conversation of all time, but I guess they can't all be. But the dull conversation had a stimulating result. A blonde girl who'd been standing nearby had overheard us. She came over and said, "Do you play racquetball?"

"Yup, just a little," I said.

Her name was Susie. "How about playing a match sometime?" she asked.

Oh yeah, I didn't need any more encouragement than that. "Sure, I'd love to. Do you want my number so you can get in touch with me?"

I gave her my phone number and went off to find Tom. It was getting late. I didn't want to admit it, but we'd both had a few too many beers to ride our bikes back to the college. After I found him, we headed back to our bikes anyway. I was feeling sleepy enough to sit on the curb next to Tom's bike. Then I lay down on the curb because I couldn't keep my eyes open. "Look out!" I heard Tom yell, as if from a great distance.

I awoke just in time to see a Honda motorcycle falling towards me. If trees and ladders weren't trying to kill me, it was a motorcycle. The whole world had become a death trap. I rolled away like a ninja and managed to avoid getting my head squashed. Tom, no soberer than I, had been trying to move his bike around to the back of the building. But once he got it off its kickstand, he was too tipsy to handle it and that's when gravity had sent it hurtling in my direction.

With the invincible bravado of youth, we stood there and laughed about the close call, how drunk we were, and the ridiculousness of the situation. I helped Tom pick his bike up, and then we managed to roll our Hondas around the back of the building and prop them up.

After arguing about whether to sleep on the concrete or the hot top, the concrete won because it was dryer. We two drunks walked to the side of the building, rolled out our bags, put our wool caps on, and slurred goodnights to each other.

Meanwhile, the party was still going on. Say whatever you want about college life, but if it's anything, it's a party that's almost relentless.

I woke first on Sunday morning. "Tom, wake up. Let's get out of here. Look where we fell asleep last night. Man, we must have been drunk." It was a pretty sorry scene, the two of us lounging on the concrete, but I (and my mild headache) knew we'd had a good time.

Tom poked his head out of his bag enough to feel the cold, foggy morning. "What do you want?" he asked irritably.

"Come on, get up. We can't stay here. It's getting light and someone might see us and call the cops. And besides, this cement is too hard."

"All cement is hard, Mark. Settle down. I'll be right with you. Just give me a chance to open my eyes."

We packed our sleeping bags and drove downtown to a small diner. It was now six thirty in the morning, and we were in the throes of post-party recuperation. A middle-aged man sat next to me at the counter and ordered a beer.

I leaned over and whispered, "Tom, did that guy order what I think he did?"

"Yup, he sure did."

I got a funny feeling in my stomach as I watched the man drink his beer. "How can you drink beer so early in the morning, sir?" I couldn't help but ask.

"Oh, it's good for you. It settles your stomach," was all he said. Then he took another swallow.

Maybe he was an alien visitor and had a different gastrointestinal constitution than we earthlings, but you couldn't have paid me to drink another beer that morning.

Pondering the mystery, we ate the eggs we'd ordered for breakfast and drove back to the college campus. We played some tennis and felt our bodies come back to life. Later that afternoon, we found Steve in the student lounge watching a football game on the super-screen television.

"Steve, who's playing?" asked Tom as we walked over and sat down.

"The New England Patriots and the Buffalo Bills, and the Patriots are killing them!" We spent that afternoon watching football and only left to get a bite to eat at the school snack bar. Honestly, we weren't capable of much else.

Around nine, I realized that we needed to check in with Bill. I called him from a payphone in the lobby. "Hello Bill, this is Mark. Is it alright if we come over?"

"Sure it's alright, but don't get here too late," he said.

"We'll be there in half an hour," I said.

We got our bikes and drove out to Bill's place, stopping on the way to buy some ice cream for him. The country roads in Virginia are unlit and, at times, very narrow. The two-lane roadways are usually full of curves and rolling hills, with beautiful sights of open farms and cattle land on each side of the road. They're fun to drive on, but if you break down, forget it; you could be there until the next morning before someone passes you.

Monday morning was a dark, drizzling day, but we went to work anyway. But by nine it was too wet to work, so Mr. Wrenn called it a day. "See you all tomorrow," he said. "It's too wet and someone might get hurt." Ha! Not that I'd managed to stay safe when it was dry, but I wasn't complaining.

We spent the whole day reading and splitting wood for the stove. After supper, one of Bill's old friends came over and they played cards and ate popcorn.

The next two days were regular work days without rain and nothing special happening. I even managed to avoid falling out of trees.

On Wednesday night, I called Susie, the girl I met at the party, and asked her if she wanted to play racquetball. I told her I was bringing Tom as well.

"No problem. See you at seven," she said.

I hung up. "Come on, Tom, let's go change and take off in half an hour," I said.

"No, that's okay. You go play with her. I'll only get in the way. Three's a crowd, remember?" said Tom.

"Hey, don't talk silly," I said. "I don't mind if you come and I'm sure we'll have a good time. Besides, she must have some friends. Hey, where's Steve?"

"He's over at that girl's dorm watching television with Cathy."

"Well, he's all set. Let's get down to the gym," I said.

After one good hour of racquetball, Susie, Tom, and I went back to her dorm to chat and meet her suitemates. It was an all-girls dorm and all males had to be out by midnight, so we were determined to make the most of the time we had.

"Hi, girls!" said Susie excitedly. "I brought home a couple of good-looking guys. This is Tom and Mark. You girls introduce yourselves."

We all sat and talked until the Resident Assistant came in and told us we'd have to leave. Susie called her friend Jon, who lived in a guys' dorm. Jon said it would be alright if we slept there, so after Susie gave us directions, we ended up unrolling our sleeping bags on a lounge floor in the guys' dorm.

The next morning, we woke up at six thirty and found it was pouring rain. "Well, we might as well forget work today," I said with a sigh.

"Good," said Tom. "I didn't feel like working today anyways. Let's get some more sleep."

It rained all day Thursday as well. We puttered around and hung out with the girls. By Friday it was still pouring. But even though the day started slowly, it ended with a bang as we found ourselves at a college mixer.

"Debbie, come on, let's dance," I said to a pretty girl shortly after arriving. "Steve, get Carol and get her out here. You too, Tom. I'm sure Heather would like to dance." I shouted my commands while I spun Debbie around, like I'd been made the Prime Minister of Making Everyone Boogie.

The dance floor was really crowded, and it was hard to move without bumping someone. The rain outside had cranked the humidity indoors up by about a million.

"Steve, I'm soaked!" I said when we passed each other on the dance floor.

"Yeah, I'm sweating, but it doesn't bother me as much as this big oaf dancing behind me," said Steve. "He's not watching where he's dancing and keeps smacking into us. He already crushed Carol's foot and caught me in the head with a couple of his elbows which are swinging all over."

I could feel something starting. "Well, move over towards us."

"It doesn't matter," said Steve. "He seems to follow the vacant spots we leave."

Towards the end of the dance, Steve moved down to the guy and asked him to take it easy. He was respectful. The oaf was not. "Hey, you hippie punk," he said, grabbing Steve by the front of his shirt. "Don't tell me what to do. Go find another spot to dance, you jerk."

Without saying a word, Steve reached downtown and brought up a left hook into the guy's big potato of a nose, knocking him back into the other dancers. The guy hadn't had enough and charged at Steve with his head down. Steve quickly grabbed his head and brought a knee to the guy's face, which drew blood. Before Steve realized what was happening, two guys jumped him and started whipping the hell out of him.

"Tom, come on!" I yelled. *Oh man, here we go.*

Tom saw what was happening, and together we pushed our way through the crowd. Each of us grabbed a guy and pulled him off of Steve. Tom took his man by the arm, swung him to the floor, and dove on him, punching away. The other guy was slightly bigger than me, but I grabbed him anyway, yanking him by the hair and pulling him off Steve. Before the dude knew what was happening, he had a combination left and right fist to the face, which left him with a front tooth knocked out. He had it coming. Attacking one of my friends is no different than attacking me.

"Mark, behind you!" yelled Steve.

I spun around just in time to grasp the guy's hand, which was about to connect with the small of my back. I flipped him to the floor with a thud. By now, the whole place was fighting, just like in a movie: guys swinging away at each other and girls screaming and trying to get out of the way. Tom stopped brawling for a moment and ran to where Steve was brutally choking a guy on the floor.

"We better get out of here before the cops come or we get hurt. This place has gone crazy," said Tom.

"Where's Mark?" asked Steve, dropping the kid. They both looked around and then saw me on top of a guy on the floor.

"Come on Mark, let go of his arm, you just broke it. We're getting out of here", said Tom.

Just then, the campus security team, wearing helmets and carrying big sticks, broke into the crowd and started hauling kids away. We made our way to a side door where there were only two guards. While the guards were busy breaking up the fight, we swiftly sneaked out the door and ran all the way back over the hill to Sue's dorm. Once we got upstairs, we knocked on the girls' door.

"Hey, it's us. Let us in," I said in between puffs. Debbie opened the door and was visibly shocked to see that we'd all made it back in one piece.

"Come in," she said. "Are you guys all right? We couldn't find you in the crowd, so we came back here before we got hurt."

Susie called out, "Why did you guys fight?"

"It wasn't us," said Steve. "This dude was dancing too rough and got offended and grabbed me when I asked him to take it easy."

"They ganged up on Steve, so that's when Mark and I stepped in," said Tom. "The next thing we knew, the whole place was fighting."

"Look at you guys," said Heather. "Tom, you and Steve have good-size cuts over your eyes. And Mark, your upper lip couldn't get any bigger."

I'd take any number of fat lips before I'd let someone rough up a friend without helping.

On Saturday, next day, no one got up before eleven thirty. The rain was still coming down as heavy as ever. It was a day for recovery. The rain kept everyone in watching TV and relaxing. That night, the girls had a little party on their floor. We got to stay past midnight because we were quiet and the RA didn't know we were still there. But at two thirty in the morning, Tom and Steve started getting silly with a couple of the girls and making a lot of noise. I was in another room partying and putting the moves on Debbie.

We made enough noise that the RA, who was an upperclassman, knocked on the door and walked in. "Okay, girls, let's get the guys out of here," she said. "You know the rules, and if you were quiet, I wouldn't be here. But you blew it and now I have to do my job."

We got dressed and walked out, really angry at the RA. Of course, we weren't mad at ourselves for being noisy; it was just easier to blame someone else for ruining our good time. Self-awareness can be hard to maintain in the middle of a party. We headed for the guys' dorm once again. Tom and Steve knew I was mad at them for getting them kicked out of the girls' dorm, especially since I'd been so far along with Debbie, but they knew better than to talk to me about it.

Sunday morning was cloudy, but no rain—finally! Steve got up first and looked out one of the tall dorm windows. "Hey guys, wake up. It's ten thirty and I'm hungry."

While we were eating, Steve asked why I was being so quiet, as if he didn't know. "Are you mad at us for last night, Mark? It wasn't our fault."

"Then whose fault was it?" I said. "I told you guys to cool it twice, but no, you had to keep fooling around until you got us kicked out." Yeah, I was mad, but I didn't want to stay mad. That never did any good. "Let's forget it and eat breakfast. Talking about it isn't going to help."

When we went back to the dorm, all the girls were sitting in the lounge. "Debbie, have you got anything to do? How about going for a bike ride to the West Virginia line?" I asked.

With a big smile, she jumped to her feet and got her jacket. She ran past me, saying, "I'll beat you to your bike."

We raced down the sidewalk to the parking lot where the bikes were. "I hope it starts. It's been sitting out here for three days in the rain," I said. But there was no problem. I started the engine and let it warm up for a couple of minutes. Then Debbie climbed on behind me, and we took off for a long country ride.

After supper, we went with the girls from Suite 6 to see Jeremiah Johnson at the student center. Later that night, around midnight, the guys said their goodnights and walked over to the guys' dorm to sleep. Before we turned in, we rehashed the week. There had been more packed into those seven days than possibly any other week any of us had lived.

And we were just getting started.

# CHAPTER FIVE:
# The Celebrities

October 4 was a cloudy Monday in Virginia. We got up at eight and prepared to head to Knoxville. We hadn't gotten anything like enough sleep, and it showed in our drowsy zombie trudge as we left the dorm where we had spent the night.

"Let's go get our gear," I said to the guys. Most of our stuff was still in the girls' suite. After scaling two flights of stairs, which felt more like Everest in our sleepy condition, we found Diana and Marsha cramming for an American History exam that was only about two hours away. We let them drill their questions while we gathered our things.

"I want to get a picture of you three guys before you go," said Diana.

I sat on the floor, with Tom and Steve sitting behind me on the couch, their helmets displayed proudly in their hands like the skulls of vanquished foes.

"Okay, you three bums," she said, "I got you on film."

We headed out to the orchard once more to say goodbye to Bill and Mr. Wrenn. They were two of the most upstanding men I'd ever met and I wouldn't have felt right about not seeing them one last time. It took us twenty miles off course, but I wanted to shake their hands and let them know they'd done right by us.

When we got to Singers Glenn, Mr. Wrenn spotted our headlights driving down the dirt road leading into the orchard and waved to us from his tree.

We parked next to where the men were picking and got off the bikes. "Hi boys!" called Mr. Wrenn from his perch up high. "Come back to help pick some more of these golden delicious apples of mine?"

"Well, no, Mr. Wrenn," I said. "We came to say goodbye."

"And to say thanks to you and Bill for everything you've done for us three," said Tom.

"We'd appreciate it a great deal if we could get a picture of you and Bill posing on the ladder picking apples," said Steve. "And we'd love a picture of you alongside us."

"Where is Bill?" I asked.

"Well, he was just here pruning those lower branches," said Mr. Wrenn with a puzzled expression.

Bill's voice boomed out. "Well, here I am, by golly! I thought you boys would be long gone into West Virginia by now." He smiled, but there was sadness in his voice, like he was trying to be overly cheerful. I could tell he didn't like the idea of us leaving. We'd been good workers, but we'd also been good company for a lonely man. Sometimes you can forget you're lonely until you have company, and when the company leaves, they can leave you lonely all over again. "By gosh, if you all need a place to stay, you know you're welcome. I even have a couple dozen eggs for you three this morning. I just need to cook them up for us all."

"Bill," said Steve, "we'd like to, but we don't want to run into Old Man Winter. It's not like we've got the convenience of a heated car on this trip. But we never want to forget you two," he added. "Bill, can you climb up on that ladder and pose?" He gestured with his camera. While he focused his lens, Tom and I sneaked around back and under the ladder as Bill positioned himself on a large branch.

"Okay, you two, look this way and give me a big Virginian smile while you put an apple in the half-bushel basket," said Steve when he almost had the lens in focus.

Tom and I were now in position. Tom took hold of Bill's ladder, and I grabbed Mr. Wrenn's. We gave Steve the ready signal and then gave the ladders a good shake. Bill and Mr. Wrenn, unaware that we'd sneaked behind them, grabbed their suddenly shaking ladders and looked down to make sure they were safe. As soon as they saw us, they pointed and smiled at us, and that's when Steve snapped the picture .

"Okay, I got it!" said Steve. "Great! That's one way of getting you two both smiling at the same time. That'll add some character to the picture."

Mr. Wrenn gave us a bag of apples and then we were off and rolling by midday, heading towards the glories of West Virginia, the land of lovely mountains, kind people, and gorgeous scenery.

With half the day gone already, we had to make serious time to get through West Virginia by nightfall. After a few stops for gas, we finally passed the border. According to my watch it was three thirty in the afternoon. Up ahead were spacious clearings, enormous skies, and majestic, purple mountains, just like someone had written in the song.

West Virginia is a mountain man country. To make it out there in those peaks, you'd have to be as tough as a grizzly bear. In the winter months, the chilling winds in the icy wilderness could have driven a normal man crazy with fear and frigidity. But while that normal man would be afraid of dying in the harsh environment, the mountain man could survive even the worst winter storm. It was fun to think about how I'd cut it if I tried to make it through a winter out here on my own. I can't say I was planning on trying it, but it's fun to measure yourself against people who have qualities that you admire.

We made it to a cozy restaurant in White Sulphur Springs that any self-respecting mountain man would have scoffed at, but we weren't complaining. I guess we weren't any self-respecting mountain men. While Steve cut into some pork chops, Tom and I talked about something Mr. Wrenn had said we should see while we were here.

"It is called Greenbrier," I said while staring at a waitress. "It's supposed to be a rich resort hotel with three golf courses, tennis courts, very big and classy." I raised my hand. "Excuse me," I said when the waitress passed, "could you tell us where the Greenbrier Resort Hotel is located? We just rode into town and need a good hotel room for the night."

She looked skeptical. "You guys must be strangers. You have to be an invited guest or a member of a large convention to stay there, sugar. I mean, money has to be your first, middle, and last initials. See that large picture hanging over there on the wall?" She pointed to a three-foot long colorful painting of a large estate. "There is everything a person could want there. I guess you could call it a rich man's paradise out here in the sticks and mountains of West Virginia."

That sounded like something worth seeing. It wasn't that far from the restaurant, so after thanking her and finishing the meal, we headed out to see what all the fuss was about.

A guard let us walk through the front gate and stroll through the grounds. We took a few pictures. But in our jeans, heavy woolen shirts, and desperate need of a thorough shower, we stuck out like weeds in a bouquet of roses.

What a place.

Greenbrier Resort Hotel was equipped and ready for any emergency. That place could fulfill any man or woman's desire. For the twelve hundred guests, they had twelve full-time doctors, a fire station, security, police, a barber shop, beauty salon, plenty of clothing and jewelry stores, places where you could rent tuxedos and evening gowns, photography shops, and a nursery for young children so mom and dad could play tennis on one of the twenty clay courts or golf on one of the three golf courses. There was also platform tennis, Olympic-style pools, horseback riding, flying, and not to mention the evening format with dining and dancing pleasures. Live entertainment was regularly flown in from Hollywood and Vegas.

Some people called it the Garden of Eden. You could certainly do worse for a name.

Just inside the front entrance, a glittering chandelier hung from the ceiling. It must have cost $5000 on its own.

There were stairs leading down and stairs running up, all decked with different colors of plush carpeting. Now I saw that there were actually a few people dressed more casually. Some of them were in tennis outfits, but there were also a lot of elegant people engaging in some very formal prancing about the hallways. They passed by us without even noticing our stares. For all I know, they were so used to being stared at that they expected it. Or maybe they thought we were on the help staff and were trying to pretend we weren't there.

A doorman was studying us with curious eyes. He didn't seem to love the idea of us being there, but I couldn't help looking back at him with the same sort of curiosity.

"Mark," said Tom, "I think that look means for us to go."

I thought he was right. "Steve," I said, grabbing his arm and breaking eye contact, "let's get out of here before that doorman asks us to leave." Me grabbing his arm broke his concentration, which was focused like a laser on a beautiful blonde.

"Okay, okay," he said. "I'm going." He grinned. "This place isn't expensive enough for our taste anyway. Let's go."

"You're right," I said, wondering what taste even more expensive than this could possibly look like. "Let's find a place to settle in for the night. What do you say, Tom?"

"Right as always, gentlemen," he said. "Right this way to the limo, which will then take you two dignitaries to anywhere your heart desires. I do hope you enjoyed your visit."

Alas, there was nothing so posh ahead in our evening. We drove down Route 60 looking for potential spots to sleep when Steve noticed a guy in front of his home, working on a motorcycle. But we didn't know he'd seen the guy until we'd gone way past the man's house. Then Steve flicked on his blinker, and we pulled over to talk.

"Mark," he said, "remember what you said about asking a homeowner or farmer if we could pitch a tent on his land if we cleared out by morning? I think I saw a spot where that might work."

We went back and Steve made his pitch to the man while Tom and I waited.

"He was really nice," said Steve when he returned, "but he told me he's got some bulls running free on his field. He thinks that if they saw the tent they might destroy it."

*And us*, I thought, imagining being woken in the middle of the night and lifted into the air on some wild bull's horns, tossed up, silhouetted and screaming against the moon.

"He also said he's got a bunch of rattlesnakes in his backyard."

Well, it was as close to the opposite of Greenbrier as you could get. What else did he have on the premises that was lethal and just itching to take a crack at biting or goring or smashing us?

"So much for that idea," said Tom. "Did you ask him about a nearby state park or campground?"

"Yeah, he mentioned Greenbrier State Park. Said it's about six miles away and supposedly it'd be free for us as campers."

We decided to go check it out. If it looked good, we'd go eat and then bed down for the night.

The road into the state park was now pitch-black, lit only by our head-lights. The mountain tops were massive and jagged against the millions of stars that seemed impossibly bright. The road wound and bent ever deeper into the woodlands. When we finally reached the campsite, we killed the lights and motors and listened to the sounds of the night.

On the way in we'd passed a ranger. About two minutes later, he appeared to register us in his log and ask for the $3 fee for the site. So much for free camping. But we paid the money, signed the forms, and headed back out to a store for grub. After that, we were in bed by ten thirty, which was insanely early for us. But it had been a longer day than most, and when you're done, you're done.

The next morning I did some calculations. We'd been on the road for twenty-eight days. We spent the morning making breakfast, showering, and relaxing, and left the campsite by one fifteen that afternoon. The road took us through a tiny bit of Tennessee, but we were back in Virginia by four.

Off I-195, we saw a man washing his pickup truck outside of his house. We stopped to ask him where we could pitch a tent.

"How about the front lawn of my community church?" he said. "There's no meeting tonight so it's fine if you want to use it. Anyone bothers you, you tell them that Bert Parker said it was okay. Tell them you spoke with me and that should set them straight."

We thanked him and pulled up to the Cedar Bluff Community Church shortly after, hoping that the name Bert Parker would ring out with the authority he seemed to think it would. The church was a new, small brick building set up on a hill out of sight from all civilization. In the field below was a Virginia-style burial ground. Mortuaries, they called them. There were no tombstones marking the graves, just small bunches of flowers laid on the final resting places, or glowing candles encased in red glass, accentuating the graveyard with an eerie loveliness.

Now that we'd seen the place and knew it would work for us, as long as no ghosts bothered us in the night, we decided to go to a store to buy food. I noticed three older women checking us out in the market, but I didn't think much of it until they followed us into the gas station as well. After we filled the small gas containers we used for our stove, we left, but they pursued us out onto the road before pulling up alongside us and waving us down a side road to talk. We told them where we were camping and said they were welcome to come visit. There was no question of going to their places. Two of them were married, and the third had a sister who was staying the night. They said they'd see if they could sneak out later and they'd love to see us, but I wasn't anticipating that. Still, it was disappointing when they didn't show up.

The next day we passed into Tennessee at Kingsport, where the air was warm and the highway was dry. It looked like the only spot on earth where it hadn't yet rained, I thought. I flicked my right blinker, signaling to the guys that I wanted to pull off.

"Hey, you two," I said, "since the temperature has gone back up, if it's not going to rain we should take our jackets off and stow them. Let's save them when we can."

Cruising at a tranquil fifty-five miles per hour, we felt the warm breeze stir the bristles of our beards at every inch of that gentle country road. We were seventy-five miles from Knoxville—where Steve had a good friend named Bill Hanley who was attending the University of Tennessee—when I decided to stop before the next exit ramp.

"Why are we stopping here?" asked Tom.

"Didn't you guys see that road sign back there?" I said. "It said Davey Crockett Tavern next exit. This is the next exit. If you both want to move on, I'll meet you at UT, but there's no way I'm passing up the Davey Crockett Tavern."

"No, we'll all go," said Steve, "but if we find out that it's twenty miles inland from 81, it's getting pretty late, and if there's a good chance of rain, we'll have to turn back."

"I agree with Steve," said Tom.

"You're both forgetting the purpose of this trip," I said. "Even if it's twenty miles farther, we just traveled nine hundred miles, so why should we pass by it now? It might not even be twenty miles away!"

"Hey, we'll go, but we're wasting time arguing," said Tom. "Let's just ask someone at the next store for directions."

At the first gas station I saw, I went in and learned that we were only seven miles from Morristown, Tennessee. As we continued down the road I sang, "Davey, Davey Crockett, King of the Wild Frontier," at the top of my lungs.

When we got there, I took some pictures of Davey Crockett's house. The iconic King of the Wild Frontier had spent his childhood in a two-story four-room wooden house. An elderly woman in an old rocking chair was reading a book when we walked in and obviously surprised her. She jumped up and invited us in, just like I expected any Southerner to at that point. But she was into her sales pitch before I could even blink.

"Hello, boys," she said, "it's one dollar for the tour and next you sign your name to this register." She didn't even ask if we wanted to take the tour, and we were helpless to resist her. She went to the window and got a look at our motorcycles. "Where are you boys coming from?"

Before I could answer, a newlywed couple walked in for the tour.

"We're from Massachusetts," I said.

"That's a long way, isn't it now?" she said before turning her attention to the newlyweds. She told them the same thing she'd told us. Then she took us through the ninety-minute tour, which was an incredible length of time for such a small home. I knew that she must have given the tour so many times that her folksy sayings and jokes were probably watered down from their original form, but she knew her stuff. There wasn't a second during those ninety minutes when she was less than knowledgeable or charming. It had been well worth the small detour and minor argument with Steve and Tom.

The skies were filling up with clouds again when we left to get something to eat. Just after dinner, sure enough, it started to sprinkle. We put on our bright rain suits, covered our gear, and hit the highway. For thirty miles, the drizzle stopped and started in fits. Then it was like God reached out with his mighty hand and squeezed those clouds over our heads until they were bursting.

At least the air was warm. But over the next forty miles, we slowed down to thirty miles per hour. At four forty-five, it was already dark as night, like the dark rain clouds were a lid on the world that had shut out the sun. I finally pulled over to see how everyone was doing. My boots were so soaked that it was like I was wearing puddles on my feet, and I doubted that the guys were faring any better.

"Do you guys want to go the last ten miles or stop and wait out the storm?" I asked.

"Let's finish it," said Tom. "We'll just go slow and take our time. We'll still make it by seven fifteen or so. Besides, I don't think this is going to let up."

"Okay," said Steve, wiping the rain from his visor. "Then let's go. The sooner we start, the sooner we'll be standing in a hot shower."

The last thirty miles were brutal. It was bad enough for the roads to be slippery, but the rain dripping down our faces made our visibility terrible as well. With night falling fast, it was only going to get worse. Hydroplaning at that speed would have been like driving on the smoothest, glassiest ice. We had to be able to see, and since that wasn't happening, we crept along at the safest speeds our sanity could handle.

Those final miles were so tense and torturous that, when we finished, I felt like I'd been wrung out like a wet towel. Cars passing on the left never failed to drench us in a blinding cascade of dirty road spray. Trucks were even worse. Every time a truck needed to pass, we got into a single file line just to allow them to get ahead of us that much quicker. Then we realized that the single file formation was safest, and stuck with it. That way we wouldn't accidentally jostle each other, and could keep an eye on one another.

I never thought it would end, but we made it. Shivering, tense, exhausted, a bit the worse for wear, hands cramping from our white-knuckled grips on our handlebars, and possibly not at our sunniest dispositions, but we made it.

We drove to the student center at the University of Tennessee hoping to find Bill Hanley's address and phone number. We took off our rain suits and trotted into the student center in a symphony of squeaking boots that everyone noticed as we looked for a student directory. It was already seven thirty when Steve found Bill's information. He called him from a phone on the wall.

"He's going to go crazy when he hears that the three of us are here to visit him all the way from Massachusetts," said Steve as the phone rang. "He'll just shit."

I couldn't picture anything more absurd than someone shitting because he heard Steve's voice on a phone, but the image made me laugh.

"Hello?" said a voice on the other end.

"Yes, is Bill there?" said Steve, wiping sweat from his brow.

"No, he's out studying and I don't expect him back until at least ten. Can I take a message?"

Steve said no, that he wanted to surprise Bill and that he'd call back in a bit. He turned to us. "What do you guys want to do?" Ah, the eternal question of three young drifters on the road.

"There's a movie showing in the auditorium," I said. "We've got two hours to kill. Let's just walk in and watch it."

We walked into the movie during a loud scene, which was great, given that our wet boots were still squeaking. Tom and Steve noticed that it was a Disney movie: *Fantasia*. And it was almost over. The next one was another

Disney feature called *Island in the Sky*, which I'd never seen. We sat there and dried out and relaxed. It felt so good to not be in motion. Or cold. Or terrified about the storm. Or getting drenched by those stupid passing trucks. After the movie, Steve tried to call Bill again, but he still wasn't there. This time, Steve got directions to Bill's dorm, and we headed that way.

It had stopped raining by the time we got inside. We stopped at one more dorm for yet more directions and got sidetracked by some noise from a TV room.

"The presidential debate between President Ford and Jimmy Carter was on tonight," Tom whispered. Since we had yet more time to burn and there were a few seats available, we decided to sit down and finish the debate before trying Bill again. Finally, this time, Bill walked in just as the guy who answered the phone was telling Steve that he still wasn't back.

"Hello, Bill!" said Steve. I could hear some anxiety in his voice.

"Oh, great," said Bill. "I'm lousy at making someone's voice out over the phone."

"Oops," said Steve. "That doesn't sound like Bill Manley. Is this Bill Manley from Wayland, Massachusetts?"

At this point, Tom and I jumped up in bewilderment. Long story short, it was the right number, but the student directory we had consulted was a year old, so Bill Manley hadn't been there in who knows how long.

"Wait, your name is Bill, too?" said Steve, as if he couldn't believe there was another Bill in the world. Of course, it was a hell of a coincidence given the way it had all happened. "I've been trying to get in touch with him since seven thirty! Do you have any idea how I can?"

Mysterious Bill gave Steve the number for student information, and then the number for the Holt dormitory information desk, which is where we were. He said they might know if Steve's Bill was actually here but had just been shipped to another floor or room. That's all it took, and about three minutes later, Steve learned that Bill—Bill Manley—was in room 402 of that very dorm.

When Steve finally got him on the phone, Bill almost immediately said, "Why didn't you call earlier?" Steve laughed and told him the story. Bill wanted to go out for beers, which Steve agreed to immediately. Ten minutes later, Bill opened his door and saw not just Steve but all three of us. He grinned. "You guys are something else," he said, shaking his head.

That's how nearly everyone reacted to us. Like we were *something else*. I liked the sound of it, because that trip meant we were doing *something else*, something totally out of the ordinary.

We decided to go out for just one pitcher of beer at the local college tavern. Tired and beat, we changed out of our wet clothes and into our only other dry set. We replaced our wet boots with tennis shoes and went back out into the rain, prepared to drink with Bill, our tall, proud friend. But just one pitcher.

"Who knows?" whispered Steve. "We might all get a gorgeous Southern belle who's looking for a good ol' fashioned Yankee to tie up with tonight."

I'll drink to that. And of course, I did. We all did.

The next morning, we were passed out and felt nearly drowned from our late night of drinking and banging it up.

"Hey, get up, you three," said Bill. "I've already done a morning's worth of classes and here it is noon already and you guys are still laid out."

"Hey," said Tom, "I lost count after the sixth pitcher."

"Was it six?" said Bill. "That's way more than the one pitcher we talked about."

It sure as hell was. I tried to focus my eyes, with mixed results, but I saw well enough to find Bill and Tom looking at me, ready to smile at my agony.

"Welcome back to the twentieth century, you two," said Bill.

"What the hell time is it?" said Steve.

"A little past noon." Bill laughed.

That's when a guy named Jon walked in in his Jockey shorts with one eye open and one eye squinting. "Hey, everyone, what's going on?" Jon was one of the three guys Bill shared an apartment with. He talked like such a Southerner it was almost like he was doing a parody.

"You cut your nine o'clock class, did you, Jon?" said Bill.

"I cut my alarm clock off as fast as it went on," said Jon. "But it's no problem. I'll get the notes from this chick in class. Speaking of," he said, looking at Steve, "that was some nice little number you were talking with last night. Tell us about her."

"I think I'm in love," said Steve. "She was pretty, wasn't she? Soft. Lady like. Talked with a nice sexy voice. An old-fashioned country girl from Pulasku. I think I was dreaming about her. I had her cuddled up in my bag when Bill here interrupted. And the next thing I see is not Debbie, but four ugly faces staring down at me."

"What!" yelled Bill. "Pile on!"

Steve hid his head in his bag while the four of us obeyed Bill and piled on top of him. A pile-on was a time-honored pastime in fraternities. During pledge weeks, pretty much anything someone did who was trying to get into a frat resulted in a bone-crushing, breath-stealing pile-on. Bill was a frat boy and apparently liked to run his dorm room the same way, meting out severe punishments for the slightest infractions. When a pile-on was done just right, the man on the bottom would think he was suffocating. You got a sense for knowing when he needed to breathe, so you'd let up just a tiny bit to give him some air, but without relieving the crushing pressure on his bones and muscles. Finally, when he'd managed to scream that he couldn't breathe, everyone would roll to the side and let the poor sucker up, just like we finally did with Steve.

As he gasped, I walked to the window and saw that it was still raining.

"Okay, let's hurry up," said Bill. "I got you guys three meal tickets while you were sleeping."

After we ate, Bill told us where the racquetball courts were. He got us some rackets and balls with his ID, and we got in a couple of hours of exercise. At dinnertime, Bill produced another three meal tickets, and we ate until we were bursting. All that free food was hard to resist. "Bill," said Steve, "all the things we used to take for granted, like riding in a car or three meals a day, plenty of clothes to wear and girls everywhere, they're like luxury items to us now. And when we get them, we're grateful."

He was right. I felt like before the trip I only had the concept of gratitude in my head, without really knowing what it meant. The trip was teaching us what it was like to go without certain things. Everything that happened to us on the road was a lesson I wanted to remember. The journal I was keeping had never seemed like a better idea than it did right then.

"I'm going to give Debbie a call and see if she can get together tonight," said Steve. "What are you guys going to do?"

We decided to go back to the Falcon, the bar from the night before. Steve came with us after making arrangements to see Debbie at eleven thirty. She was taking a one-hour break from studying, and Steve was determined to make the most of it. When he asked Bill if it was all right to take Debbie to his apartment, Bill gave him the keys and said, "But don't get my sheets dirty."

"Ah, don't worry. We're only going to talk. Thanks for the keys."

Only going to talk. Uh-huh.

Two hours later, we made our way back to the apartment. Debbie and Steve, just leaving, greeted us at the door. "Hi guys. You remember Debbie, don't you? She's got to go study a bit more for an American Lit exam tomorrow."

When Steve returned from walking Debbie back to her dorm, we bombarded him with questions. Bill checked his bed and saw that, curiously, the sheets weren't even wrinkled. It turned out that just when Steve was about to take Debbie into Bill's room, Bill's roommate Will had walked in. He said hello and good night in the same breath, went into the room he shared with Bill, and closed the door behind him. We all laughed, including Steve. Then we strategized about the following weekend. We were going to throw a huge party the following Friday night, and then go to a Chicago concert on Saturday, taking Debbie and anyone else who wanted to have a good time.

It was two thirty in the morning before we even started trying to sleep.

The next morning I was up early. I wanted some alone time, so I walked to the YMCA to be with my thoughts. Then I went back to check on everyone and see what the afternoon and evening would bring.

Saturday night was prime time for the University of Tennessee's social scene. All the bars were slammed with college students and locals out looking for an evening of fun and frolics. The guys were out hunting for girls to score with. The girls were a little more serious and were out looking for husbands to nab. But the night life didn't really get going until around ten. That afternoon, we took in an early movie, a comedy called *The Four Musketeers*. By nightfall, as we started hitting the taverns, we yelled, "All for one, one for all, and don't any man forget it!" so many times that we started getting hoarse.

After downing a few beers at one of many stops, Bill suggested we try a place called The Last Chance Saloon. "It should be hopping by now. Let's go, musketeers. Drink up."

"Yes, we'll find our fair maidens elsewhere," said Steve, putting his empty mug on the counter and wiping a foam mustache from his lip with a swipe of his forearm.

When Bill pulled his Cutlass Supreme into the parking lot at the Last Chance Saloon, he and Steve noticed a beautiful blonde sitting in a white

Volkswagen, wearing a white faux fur coat. Her window was rolled down, and she seemed to be looking for someone.

Bill stopped his car so Steve could say hi to her.

Her name was Jan, and she was friendly and all smiles. But it really was obvious by the way she kept looking around that she was waiting for someone. Even so, Steve and Bill wanted to keep talking to her, so Tom and I went inside to try our luck.

There was barely even elbow room in that place. In one corner, a bunch of frat guys were bellowing out their house's songs, competing with the jukebox in another corner. The faint smell of marijuana hung over everything. People jostled each other and laughed and drank, and it was a hell of a fun scene.

Soon all four of us were at a table. Steve's mystery woman in the white Volkswagen had been a bust. He said she'd gotten so preoccupied that she'd left all of a sudden. Then, as if she'd sensed that someone was talking about her, she appeared in the bar. In that coat, I immediately started to think of her as Foxy Lady. Steve saw her and waved her over.

"I changed my mind," she said. "I didn't want to ruin my whole night."

The evening wore on. Steve and I asked Foxy Lady if she wanted to go back to Bill's place for a few beers. She was a hot one, married and divorced at twenty-six and looking for a good time. Bill gave us the keys and said, predictably (and understandably), "Just don't dirty my sheets."

"If they get dirty," said Steve, "Mark and I will wash them."

After spending some time with Foxy Lady at Bill's, Jon and Bill came back. They immediately started a late-night, for-no-reason-really fight over nothing. Whatever they were mad about was a mystery to me, but we got out of there so their tempers could burn out and we could avoid getting involved in their spat. Foxy Lady dropped us off at a breakfast place, made us promise to call her, and then took off.

When we got back to Bill's room, we were locked out. He must have been mad at us too, because he knew we were coming back. We hadn't done anything wrong, but there was no other reason to lock the door. Anyway, it was his place, not ours. We didn't want to aggravate the situation.

"Let's go down to the lobby and see if we can find a soft couch," said Steve.

We walked to an adjacent dorm and asked the girls working at the desk if we could sack out on the couches in the lobby for the last few hours of the night. They sympathized with us when we said we'd gotten locked out, and we tried to lie down and get some shuteye. But after an hour of listening to them crack jokes at the desk, the situation was desperate.

"Let's try the hallway," said Steve. "At least it'll be dark and quiet down there."

"We're going to be hurting tomorrow," I said, eyes half open, crawling off the couch, and heading towards a dark hallway that was looking better to me every minute.

It was nine thirty when Steve woke up. "Hey Mark, I'm going to go down in the lobby and call Bill. The phone is right next to Tom's head. He'll answer it fast and that way it won't wake anyone up. I'll tell him to unlock the door."

The plan worked. After Tom let us in, he told us about Jon and Bill's fight. Apparently it was something that had been brewing for a while. It hadn't had anything to do with us. "The door must have been locked by accident," he said. "But how did you sleep on that hallway floor?"

"Well, when your body says to stop and sleep now, you do it, even if it's on a hard floor. It had a rug on it."

Tom didn't look like he thought the rug sounded all that pleasurable or comfy.

We spent the next three days recovering, relaxing, and recuperating. Then it was off to the Smokey Mountains National Park, which lies on the eastern boundary of Tennessee. Half of the park is in Tennessee, and the other side's in the northwest corner of North Carolina. An old-timer on the road had told us it was the prettiest country you'd ever want to see, and we couldn't wait.

We left quietly and managed to avoid waking anyone up. There we were, loading up for another adventure, and everyone else we saw was walking to class with books under their arms. As if he could tell what I was thinking, Steve said, "We did our time already. Now we're out having some fun."

The Great Smokey Mountains were only about an hour away. At the base of the mountain range, we rode into a small resort town called Gatlingburg. It was packed with tourists. Traffic was bumper to bumper everywhere I looked. There was a big gondola ride going up the side of the mountain next to the town and a beautiful mountain stream running through the town between the alpine-style buildings. The whole thing was just as charming as could be.

We made our way through and headed to the park. The ranger and information station was packed as tightly with people as the town had been. It was mid-October and everyone was out to see the foliage, which was at its most colorful.

We spoke with a ranger who mapped out a good three-day hike for us. It followed a park road that was nothing but hairpin turns and steep climbs. A clear, noisy stream gurgled and flowed alongside us. At times, the road grew anxiety-inducingly narrow, and at one point, it even went under a low overhanging ledge that could have given someone a bad knock if they weren't paying attention. But we managed to keep our heads.

It took an hour of gorgeous riding to reach the park store, an A-frame building with picnic tables on both sides. We bought groceries, divvied them up so everyone was carrying his share, got our bikes stashed, and hit the trail.

Fall days for hiking don't come any more perfect than that. The sun was shining like it was there only for us, the temperature was cool, and the leaves were like the most intense watercolor painting you've ever seen. It was nature demanding an audience. We kept a moderate pace as we made our way up the trail, determined to reach our designated campsite by dusk.

We took short, five-minute breaks every twenty minutes or so. This was one of the many times on the trip that was great for the background Steve and I had as physical educators. We knew how to keep our bodies running, which was even more important on the trip, as it could end in a hurry if we didn't stay healthy.

I hustled up ahead of them, and then turned and snapped a quick picture.

"Boy, I'm glad we've only got two miles to go," said Steve. "I'm starting to get hungry." It was now three thirty in the afternoon, and the sun was getting low. If we couldn't get to our site before dark, setting up camp was going to be uncomfortable. But we made it to Campsite 10 without trouble.

I started building a fireplace so we'd have something to cook with. Cooking in the woods was always a hassle. The pans were small, you were always hunched over the fire, smoke was in your eyes, you have to cook and eat while sitting on the ground, and then you wash the pans with whatever limited water you have, not to mention that the food, whatever there was of it, was often lousy. But we were still happy to have it, and I'm not sure which of us was the hungriest that night.

After dinner, I sharpened my hatchet and knife like a Viking preparing for battle, while Tom stared into the fire. Later we played cards, toasted marshmallows, and said goodnight.

The next morning I was up at eight thirty. I made breakfast and got my pack ready for the day's hike.

"Why'd you get up so early?" asked Tom when he and Steve opened their eyes about an hour later.

"I wanted to get on the trail early today," I said, "but you guys took care of that."

Before Tom could respond to my sarcasm, a middle-aged couple hiked by our site. We offered them coffee, but they said they had twelve miles to get through that day and couldn't afford the time. While Tom and Steve got their gear ready, I read a few chapters in a paperback that I'd brought. The guys were ready to go by eleven o'clock.

"What trail are we taking today, Tom?" asked Steve as he swung his pack onto his back.

"I don't know. Ask Mark. He has the trail map."

I was a regular Lewis and Clark as I plotted our course. "We have to stay on the Anthony Creek Trail until we come to the Russell Field Trail, and then one more mile to the shelter. Once we're there, we can relax for a while and sit in the sun."

The trail wasn't too bad. It was very narrow in spots, but the climb wasn't too steep. The forest floor was thick with vegetation, and the trees were wrapped in vines. The largest hemlock tree in the world—19'20" in diameter—is in the Smokey Mountain Forest. We hiked in single file at a moderate pace for about twenty minutes before stopping for a quick rest, water, and some hard candies for energy.

We headed up the trail again. Soon I asked Steve to let me get ahead of him.

"What are you in a hurry for?" he said with a frown.

"It's not that," I said. "It's just that it's more comfortable for me to hike at my normal pace. Every time I get on your heels I have to put on my brakes, which expends energy, see?"

The trail grew steeper and rockier. Then there was a small, very muddy stretch because of a mountain brook that decided to turn everything to muck.

"Watch the mud," I called back. "It's very slippery."

The trail cut right into the side of the mountain as it continued upward. On one side was the uphill grade of the mountain while on the other was a steep drop that would have given nightmares to anyone with vertigo. The Great Smokey Mountains have good tree coverage from top to bottom, so even up there at the five-thousand-foot peaks, there were trees growing.

"Hey, Tom, Steve, there's a clearing up ahead." I got out the map to see if it was Russel's Field, our destination.

"Is it marked on the map?" asked Tom, catching up.

We hiked a little farther and found the Russel's Field sign. "That means there should be an overnight shelter a half mile farther up the trail," I said. "Let's keep going until we reach the shelter. By then it should only be about twelve forty-five and we can rest."

At the shelter, we stripped off our heavy packs, got out some salted peanuts, and lay down in a small grassy clearing in front of the shelter like three content dogs who'd found the perfect sunbeams to nap in.

The rangers had done a great job building the shelter. The fieldstone walls and log roof made it look about as sturdy as a fortress. They'd even put a heavy chain-link fence across the entrance to make it bear-proof.

"Why don't we sleep here tonight?" said Steve. "That way we wouldn't have to pitch the tent."

It sounded fine to me.

"Might as well," said Tom. "We can just sit up here all day and relax."

Except that, while we were lazing about in the sun, reading and resting, Tom and Steve decided to have a heated argument about a financial problem that hadn't been settled earlier in the trip. Why they needed to pick that moment I'll never know. I guess the scene had gotten too picturesque for them. There were times where it was like they just couldn't abide a few minutes of tranquility.

"Mark, don't you owe me fifty-five cents?" said Steve all of a sudden.

I couldn't remember, but he could have been right. "I'm not sure. Do I?"

"Yeah, you do, and we should straighten our money matters up now so we're all even."

Now? Up on top of a gorgeous mountain where we couldn't have spent any money even if we had a trillion dollars? Why now?

"Wait a minute," said Tom, who was sitting behind Steve. "If you want to get down to the nitty gritty     stuff, what about the $18 you owe me for last month's phone bill in the apartment? You were supposed to balance that out with me on the first day of the trip like Mark did."

"I don't have that kind of money now. I'll have to pay you when we get our next job," said Steve, hoping Tom would simmer down.

"No, I need the money now!" Tom yelled. "I used some of my trip money to pay your bill and I think you should have thought enough to bring extra money to cover your debts."

It occurred to me that this might have been the only conversation like this that had ever taken place in this serene setting. Put three people together, and someone can always find something to fuss over.

"Well, I don't have enough now," said Steve.

"Then you'll just have to wire home for some money, Steve, because I need the money, too. You just got done complaining to Mark about the fifty-five cents he owes you. I think you should stop and think a little before you say anything."

"Okay, don't get all riled up," said Steve, as if Tom was the one who had started this argument. "I'll write home and ask my mother to send your mother a check."

"No, that won't help out here in the wilderness. Tell her to send it to our next destination, which should be Nashville."

I just sat back trying not to get involved.

Steve had an uncanny knack for saying the wrong thing at the wrong time, and often in the wrong place. He could always find a way to hurt peoples' feelings. Ever since our apartment days, Tom and I were forever trying to help Steve with his problems without yelling or arguing. We'd always try to explain what was right and wrong, and why sometimes he didn't need to say everything that popped into his head. I usually argued with him more than Tom did, but given the trip and our constant and close proximity to each other, Tom had been pushed to the limits of his tolerance.

I listened until the limits of *my* tolerance were exhausted, and then called for a truce. They settled down quickly, which made me wonder again why the dumb conversation had needed to happen at all. When Steve got a thing in his head, it nagged at him and always found a way to come out. Hopefully we'd seen the end of that for a while.

At about three thirty, a ranger on a big black horse galloped into the clearing. "Hi, boys! How was your hike?"

"Okay," said Tom from the ground without looking up.

"I suggest that you boys camp here for the night," said the ranger. His voice was kind, but it didn't actually sound like a suggestion.

"Why?" said Steve.

"We've had reports that there's a rogue boar roaming around this area of the park. We've already got reports of a missing girl; there's no sense asking for more trouble. You should be safe if you sleep in the bear-proof shelter.

Just make sure you secure the door. Oh, and before I leave . . . do you boys know what a wild boar looks like?"

I pictured tusks and bristles combined with a hot temper and murder in its heart. I was pretty sure that Old Yeller saved the main character of that book from a bunch of wild boars that had run him up a tree. "Yeah, we've got a pretty good idea," I said.

But that wasn't enough for the ranger, so he gave us a more detailed breakdown. "A wild boar looks like a big hog, only with black fur all over his body and big sharp tusks sticking upward from the sides of his mouth. They're generally very mean, very strong, and can rip you to pieces with those tusks of theirs. This boar happens to be on the rampage for some reason. We've found some small trees torn up by the roots, and some of our shelters have been damaged, and I told you about the missing girl . . . So have fun, but keep your ears and eyes open."

Now I was picturing a boar wild enough to dig a tree up by the roots, before deciding to go kidnap a girl!

We thanked him for the advice and watched him ride away.

"What do you think about that?" said Tom with anxiety in his voice.

"Well, for one, it reaffirms our plan to stay here tonight," I said. "I'm not traipsing around in the dark with some savage hog looking to slice me up."

Time had slipped away from us. It was five o'clock, the sun was setting, and it was getting cold. I went to get some firewood for the stove we'd use to cook with in the shelter. When I got back ten minutes later, Steve and Tom were cooking chili. "How's supper coming along?" I asked. "That chili don't smell too good." It probably smelled about as nasty as a wild boar, truth be told.

"It'll have to do," said Tom, "because we don't have anything else."

Steve put a spoonful of chili in his mouth, made a face, and said, "Damn, this stuff tastes awful."

Just then a hiker walked up to the front of the shelter. "Hi, mind if I join you?"

We didn't mind at all. The stranger opened the chain-link door and squeezed through the opening with his pack still on his back. "My name's Jim," he said.

We introduced ourselves, and then offered him supper, hoping to give some of that awful chili away.

"No thanks," he said. "I have some food I'll cook up as soon as I take off my pack. I've been hiking up here for three days now. Sure is good to see some people. How long have you guys been in the backcountry?"

"Only two days," I said. "We met a ranger today who told us to be careful while we were in this area because there's a wild rogue boar roaming around."

Jim frowned. "I haven't bumped into anyone for two days, so I don't know about the boar. He's probably off in some other area of the park by now." He excused himself to get some firewood outside for his own cooking. After he came back and prepared his supper, I asked him how he liked hiking alone, because I couldn't imagine doing it myself. There just aren't those many experiences I can think of that aren't improved by *sharing* them with someone, and hiking is definitely one.

"It's not bad," he said as he stirred a vegetable soup that put our chili to shame. "But it does get lonely sometimes. It's peaceful being alone, but it's comforting to bump into friendly people once in a while."

After supper, all four of us got in our bunks and talked and enjoyed the fire. "Before we turn in," said Jim, "we should hang our packs from the rafters."

"Why?" I said.

"There are field mice in most of these shelters. They like to raid peoples' food, and these little guys are smart and agile. Later I can show you guys how to mouse-proof your packs. A guy at another shelter showed me."

Steve jumped down and got out some marshmallows. "Who wants one?"

Of course, we all did. Everyone got down to sit by the fire, which had now dwindled to hot red coals. After we were done and the embers were nearly invisible, Tom stood up. "I'm going to brush my teeth and take a leak," he said, as if he were Napoleon announcing a charge into an enemy's flank. I joined him a few minutes later to clean my teeth and salute a bush.

"Hey, Tom," I said, "beautiful night, isn't it?"

"Shush." Tom looked around.

"What's the matter?"

"I thought I heard something in the bushes behind me," he said.

"Probably just a raccoon or an owl."

But then we both heard the same noise—something sizable, moving fast, and what might have been a grunt or a growl. We rushed back to the shelter and slammed the door behind us.

"What's the big rush, guys?" asked Steve from his bunk.

"While we were brushing our teeth, we heard some heavy rumbling in the bushes out to the right of the shelter and didn't stick around to see what the hell it was," said Tom, panting.

"It could be that rogue boar," I said. Boars outside, maybe. Mice inside, maybe. It was turning into a regular zoo. Maybe the animals had a plan to tag-team us and ruin our night.

"Well, we'll be safe in here," said Jim. "If it is that boar, it's probably the smell of our supper that attracted him."

It certainly wasn't *our* supper that attracted him.

"More than likely," Jim continued, "he'll wander away by morning. Let's hang our packs up. You'll need some good line and an aluminum pie pan or piece of flat cardboard. Punch a small hole in the center of the pan and run the line through it. Then tie a knot bigger than the hole beneath the pan, about a foot over your pack. These mice can climb down, but when they reach the pan they try to get around it and fall off." We followed his instructions, and then hit the sack.

It got cold that night, which made the hot oatmeal in the morning a pleasure. After breakfast, we washed our pans in the stream and prepared for the day's hike out of the backcountry. Jim wasn't leaving yet, so we said our goodbyes and hit the trail around eight thirty. The trail was easy, and we were back to our bikes at the ranger's house in no time. By four thirty, we were headed back to the University of Tennessee, and we were back in Bill's apartment shortly after five.

"How was the hike?" he asked. "Did you run into any bears?"

We made short work of describing him the hike as we were in a hurry to rest. The three of us then went to sleep quickly so we could be ready for the party that night. Bill woke us up around seven thirty to see the pep rally taking place in the courtyard between the tall dorm buildings. Getting up was a task that would have fit into the Labors of Hercules, but we managed, grabbing one beer each before heading outside for a look. The courtyard was filled with kids yelling and chanting, "BEAT BAMA." There were banners hanging from dorm windows, kids carrying big signs saying, "Go Vols—Beat Bama," and a dozen other slogans. Cheerleaders cheered over a PA system, and a giant yellow hot air balloon from Wendy's Hamburger stand was hovering over the crowd. The rally went on for an hour before breaking up so everyone could allegedly go back to their studies.

"This should be a good weekend," said Bill. "One of the biggest games on our schedule will be nationally televised Saturday and then that night Chicago is playing at the Stokely Athletic Center. I've already got tickets for you guys."

"That sounds great," said Steve. "How much did those tickets cost? We'll give you the money now."

"Don't worry about it," said Bill. "You guys are a riot to have around. And everything's all set for the party, including the women."

Bill drove us to the supermarket in Knoxville so we could buy the foods we needed to cook the big Italian dinner that was going to dazzle the partygoers. Back at the dorm, Steve divided the bill and then got right into making the meatballs, while Tom and I started on the sauce. Bill thought cooking was woman's work, so he just watched us and sipped a beer.

The party couldn't have gone off better. We each had a pretty Southern belle to ourselves, the food was marvelous, and those women couldn't believe the way we New England men could cook and present a dinner. It was a riot of food, laughing, dancing, and all sorts of other shenanigans.

But Saturday was when things really got going. I got up at eleven and had breakfast at the Torch Restaurant with one of Bill's roommates and his girlfriend. You could feel the thrill of the big game everywhere in the town. I love sports, but these people were fanatics. The game was all anyone was talking about. Students in bright orange were parading around, and alumni were pouring in by the hundreds. We were on our way back from breakfast when I got the idea: we should wear our orange plastic rainsuits to the game. I told Tom and Steve the idea as soon as I got back to the apartment. "We can put something across the back and get on TV," I said. It sounded so simple, and I thought it could really be that simple. I had something orange to wear, and I had the stubbornness to make it happen.

"You don't really want to do that, do you?" asked Tom.

"Of course I do! Who wouldn't? Have you forgotten how many times we've talked about getting on the tube? Well, here's our chance!" I knew it would work; I just knew it. And I either wore them down or won them over, but they agreed in the end, even if it was just to get me to back off.

We went and played tennis for a while, and then got ready for the game. "I'll get the rain gear," I said, "but what can we use to put a sign on them with?"

Steve thought for a moment. "How about the white medi tape in our first aid kit?"

Fantastic. It's not like we had needed it for any injuries. Might as well use the first aid kit for something.

Bill and Jon were watching us, shaking their heads. "Look at those nuts. They'll do anything," said Bill.

"I'm psyched!" I yelled. As if they couldn't tell. But I couldn't believe how excited I was. It was like I was made of electricity.

Once our suits were on, we used the tape to make letters across our jackets, spelling out "GO VOLS" across the front of all three. Across the backs it said "HI ABC." *That ought to get their attention*, I thought.

Then Tom made a big sign that said "HI MOM IN BOSTONABC #1." "Hey," he said. It was three thirty. "We gotta get going if we're going to make the kickoff."

"Man, we are getting on TV no matter what," I said for the millionth time. "I did not get dressed up like this for nothing."

The streets leading to the stadium were like rivers with people and noise and wildness all flowing to the gates. We rode the wave that I hoped would toss us right up onto the biggest stage yet.

Lots of people stopped to look at us, and plenty of them waved and chuckled as we passed. "You guys walk ahead of me," said Bill, grumbling. "I don't want my friends to see me walking with three nuts."

"Come on, Bill," I said. "It's all in school spirit. Look at those alumni walking down there. They've got orange and white shoes, and some of them have painted their teeth orange."

We made it to our seats, but it didn't take long for us to realize that we didn't like them and they weren't going to work for my grand plan.

"We can't sit way up here," said Steve. "We're so high up we're going to get nosebleeds. And we'll never get on TV from here."

"We're only ten rows from the top and there are eighty-two thousand people here," said Tom. "There's no way we're getting on TV."

"That's what you think," I said, rolling up my plastic pants so my legs would stop sweating. "We'll figure it out." I felt like I was walking around in an oven.

The game kicked off at four. I stewed, and planned, and schemed, and then, after the halftime show, I saw that it was time to make our move. "See that section down there?" I said, pointing straight ahead to a spot close to the field. "If we want to get on TV, we've got to get down there."

"There's a guard down there," said Bill. "And you need special tickets for that section. You guys can't get down there."

"Watch us," I said. "Let's go, guys. We're going to have to move fast. Don't hesitate. Look like you know exactly what you're doing."

As we hustled down the steps, Steve turned around. "We'll wave to you from down there, Bill," he said, pointing to a section right on the fifty-yard line.

Bill shook his head.

We worked our way down a maze of ramps from the upper tiers to the lower seats. The crowd was so thick we had to go in single file. Steve led and ran interference. When we made it to the guard, it took a little conning and a lot of charm, but he let us in. He knew that everyone in there was going to get a kick out of us, and it was the section of the field where there was a cameraman whose only job was to scan the crowd for fan footage.

I ran down to the first row of seats to try and get the cameraman's attention, while Tom and Steve hung back in the aisle holding up our sign. It was no use! The cameraman didn't pay any attention to me. He was starting to head back up the aisle when the captain of the cheerleaders called to him, "Hey, you guys look pretty good dressed up in those orange suits. Call your friends and come down on the field! We'll get you guys on TV." It was like hearing the voice of an angel.

I looked up to where they were standing and waved them down. We all ran down the stairs like we were being pursued and jumped the fence. Suddenly, we were right out there on the sidelines surrounded by cheerleaders. If I hadn't been wearing a hot-orange rainsuit and sweating like I had landed in Hell, I might have thought I'd arrived in Heaven.

"Hi, my name is Nancy," said the cheerleading captain with a pretty smile and beautiful blond hair.

We introduced ourselves in unison.

"I want you guys to stand and face the crowd so they can read what it says on you."

Our hearts were pounding so wildly it almost felt like we were choking. My dream had come true, and it had come through big. I knew I could get us there. We never quit, and that relentless effort had paid off. *I strongly believe that a person can reach his/her goal if he never gives up dreaming of it.* I couldn't have been more excited if I'd been on the field throwing the winning touchdown. And we weren't just on TV; we were right there on the sidelines doing cheers with the cheerleaders in front of more than eighty thousand people for the whole second half of the game. Wow!

I'm not sure I've ever had more fun, and the best part of it might have been when we took picture after picture with the cheerleaders, who were treating us with all the care and attention any man could ever want.

There are people who complain when their dreams don't come true. I was never going to be one of them. I saw my dreams, and I made them happen. Sometimes I dragged my friends along, kicking and screaming. I'd hear the sound of those cheers in my head for a long time. If I try, I can still hear them now, and my heart starts to pound just like it did when we made it to the sidelines.

CHAPTER SIX:

# Nashville

Nashville was home to the Grand Ole Opry, the roots of country and bluegrass music, and most importantly, it was where I had an address for a girl: Terry. She had moved there with her parents from Massachusetts, and now we were closing in on her location.

It was October 19, and we'd been on the road for forty-two days. We'd put approximately eleven hundred miles of wear and tear on our bikes, nearly as many on our bodies, and probably as many smiles on our faces. Luckily, we hadn't had to deal with any major trouble. That was about to change in Nashville. At some point, your number's up.

We pulled into a parking lot for quick talk before heading into the city. We decided to go to the YMCA so we could get a workout and I could talk to the physical director before hopefully seeing Terry that night. Since I had worked as a physical director of a YMCA in Massachusetts, the YMCA's would let us use their facilities for free. That helped us get a few extra showers.

"You think she'll be as surprised to see us as Bill was?" asked Steve.

"Are you kidding?" I said. "She'll be tickled pink." And I hoped that she'd be so tickled pink that she wouldn't be able to resist making our visit a memorable one.

We found the address for the YMCA in a directory and headed straight for it. Before we started playing a hectic game of three-men cutthroat racquetball at the Y, I gave Terry a call. Minutes later, we were all set for the night.

Terry and her parents were going to stop by the Y around nine. She only lived about fifteen minutes away, and her parents had said we could stay there.

"That's great," said Steve. "Too bad she doesn't have her own place, though."

Maybe, but I wasn't complaining. We were going to have a roof over our heads and zero chance of wild boars sashaying through the place while we tried to sleep.

We were still full of energy after racquetball, so we played some basketball as well before taking a steam and a shower. I was feeling so content, so happy. And it got even better when we hit the lobby at nine and there she was, looking as pretty as ever, so nice that she barely seemed real.

As soon as Terry saw me, she jumped out of her seat and threw her arms around me. "You three are beautiful!" she said. "I can't believe you're here!" She couldn't stop hugging us, and we weren't about to get her to try.

"We're just as glad that *you're* here," I said. "I hope we're not putting your parents out. I know it's really last minute."

"Are you kidding? They're as thrilled as I am!"

That was welcome news. I couldn't wait for the night to get started. When we got outside and Terry saw the rain, her face fell. "Can you guys ride your motorcycles in this awful rain?"

I had to laugh. She had no idea what we'd been through as far as nasty weather went and how we'd learned to ignore it. "We'll be fine. Just don't go too fast," I said. "We've got our rain gear and we'll keep you in sight. Just give us a few minutes to get ready."

Terry's parents' house was gorgeous, but I wasn't surprised. Her dad was a public relations man for a telephone company in Nashville and had done pretty well for himself. Rolling out our bags on the thick, white, shag carpet of the living room was heavenly after so many nights on the ground. Just before we lay down to sleep, Terry said she had a girlfriend who had her own place. Tomorrow she planned on asking her if we could stay there for a bit while we were in Nashville. Terry wanted to party with us, and it sounded like an ideal set up.

The next morning was Steve's dad's birthday. Steve woke up and realized that he'd forgotten to send him anything. He decided to write him a long letter thanking him for all of his love, advice, and excellent judgment. When I looked at the kind of man Steve was, I was grateful to his dad as well. A good father is a blessing you can't buy.

Terry was up early preparing a breakfast hefty enough to stuff an army. We were planning on tagging along with her and then hanging out on campus while she went to school. We'd meet up when she finished and be with her friend by six thirty.

"I'll have everything set by then," she said. "Be ready to party. Well, I guess I don't have to tell you guys that."

No. No, she did not.

After saying goodbye, we decided to go do laundry, a task that reminded me of Sisyphus rolling the rock up the hill in Hades, a chore that never seemed to end. We'd let some things slip over the past two weeks, and it was a good day to play catch-up. We started by writing letters. I put on a pair of headphones so I could have a soundtrack of RCA Victrola originals to inspire my writing. Steve did one better. In the opening line of his letter to his dad, he said he was writing under the influence of Beethoven's fifth symphony and so his dad had better be prepared for a mood-changing letter.

I wasn't in the mood for classical, although I'd wager I could write a letter every bit as mood-changing as Steve. It was country-style Dixie for me. Dixieland tunes are happy, fast, lively party music full of clarinets, banjos, trombones, and pianos all jostling for their spot on the stage. My pen was soon tapping up and down the page with all the speed of a master fingerpicking a banjo. But I knew that, no matter what the mood, and no matter who we sent our letters to, the message was always the same: everything's fine, we're doing great, it's a trip full of rich rewards, we're grateful for you, and nearly everyone is as helpful as could be. We always closed in the same way when we wrote to our parents: "Love, your three sons, Mark, Tom, and Steve."

There was no other way to do it. We felt like brothers. It was a role we'd play all the way out to California. It might as well have been true.

When we got back to Terry's school, she was ready to go. It was very cold, and the overcast skies would have been threatening to people who weren't as ready for a party as we were. I think we would have ridden our bikes on the edge of a live volcano if it was the only way to get to a party.

We bundled up and followed Terry, who had the luxury of driving a warm car. Her friend's name was Sid, and Sid lived about twenty-two miles west of Nashville. She was divorced and was also the proud mother of a ten-month-old baby.

When we arrived, Sid had a visitor that she was obviously tired of. It turned out that she'd been trying to get rid of him for nearly half an hour. It was also obvious that she was bewildered and didn't know what to try next. I only had to talk to the guy for about five seconds before I realized why he wasn't taking the hint. He was twenty-two, married, separated from his wife, and had three kids to support. Sixth grade had been his final stop in school. It broke my heart to hear that he couldn't read or write. There are certain ruts that, once you're in them, only get deeper. He was in a bad one and couldn't see his way out of it. No wonder he wasn't happy! It must have been hard sitting there with us. We weren't rich sultans or anything, but we were resourceful, pure potential, doing whatever we wanted and taking a grand tour of the country. But that reading and writing . . . it made me want to cry. I can't even imagine that, in this rich, powerful country, a man can still become an adult without ever having learned to read and write. How was such a man supposed to transcend his limits, when his limits were so drastic?

People would be able to take advantage of him without his knowing it. In a city he'd stick out like a sore thumb. So, instead, he was living a sheltered life, rather that risk exposure. I hated the thought that our freewheeling ways and adventurous spirits might be hard for him to be around, but there's no point in changing who you are to make someone else comfortable.

He wasn't fitting into the conversation. And no matter what we tried, it was obvious that we weren't going to figure out *how* to fit him in. He grew noticeably uncomfortable, fidgeting and avoiding eye contact. I hoped that our growing embarrassment wasn't as noticeable as I felt it might be. Finally, he abruptly stood and said goodbye, and then walked home to whatever awaited him. But I knew what awaited him: more of the same.

As soon as he left, I learned that I hadn't been alone in my feelings. "He chose to live the way he has," said Sid. "It's partly his own fault." Yeah, but it's still a brutal thing to see someone suffer, no matter what the reasons might be.

The next morning, Steve was lying on the couch wrapped up with Sid, Steve was lying next to Terry, and I was stretched out on the couch with my head hanging off the edge when there was a loud, echoing knock on the front door.

Sid and Terry immediately jumped up, almost like they'd been expecting it.

"Open up, quick," said a voice on the other side.

Sid opened the door, revealing Marty, her younger sister. "Mom's coming right over," said Marty. "I got here as soon as I could to warn you."

All business, Terry turned to us. "Guys, I hate to do this to you but we've got five minutes to move. Please take your stuff and go into the kitchen. My mom's coming to pick up Jessy for the day. As soon as she leaves, you can go back to sleep."

We got our sleeping bags and jackets and stood in the kitchen, still half asleep, hoping that all that Sid's mother would want would be to take the baby and go, fast.

Marty was peering out the bay window when she whispered, "Here she comes!"

"Okay, guys," said Sid, "be quiet. "We'll try to get her back on her way."

It's not like we were in there wrestling. We wanted this to be over as soon as possible. We weren't going to make a peep.

"Hi, Mom," we heard Sid say.

"Where's my cute grandson?" said a voice that was way too exuberant for how early it was. "Are you ready to come with your grandmother today?" It was quiet for a moment, and then we heard her say. "Marty, why did you leave in such a hurry this morning?"

It was hard not to laugh, knowing that she'd been racing over here to stash us in the kitchen, but we managed.

"I just wanted to see Terry before going to school."

"That's all?"

"That's all."

Maybe I was paranoid, but I felt like we had to move. We hurried out the back door, and hunched down on the cold, wet ground under the kitchen window with our gear in our arms. It felt like the scene in Jurassic Park where the kids are hiding from the velociraptors in the cafeteria. From our hiding place beneath the kitchen window, we heard Sid's mom asking if anyone had come over last night. Whatever her suspicions, she couldn't turn up any evidence. Five minutes after arriving, she was gone.

"That was too close," said Steve.

"The coast is clear," said Sid, appearing at the back door. "That was some quick thinking, coming out here." She waved us in. "I'm sorry, but I can't have you guys staying here tonight. I'd like to, but I'm pretty sure she's suspicious."

"You guys didn't even make a sound going across that floor," said Terry, eyeing the linoleum in the kitchen. It was obvious that she felt bad that our brief stay with Sid was already ending. "What are you guys going to do tonight? You'd be welcome back at my parents' house."

"We appreciate that," I said. "Tonight we're meeting two guys from the U of T at the Friday Night Club. How about if we meet you there? One of the guys is from Nashville. We might be able to stay at his folks' home as well."

Terry agreed, but said she had to be in by eleven. Yikes, her school had a strict curfew.

"How can you stand to be told when you have to be in for the night?" asked Tom. "It's college, not high school."

"Ah, it's only two more semesters," she said. "It's not that bad, but I can hardly wait to finish."

Plans made, crisis averted, the girls hopped in their car, and we got on our bikes and began the twenty-two miles back to Nashville. When we got there, we went to the post office. Back in Knoxville, Steve had written to his parents and asked them to send a $50 money order. If they sent it to the main post office, they'd hold it there for Steve for ten days. This would let him pay Tom back for the apartment money they'd squabbled over in the woods, and also let him replace a few worn-out items he'd been making due with.

I'd asked my three aunts to send me flashlights and batteries. They worked at a Ray O Vac in Clinton Massachusetts, and got deep discounts. The man at the general delivery window went to get our packages and came back with a big smile on his face. He had a package for Steve and an envelope for me.

"Let's see what our friends back home think about our trip," I said, tearing it open. Two flashlights with batteries fell out.

"Now you'll be able to go night-crawling again," said Steve, cracking us up. "Those worms will never see you coming."

We disbanded for a little while. I had to get my sleeping bag dry-cleaned. Steve went to a laundromat to wash some of our stuff, and Tom went to find a pair of sunglasses. Across the street was a Naval Surplus store. Steve thought he might be able to get a good pair of boots in there. The soles of his current boots had been worn down so smooth he could practically feel every tiny pebble when we were hiking.

When he walked back out of the store, he was at least two inches taller.

"Say, shorty," he said to me, "what's it like down there among the ants?"

"Take those high heels off and find out, lady," I said. They weren't quite high heels, but they were pretty tall.

We rolled up our bags and gear and got going again. Inside the laundromat, a small, slender woman was watching us, but she looked curious more than anything. "Hi, boys," she said when she finally approached. "I just had a question about your trip. It must be interesting to travel by motorcycle. Where are you from, and where are you heading?" She was probably in her mid-forties, dressed conservatively, and was as friendly as anyone we'd met yet.

Steve and I stopped packing and talked to her. It made me laugh that she kept commenting on our manners and how clean we looked. "You're so nice! You're so clean! You're so well-spoken!" I don't know, maybe she had a different notion of people who rode cross-country and would have expected us to be more like goons with beards or something.

"My name is Mrs. Rose," she said, "and I think what you boys are doing is something. I bet you could use a home-cooked dinner, Southern style. Why don't you come eat with me and my son tonight? He's twenty-three and also has a beard." It made me feel like anyone with a beard was in some sort of secret, privileged society, and that we were all supposed to get along just because we had hair on our faces. "He's going to engineering school and would love to hear about your trip."

It was heartening to know that her son had qualities other than a beard. "We've got another friend," I said. "He'll be meeting us here around three. He looks a lot like us," I said, just in case the thought of yet another guy with a beard would thrill her heart.

"He's welcome also," she said. "I'll make ham, sweet potatoes, squash, biscuits, and show you how us Southern people eat. Does six sound okay? If you want to shower first, you could come by as early as five, too."

I looked at Steve. Like he was reading my mind, he looked at Mrs. Rose. "That's very nice of you to offer. We wish there were more people like you around. People up north wouldn't be doing what you are, stopping to talk and asking us over for dinner."

"Well," she said, "I don't go asking everyone. But you two are nice and decent boys. I can tell you've got good heads on your shoulders and I do want to hear more about the trip, so don't forget that there's something in it for me."

She gave us her address and phone number and then hurried off to tend to the business of her day. My goodness, I'd always known that we were nice people, but this was a masterclass in just how much it could pay off to just be decent. In a way, it was kind of sad to think about how well people responded to us just because we were nice and friendly. It made me realize how tragically rare it can be, when people are surprised just because you treat them well.

Tom was as excited about our dinner plans as I thought he'd be. "Wait, you guys charmed an older lady into cooking us a hot dinner? How'd you manage that?"

Same as always. Simply being nice must be the poorest kept secret in creation!

Little did we know that one of the stranger nights of our lives was about to begin.

After heading to the Y like usual for a workout and showers, we headed to dinner. At six o'clock, we showed up at Mrs. Rose's place. She and her son—a polite young man who listened well and did indeed have a beard—were so delighted by our reaction to the dinner that it was almost like we'd done *them* a favor, despite the fact that she'd obviously put serious time and effort into feeding us. The main course was a succulent ham with baked pineapples, trimmed with home-cooked candied yams, warmed apple sauce, salad with several dressing options, biscuits topped with rich butter, three different plates of steaming vegetables, and more. They can't eat any better in Heaven, although I guess I'm not sure if they eat in Heaven at all.

When we were done, we were so full we could barely move, but we had enough energy to compliment her up and down. I would have thrown her a parade if I could have. Before we could leave the table, Mrs. Rose vanished for a moment, and then reappeared with a bunch of apples, nuts, and cheeses. Finally, she gave us each an apple cider and took us into the TV room to watch the end of the last game of the World Series. The Cincinnati Reds would wallop the Yankees in four straight that year.

I asked if we could help with the dishes, but Mrs. Rose wasn't having it. "You boys are my guests and it gives me something to do!" Since I was pretty handy with tools, I asked Mrs. Rose if she needed anything repaired, and she said she had a door and section of fence that needed fixing, so wanting to repay her for her kindness, we made the repairs for her and she expressed her gratitude. We said goodby and thank you, to her and her son, and with that we were off!

We stopped and asked for directions to Friday's, where we were going to meet Bill and Jon at eight thirty. It turned out to only be about four blocks down on the same street. As we headed down the hallway to the door, we thanked her profusely. Steve promised to keep in touch, now that we had her mailing address and phone number.

"We'll be waiting for that first letter," she said. "God bless you boys."

Mrs. Rose had fed us and treated us like gold, like we were her own sons. It was a shame that her husband had died. I was glad that she had her son, but I wished that she hadn't lost her husband.

On the way to Friday's, we stopped at a red light. Steve told us that Jon owed him some money and he planned on collecting.

We found a good parking spot in the Friday's lot, under a bright street-light. That way we'd be able to keep one eye on our bikes while we were inside. Nothing would have derailed our trip faster than coming out to find that our rides had been swiped.

Friday's was classier than your typical college juke joint. The doormen who sat us at our table wore fancy leisure suits. You could order dinner, but you didn't have to. If you wanted, you could just sip a drink all night while listening to the tunes. The tables were full of prime prima donnas. In short, we stuck out about as drastically as three skunks would have, with black and white stripes painted down our backs, primed to lift our tails and spray all the beautiful people with our wretched stench.

After a quick survey of the scene, Jon, Bill, and Terry were nowhere to be found. We went back outside to discuss options.

"Are we early?" said Tom. "It's only eight fifty."

"Knowing Bill's rocket-like pace," said Steve, "we'll probably have to wait until ten."

"Hey," said Tom before our annoyance could creep any higher, "isn't that Terry over there by our bikes?"

One out of three of our friends on site wasn't bad, especially when the one was Terry. She was locking her car door when she saw us. "Hi, guys. Sorry I'm late. I had to cash a check and gas up. How's Friday's? Did you meet your friends yet?"

"No," said Steve. "And we feel a little underdressed in there. No Bill and Jon. So here we are at nine thirty and no place to stay yet." He obviously hoped Terry would have another wild idea and an even wilder friend.

"I know another girl," she said. "Let me call her. She might already be out partying, though."

This mysterious lady had already headed out, but the person Terry spoke with on the phone said that she'd gone to Fanny's nightclub. Terry asked us to follow her to Fanny's and then we'd see what was what.

When we got there, she went inside to see if her friend was there.

Ten minutes later, she returned with disappointment on her face. "Sorry, guys. She already left with some dude."

"She must be a fast worker," said Steve. I couldn't tell if he was annoyed or disappointed. Maybe a bit of both.

"It's almost eleven," said Terry. "My curfew's coming up. I'll call my parents. Just go stay there. I'll tell them you're coming."

"No, that's all right," said Steve. "It's too late anyway, and it's three miles away. We're bushed. Don't worry, though; we'll find a place to stay."

I didn't know where, but he was right. We always did.

"We'll find someone to put us up in Fanny's," I said. "We'll see you tomorrow."

Terry got in her car and drove away. We turned to go inside and hustle up a place to stay, and hopefully a little fun. Or a lot.

Steve took off his long johns. Now that we weren't driving around in the cold dark, we'd warm up fast inside the joint.

Right after we got inside, we ran into the doorman. He was tall, 6'4"at least, with shoulders as broad as a refrigerator and a chest that looked as solid as rebar. Some of his front teeth were missing. I had no doubt that they'd been knocked out in a fight, or several of them. When he took a step, I noticed that he had a slight limp in his right leg. His job was simple. Check IDs, don't let anyone under eighteen inside, and stop any brawls before they start. And of course, if a brawl starts, his job was to end it. He certainly looked well-suited to the task. I don't want to get ahead of myself, but we were going to learn a few things about him that night, including his name, which was Luke. Luke loved a good fight, but he loved meeting people even more. He seemed happy and relatively calm, although he told us that he'd mellowed a lot since his younger years. He was thirty-three years old and had spent nine years in prison. During a street fight, he had stabbed a guy and had been convicted without too much fuss or doubt. His marriage had failed and he had some kids that he thought about a lot, hoping that one day he'd get a chance to help them and enjoy their company. When he talked to us about his past, he sounded a little depressed, but he'd perk up quickly when he started talking about his future.

But that all came later, and Luke's seeming happiness would be cast into doubt in a drastic way before the next day began. We went inside to check the place out before we got to know Luke at all.

Fanny's couldn't have been more different than Friday's. It was bigger, for one. There was a live rock band playing on a stage and a game room set apart from the main bar. Since one bar couldn't possibly be enough, there was another one in the game room. They didn't even serve food, just liquor. The place was packed with townies, and you couldn't have found a place to sit if you'd been the pope, although the pope probably doesn't spend a lot of time in clubs.

On his way to the bar, Tom noticed that a small table had just been vacated. It was like striking gold. We observed the crowd for about half an hour. Everyone seemed to know each other. It was like when a high school band of party kids gets together to celebrate when a local boy comes home from a war. There was so much cigarette smoke in the air that it had practically replaced the ceiling. I had to get out of there and breathe. It wasn't long before Steve and Tom followed me, tired of choking on smoke.

On the way out, we passed Luke.

"Hey, Luke," said Steve, "you ought to tell your boss to do something about that smoke screen in the main lounge. It's hell on us non-smokers. Maybe he'll give you a raise for your helpful suggestion."

Luke laughed. "Yeah, I'll do that. But you boys aren't leaving us yet, are you?"

"No, not yet," I said. "Just need some air."

"Right outside that door," he said. "But it's cold. Hurry back now." He held the door wide open.

"Good old Luke," said Steve when we were outside, mimicking Luke's good old boy speech and accent.

Tom was shivering. "It's so cold out here. I'm already sick of seeing my breath. We have to find a place to stay tonight."

"Luke knows a lot of people," I said. "Let's see if he knows a place where we could hole up for the night. He might even give us a lead on some foxy chick's apartment." I put my hands, which were already chilled, in my pockets. Luke hadn't been lying about that cold air.

Steve walked over to Luke and asked him the million-dollar question. Luke was answering him when an old friend of his walked in. He came over and whispered something in Luke's ear. Luke nodded. "Ah," he said, "Ah, okay." Suddenly the guy rushed out the door to where a taxicab was waiting. Very mysterious.

"Who's that?" said Steve.

"Oh, that's Hank. He's a good old boy. He's got seven prostitutes working for him. He's just checking on them. It makes him good money." Luke mentioned this all very casually, as if everyone was running seven prostitutes and making good money off of them. "He's got a place," Luke continued. "He's hardly there, but he's got a roommate named Gil. They're only a couple of miles away. I'll ask him."

"Thanks, Luke. I appreciate it," said Steve, patting him on the back. He came back over to us with the update. None of us had any serious objections to the thought of staying out at Hank's. Better to hang out with a pimp than freeze to death.

We spent some time drinking, trying to hustle girls, and enjoying ourselves. Finally, Steve went back over to Luke to see if there'd been any progress on the night's lodging situation. It was all set. Luke was going to take us over to Hank's when he got off work at two thirty that morning.

We did our best to kill the remaining two hours in productive fashion. Last call was announced at one o'clock. It might have been the first time that the three of us were thrilled to hear that a night in a bar was ending, thinking about how badly we wanted to lie down and sleep. Even if nothing else happened, we were going to feel grim in the morning. If you want to feel real fatigue, ride a motorcycle through the cold, do a workout in the middle of the afternoon, take a sauna, and then stay up all night in the middle of a smoky room. You'll get the idea.

We went outside to the bikes shortly afterwards. Luke didn't appear until two forty-five, however. He had a story about needing to put all the chairs back in place, but it rang false. The last guests had been ushered out forty-five minutes earlier. What had he been up to? I could tell Steve and Tom had noticed the weird vibe as well.

"A bunch of us are going to Jimbo's for breakfast before heading home," said Luke. "Just follow me."

Our precious sleep was getting further and further away. "It's only three o'clock," said Steve with an edge in his voice. "I didn't want to sleep anyway."

Still, even though we had to get back on our bikes and ride the three miles to Jimbo's in the thirty-four-degree weather, Luke was still doing us a favor. We tried to feel as grateful as we could, but it can be tough when you're so tired you can barely see and so cold you can barely breathe.

Jimbo's was a small, all-night dump of a diner. The only people eating breakfast there at three fifteen in the morning were the night crew from Fanny's. That might be the first time in my life that I just couldn't get into eating. I was just so tired and done with it all. My brain wanted to sleep; my stomach wanted to sleep. I think that even my teeth were tired. But I sipped a hot cocoa and watched the people in the diner. Then I saw a guy snort a bunch of coke up his nose from a small bottle. He started beaming like he'd just heard the greatest news in the world. He passed the bottle to Steve, offering him a snort. Steve put up his hand, taking an obvious pass. The guy offered it to Luke next.

"Is that cocaine?" asked Luke.

"Sure is, man! Take a snort, Luke. Clears your head up."

The only thing I needed to clear my head up was sleep. Luke, however, had other ideas. He took the bottle, placed it in one nostril, and inhaled through his nose like an elephant sucking up stream water through its trunk. Now Luke was beaming just like the guy who handed him the bottle. "*Man*, you're right," he said. "It clears your head *up*. Here boys, take a snort. One hit of this will make you sleep like a baby."

"No thanks, Luke. I don't need that stuff to make me sleep like a baby."

"Okay, boys," said Luke.

Hallelujah. Maybe he was getting the hint.

"Before I bring you to Hank's, I just have to drop off a few people. It's on the way and nearby."

That didn't sound like getting the hint.

Tom looked at his watch. It was already five in the morning. After five more cold miles of playing "follow the coked-up leader," we finally arrived at Hank's place. It was a small cinder block house down a long dirt driveway lined with trees. In the kitchen, dishes were piled high in the sink, grimy and smelly like they'd been there for a century. In the living room, a big old brown, furry mongrel was sprawled out like he was the emperor of the home.

Luke walked in to wake up a guy named Chimp because it was time for him to go to work. "Hey, old buddy! Time to get up!" Luke flicked on a light.

Chimp was 5'4" and small-boned. He couldn't have weighed more than a hundred pounds soaking wet. He looked malnourished and pale and sickly. When he crawled out of bed, I saw that he was wearing a pair of dingy Jockey shorts that looked as if they hadn't been washed in months. The odor of mildew hung over everything.

"These three guys are from Boston, Massachusetts," said Luke. "They're traveling cross-country by motorcycle and need a place to sack out. I didn't think you'd mind. Hank said it was okay. He's working all night so he won't be in."

"Hey, sure," said Chimp. "The bed isn't much, but you guys are welcome to it."

"Chimp's a good old boy," said Luke after Chimp left the room. Indeed, apparently everyone in Nashville was a good old boy. "If you're stuck for a place tomorrow night, you can stay here again. I'm going to take Chimp to work so you can have the place to yourselves. Enjoy your sleep."

Before we said goodnight, I suggested that we fold up our pants and use them as pillows, making sure our wallets and what few valuables we had were practically under our heads. After the drama of finding a place to sleep, we were bedding down in a place that was basically an anxiety factory. "I'm guessing they don't sleep too soundly," I said. "So let's be cautious." Then, after making sure they were gone, Tom rolled out his bag on the living room couch, I did the same on the couch in the bedroom, and Steve laid out his bag on Chimp's antique bed.

Steve checked his watch and groaned. "I can't believe it's this late."

"You mean early," I said.

He jumped into his bag. "See you guys tomorrow around one."

At twelve forty-five the next afternoon, Tom was roused by laughter and voices from the kitchen. I was just waking up when he walked in, tightening his belt. "Hey," he said, "there are some people in the kitchen. I'm not sure who and how many because the kitchen door's shut. It was dark in the house because all the shades were down. One of the voices is Luke's, though."

"What's it look like outdoors, Tom?" I said.

"I just took a quick look out the front door. Blue skies and sun. We have a good four hours of riding weather. Let's get Steve up and make like the wind."

I reached over to wake Steve. "We're leaving this hole in the wall gang in a few minutes," I said. "We've got good weather and this place is getting to me. The sooner we leave, the better we'll feel. But let's go say goodbye."

After rolling up our bags, Tom and I went to the kitchen. Luke was standing, lighting a match under a spoon that held a white powder, heating the substance to liquid poison. A young girl was sitting at the table with Chimp. She appeared to be about high school age. An unopened algebra book lay on the table in front of her. She was dressed in ragged jeans and a flimsy white blouse that exposed her large breasts.

She was holding the spoon that Luke was heating up. She stared into its depths, anxious and distressed, twitchy with need, her tongue rolling in her mouth. There was also a small pile of white powder on the table. Chimp had a rubber tube wrapped tightly around his upper arm. "Hurry, Luke," he said, his legs jittering and bouncing beneath the table.

"You'll be feeling alright in a few seconds," said Luke. He took a hypodermic needle off the tabletop, and then blew out the match. The powder had liquefied to the point where he could now get it in the needle. He hadn't yet seen us watching from the kitchen door. When he stuck the needle into Chimp's arm, Chimp grimaced. His legs stopped jittering, and euphoria flooded his face when the LSD hit his bloodstream.

The girl was already preparing another batch, this one for herself. She lit another match and waited impatiently for the new dash of powder to start bubbling.

Luke turned and saw us watching. "How did you sleep, boys?"

"Like a baby. Thanks, Luke," I said, trying not to sound as uneasy as I felt.

"Hey, boys, this is the real stuff," he said. "We normally don't just give this out to anyone, but since you're new friends, we'll share with you."

Just then, Steve walked out from the bedroom to see what all the fuss was about.

"No thanks," I said. "Just wanted to thank you for letting us rest our weary bones here for a few hours." I was starting to feel sick. My stomach was flipping, and my skin felt clammy. It was such a grotesque scene. It felt like the entire house was *ill*.

Luke noticed Steve and made the same offer to him.

"No thanks," said Steve. "But I'll watch if it's okay."

Steve watched closely when the needle drew near the young girl's arm. He watched the reactions of everyone in the room. I wondered why he wanted to commit such a grim vision to memory. Perhaps he wanted to make sure that he couldn't ever forget it, that it would always be able to serve as a reminder and a warning that there are certain paths you simply can't afford to step on to. After her injection, without saying a word, Steve picked up his gear and walked out the door. We followed, saddled up, and rode away as quickly as we could.

After a while, we pulled off to talk about a plan for the afternoon. We decided to head towards the Grand Ole Opry. Not long after that, we were at a gas station. I watched Tom open his wallet. His face contorted, and he threw the wallet to the ground in disgust.

Someone in the house had stolen forty dollars from him. He hadn't put his wallet under his head like I'd suggested, but it had been right next to him on the floor. "It must have taken a lot of guts to steal it from right out under my nose!" he said.

There's no gamble that a guy with a habit won't take.

CHAPTER SEVEN:

# New Orleans, Party Town, USA

T he next morning, the skies were cloudy as we headed south. We drove until sundown before taking our first break of the day, which we had spent cruising along at a refreshing seventy-three degrees. It was seven when we stopped and made camp at a traveler park ten miles outside of Montgomery, the state capital and the home of Governor George Wallace. We all thanked God for another safe day and called it quits at ten thirty, hoping the next day would be sunny and even warmer.

When we woke, it was Sunday, October 24. There was a light mist in the air, but, as if some weather God had heard our pleas, it was even warmer than the day before. Mobile, Alabama, was 188 miles due southwest. We hit Pensacola, Florida, at around noon and headed straight for the Gulf of Mexico. After two-and-a-half days, we finally rode into a gulfport. Docked at the wharf was a double-masted fishing schooner that someone was restoring. Her name was "The Buccaneer." A gold-plated plaque on a railroad tie told us that she'd been built in Essex, Massachusetts, in 1907.

Taking Route 98 west along the gulf coast to Mobile, we sped away from the inclement weather. Thirty miles farther down the road, my bike decided to give me some trouble. I was burning gas, which meant my plugs would be loaded with carbon deposits, which compromised my top speed. I was losing power and we couldn't figure out why. We pulled a safe distance off the road so I could clean my plugs.

With my Swiss camping knife, I shaved them clean and tightened them back into the engine head. We drove a few more miles to a small town and filled up at an Exxon station. I can't remember the name of the town, but we knew that Mobile was another sixty miles away. I was still getting lousy gas mileage, and my bike wasn't doing any better. The clouds were catching up to us so we had to look for a place to camp, and fast. Since we were close to the gulf shores and it was off season, we considered camping on the beach. Because our tent was self-supporting, we could pitch it right on the sand, assuming that there weren't any unforeseen problems heading our way.

It was another ten miles to the shoreline, a relatively a short ride. Except, when your bike is running foul, you wonder how serious the problem could be and how much it is going to cost. Every additional mile you drive when something is wrong increases the chances of irreversible damage. A big repair bill would set us back some, especially if I ruined my engine by pushing too hard. It was probably something simple, but we couldn't put a finger on it. We were tired and hungry, and the weather was beating down on us like it was part of a conspiracy.

Boarded up and deserted cottages lined the road. The desolate sight made us all feel a little low. After a few miles of barren land, I slowed to a careful stop and wiped the mist from my face shield.

"This area reminds me of the Cape when they close down things after Labor Day," I said. "But I noticed some folks in a cottage a couple of miles back. Let's ask them if it would be alright for us to pitch our tent out front off their beach."

We drove on back through the dismal wetness to the only cottage showing signs of life. It was a beautifully constructed house supported ten feet above ground with steel poles that were at least five inches thick. It was raised off the ground so a rising tide couldn't wash it away in the middle of a ruthless storm.

Tom noticed that the Cadillac Seville in the driveway had Canada plates and a doctors' logo. "This guy goes south for the winter," he said. "Man, it must be nice to have a ton of money." He sighed. "This house is rich looking. It must have set him back at least three hundred bucks a week to rent. I suppose to a doctor it's peanuts."

I rapped on the screen door. Two older men in their late fifties approached cautiously. After talking with them for a few minutes through the screen door, they decided we weren't outlaws or madmen. Our intentions were clear when they saw our bikes packed with camping gear. The two men were part of a pair of couples that were there on vacation. The man with the Cadillac Seville was from Montreal, visiting his friend from Alabama. He was a doctor and made an annual visit so they could see each other. He started praising the area and the beaches to no end, like he had suddenly turned into a poet. I could see how the place would be a relief from his everyday pressures.

Since there was no one living next door, they didn't think the people would mind if we parked our bikes under their house, out of the bad weather, and pitched our tent on the beach.

"If anyone bothers you, tell them to see me, boys," he said.

"Okay, thanks, doctor. We appreciate it."

That was the first time I'd ever cooked dinner under a house. We set the stove in an old deep sink to protect it from the ocean winds. Then we left our dirty dishes for the next day and quickly walked to the beach. Now the mist wasn't as bad as the wind, which was blowing harder than before dinner. Like a toothache, a nasty wind is impossible to ignore and we were in a hurry to get inside the tent. With the strong copper cross-joints that I'd made in Virginia when the plastic ones broke, we didn't have to worry about the wild winds snapping the tent's aluminum rods in half. We placed the tent so it faced into the wind, which eased the pressure on the rods. With the front door and the rear window open, the wind passed through freely, a most unwelcome guest. The wind raced in with all its force and expanded the sides of the tent like a balloon. It was not a one-man job. While Tom finished connecting the rods, Steve and I stretched the tent out on the sandy beach. When Tom was ready with the rods, we worked quickly to fasten her down securely. Tom ran to get our gear to weigh down the tent, while Steve and I held her down at each end. No more than five minutes after we were in the tent, getting our sleeping bags and gear situated, we heard the pitter-patter of raindrops falling from the darkened sky, echoing loudly and infuriatingly inside the tent walls.

The tent was going to be tested yet again. I didn't think we needed to be concerned because the sand would absorb the excess water. We were pitched up high and at a downward angle at what I hoped was a safe distance from the water's edge. The strong winds worried me more than anything. I hoped we didn't blow away, and I hoped that the aluminum rods didn't break, and I hoped that, one day, I'd never hear or feel this much wind and rain again.

"Well, Mark, we'll soon find out," said Steve while trying to read his book by the weak beam of his flashlight. I was sick of trying to read by flashlight, so I turned in early.

A sudden shift of the wind woke me at five in the morning. It was still dark, and the rain had stopped. I crawled out of my bag and out onto the sandy white beach, which contrasted starkly with the gray skies. The wind had shifted, blowing right into the side of the tent wall, which was acting as a sail. If it wasn't for our weight holding her down, she would have blown out to sea.

When the guys woke up, we ate our granola for breakfast and returned to the tent to read, write, and sleep. There was nothing better to do on a grim day with a sick bike. But by noon, the tent was starting to feel as cramped as a straitjacket, so Tom and I decided to do laundry and buy our dinner at a store. The laundromat and store were only four miles away, so we geared up and went.

We were folding our laundry when the weather finally began to break. The sun poured down its warm rays of sunlight, drying up the earth. The sky slowly became a sea of deep blue, and by early afternoon, we had something like decent conditions. Too much gray will make you crazy, and the sun felt like an old friend who I thought I'd lost for good. We cruised west in high spirits.

Back on the beach, we played some three-man football. We had all the territory we wanted since the beaches were deserted. Our mothers would have cracked up if they'd seen their three sons playing football with a beat-up tennis ball (it was the best we could do) on the gulf shore beaches in their underwear.

After a much-needed hour of burning off some energy, Steve went and asked the doctor if we could use their outdoor showers after we took a swim. Then Steve and I took a dip in the Gulf of Mexico. The waves were between three and five feet high. We ran and swam and splashed like graceless seals.

After we showered, we were preparing to cook a hearty dinner under our new house when the wind remembered that it hadn't tormented us for a while. It was just after five, and we wanted to have dinner in the daylight, which had become a novelty.

Steve was opening a can of chicken dumplings with his Swiss Army knife, determined to get the first spot on the stove. All of a sudden, his eye caught a bright orange and blue object rolling across the shoreline, like an out-of-control beach ball.

"Hey! Our tent's blowing away!" he yelled. "Quick, let's go!"

The whole time we ran down that tent, I was imagining the worst: our tent torn and full of big gaping holes. At the last minute, Steve lunged and dove through the air, thrusting his legs as hard as he could, pressing on the earth in hopes of grabbing hold of the tent and halting its disastrous course. Got it!

"Lucky thing you looked up when you did, Steve," I said. "Otherwise this here tent would have seen its last campfire. And that wasn't a bad diving tackle."

We'd been lucky. If Steve hadn't looked up when he did, the tent would have passed by a dip between two tall sand dunes, which would have hidden it from sight. If it had made it that far, it would have made it into a gully and we may never have found it. The thought of being out in that wind with no tent made me shudder.

The warm weather, while pleasant, had betrayed us, drying up the sand, loosening the tent enough so that a strong gust of wind had been enough to yank it out of the ground.

After all that drama, we folded up the tent, and once again began our dinner. Of course, by now it was dark. "Back to candlelight power," I said.

"But we got the tent," said Steve. He looked up. "And thank God."

I looked up, too, and realized that, despite the nonsense and hassle of the day, I was grateful. It could have been worse.

We carried our bags to the house that we'd stashed our bikes under. It had an open-air porch with a view of the beautiful ocean, not to mention a view of every sunrise and sunset. The strong winds cleared out the storm clouds and produced a starlit sky. Each star looked frozen in place, flickering like a candle. As the twilight advanced, the air grew colder. With some difficulty in the brisk air and dim light, I still managed to write a few pages to an old girlfriend before getting into my bag and sealing off the top with a tug of the draw cord, ready to sleep.

The next morning was October 26. It marked seven weeks on the road, and the coldest night yet. It was wild, being on a beach and feeling as cold as those mountain men back in Virginia must have felt on those chilly peaks. How far south did we have to go to settle into some warmer climate? And as if the cold wasn't enough, my bike was still having problems. It was hard not to wonder if we'd chosen the right time of year to travel, but doubt usually creeps in when things go wrong. It would pass. We were still happy.

We had a long sixty miles ahead of us. Out start was delayed by an hour because my bike wouldn't start. Steve pulled out a Honda manual that he'd picked up back in Massachusetts. I opened that manual like I was looking through a book of codes, hoping to unlock some simple secret that would get us moving. I pulled out the plugs and started shaving the carbon deposits, thinking that maybe I'd put in a bad tank of gas and it was fouling up the plugs with carbon. My engine just wasn't burning the gas right, but why?

"Hey," said Steve, "why don't we exchange spark plugs and see if yours work in my bike and vice versa?"

"Sure," I said. "I'll try anything."

It worked! My bike started right up. My plugs blew off a little carbon from the exhaust, but after a while, it was like nothing had ever gone wrong. We got a nice, uneventful stretch of riding, but with two miles to go from the Honda dealer, my bike gave out again. We pulled into a Texaco station in Mobile. It was Tom's turn to exchange his plugs, which got us down the road a little closer to the dealership.

The people at Honda were really down-to-earth. They were a bit busy to handle three oil changes and one problematic bike that afternoon, but promised to work on them first thing in the morning. I asked the owner if we could sleep behind their building and told him about our trip. He didn't mind, but said we'd need to call and let the police know because they made a spot check on the building every night. Getting woken up by a grumpy cop at four in the morning didn't sound any more fun than getting roused by the wind.

The mechanic that was going to be changing our oil and looking at my bike overheard us and invited us to have dinner and then stay at his house. This took customer service to another level entirely. People felt safe around us, and I loved it. If you invite every stranger home, you're eventually asking for trouble, but they just knew we wouldn't be a problem.

It was two thirty in the afternoon, the skies were blue, and the sun was strong, as if trying to atone for abandoning us for a few days. It must have been somewhere in the seventies. Looking up to the blue skies, I thanked God again.

Just before five, Vernon, the mechanic, screwed off our oil plugs so they could drain overnight. We grabbed our sleeping bags and followed him to his Pinto.

When we arrived at his home, Vernon's wife Leandra had the table already set for five. There was a baby chair next to her, so their little Steve could sit and join us. He was cute and looked like a great mixture of Leandra and Vernon. Stevie wasn't old enough to be a steak-and-potato man yet, so he had to settle for beef-flavored baby food that Leandra spooned for him. Some of it even managed to get into his mouth.

They made us feel right at home. We pitched in after dinner to help clean the table off and wash the dishes. With the job almost completed, Leandra pushed us out of her kitchen so she could finish and we could relax in the living room. Vernon was forever offering us a beer, a snack, anything to make sure we were comfortable in his home. There was such happiness in this family. You could read it in their eyes, on their faces, and even in the way the air felt. It was just a good, good place, perfect and pure.

Vernon told us that he'd been eighteen when he said "I do" to a six-teen-year-old Leandra. They'd struggled for five hard years to get where they were. They lived in their own house, on their own land. Neither of then had graduated from high school, but it didn't seem to affect them in any way. However, they were attending evening classes to obtain their diplomas, which they were excited about doing together. I loved the thought of them studying side by side and checking each other's work. Between school, the baby, and Vernon's mechanic work, they had a full, simple, happy life.

Vernon had good news when he woke us up at the break of dawn. He'd started up my bike after dumping in two quarts of clean oil. Carbon had started pouring out of the exhaust pipe, and the whole thing sounded choppy. When Vernon looked inside the framework of the bike, he'd noticed a polishing rag stuffed near the intake air filter valve. After dragging it out, he saw that it was being sucked into the airtake valve, choking off the correct flow of air that needed to mix with the gas to burn properly.

He was as excited about saving my time and money as I was listening to him spelling out that the problem was a dirty rag stuck where it shouldn't have been. It had only been a night, but it was hard to say goodbye to him. We asked him to give our thanks to Leandra and to give little Stevie a tickle from us whenever he needed one.

It wasn't until late afternoon that we decided where to stop next. With the harbor near, I got the idea to go to the Alabama state docks to look for a job. Maybe we could pick up some quick money. However, it was getting late and cold, so we postponed that until the next day. We found a grassy field trailer park to camp at before eating dinner at a Hardee's Hamburger restaurant. We ate, read, and killed some time. Tom's eyes were glued to a book called *Grizzly*. I wondered if anyone had ever written a book called *Wild Boar*. I wrote the day's episodes down in my journal and laughed all the way through a movie called "The Bingo Long Traveling All-Stars and Motor Kings."

It was nearly ten when we pitched our tent under the very cool skies. I took a hot shower, and since the shower room had the only available light, I decided to read a few more chapters before hitting the hay.

The next day was gloomy and cool. It was a good morning to rest in the bedroll a bit longer than usual, but our impatient stomachs got us out of bed at nine.

After a short breakfast, we packed and set out for the Alabama state docks in hopes of finding paying work by day's end. We followed the river to an open gate, and then followed the railroad tracks into the dockyard parking lot. A large ship was emptying its cargo nearby. On the shipping platform stood a big black guy who waved us over. We turned off our bikes, thinking he needed three more guys to help unload cargo. Tom wasn't as anxious as

Steve and I; we two were mainly interested in having a new experience and another story to tell. Of course, money would be nice, too.

We walked up to the dock, where men were unloading shipments of bananas from Guatemala, nearly three thousand miles away. The crates were pushed on rollers that angled down from the ship's deck to the work platform, and then into the many trailer trucks. They could fill ten trucks in one hour's time, allowing ten more to back in and do it all again. That's when we came into the picture.

The black man's name was Tom. He was tall, lanky, friendly and had a great personality. "I wish you'd been here around seven this morning. I would have hired you immediately." The job paid $8 an hour, and they paid at the end of the day. So yeah, perfect, but too late. He said a ship could come in anytime that would need loading. Or not. It wasn't a stable business model unless we wanted to wait around hoping real hard. We watched the men work for a while, loading the banana crates that rolled fast down from the ship to the laborers below on the platform, who then pushed them through to another bunch of men who stacked them in neat rolls inside the boxcar. It was fascinating to see them work so fast and enjoy doing it. And you could tell they knew each other. Hard work can produce a lot of camaraderie.

"It looks like a lot of fun," I said.

"Oh yeah. It's not bad." He nodded at the workers. "Sometimes they start killing each other, you know, and the next minute, they can be laughing their heads off. They'll even go out to dinner tonight and laugh about their squawk they had early that day. Man, they're stupid, but very good-hearted. When someone's wife or kid is sick, everyone puts money in a collection and they give it to the man whose family is going through bad times. Dock people are stone stupid until it comes to helping another dock worker out of a family jam like that one."

We saw an old-timer named Ben who'd been working the docks for forty years. He was operating the forklift, smiling and cracking hilarious jokes to the men, and still he was outhustling them all. I could tell that everyone admired him for his stamina and loved him for his sense of humor. People came to work just so they could listen to old Ben sitting high in his forklift. Work doesn't have to be misery. Ever.

Tom advised us to search for work in Pascagoula, at the Mississippi state docks. He thought that they might be hiring. That was that. There wasn't anything else we could do.

Across the harbor, jutting up as high as a mountain across the bay, was a battleship. "Let's go see it," I said. It was enormous, even at that distance. I couldn't wait to see the immensity of it up close. We had an afternoon to kill. Tom and Steve agreed without any friction.

We took a $2 tour of two battleships that afternoon: the USS Submarine Drum and the USS Alabama. Both were WWII historical heroes. It took four hours to move through all the decks. I knew they would be big, but those battleships were *massive*, like floating cities.

The tour was worth every penny, even though $2 isn't a ton of pennies.

We headed into town to treat ourselves to an Italian dinner. I always thought it was safe to buy Italian food if it's an Italian restaurant. Well, for the first time I was wrong, and the food was what you could charitably call "Just okay." If you're on the coasts, it's a different story, but from then on, I would know that you're rolling the dice when you go into an Italian joint in the Midwest.

After that just-okay dinner, we got back on the highway in order to find a place to sleep. Off of I-90 West, Tom caught sight of a KOA campground sign advertising their location, and took the off ramp. We turned off the ramp where another sign said "KOA Next Right." It seemed like we rode forever, taking lefts, then rights, and following a never-ending stream of KOA arrows. It was another seven miles down the road. KOA is normally pricier than other options, but it was getting dark and cold out (surprise, surprise) and we wanted to get situated. More unseasonable, nasty weather was on the way.

We'd seen a McDonald's on the way. "Hey," said Steve, "let's go back to McDonald's and sit till late at night and then slip in. The office will be closed and all we'll have to do is get up early in the morning before the office opens. We can't keep paying campground fees, or we'll run out of money by the time we get to California. They won't even miss it. Besides, we won't use anything except the ground. If KOA doesn't lower the rates on the off-season, we'll have to do it for them."

McDonald's was warm and cozy. We had plenty of light to read and write until closing time at ten. Then we bundled up and made our way back, arriving mostly numb seven miles later at the KOA trailer park. We quietly rode in and drove to the back. You wouldn't want to use a revving Honda for a pillow or anything, but Hondas aren't very loud and we didn't think we woke anyone. We pitched our tent, and it was lights out.

The next morning, we fled down a footpath towards the back of the park and blazed our own trail through twenty yards of thinly settled woods to a paved street that led back out on the highway. We drove right down by the waterfront in the Mississippi town of Pascagoula. The docks were filled with fishing boats. As we drove down a side street, I saw a fishing company office.

"Let's stop here and ask if they can use any deck hands on those fishing boats," I said.

We parked the bikes in front of an old, shaky-looking building with a sign hanging over a boarded-up door: "JOHNSON & JOHNSON SHRIMP CO."

Tom looked at the rickety stairs leading up to the office door. "This place doesn't look so hot."

"Look," said Steve, "we need a job, so it doesn't matter what this place looks like."

We made our way carefully up the stairs and knocked at the office door.

"Come in, come in!" yelled a hearty voice from within.

"Here goes," I said, opening the door.

"What can I do for you boys?" asked a white-haired man sitting behind a small desk. The office was just a plain room with very little in it. There was the man's desk, two chairs, a wastepaper basket, a coat rack standing in the far corner, and a big navigational map of the Gulf of Mexico on the wall behind the man, who looked like the old man of the sea with his white hair and beard. He was small, but you could see that he had put in some serious time at sea. He was weathered, experienced, and looked like he'd be tough as nails in a fight.

"We're interested in working a shrimp boat," said Steve in a bright voice.

"The gulf has been too rough the past few days," said the old man. "There is a bad storm out there. That's why you see all these boats docked up. Besides, what experience do you boys have? This isn't simple work!"

Well, we had a lot of experience, just none in shrimping boats.

Thinking fast, I said, "We're good workers and quick learners, and we know how to swim."

"Unless you have much experience shrimping, it can be a very dangerous job. Just last week a greenhorn lost his finger in the winch. Another guy got so seasick he couldn't work and made the captain bring him back."

Well, I didn't want to lose a finger or get seasick. We thanked him and went back to the bikes. Then we went to a waffle house at the end of the street. At ten o'clock, with a tasty breakfast in our stomachs, we continued our westward journey. The skies were cloudy and there was rain in the air, so we took I-90 West and drove eighty-one miles to Biloxi, Mississippi, where we looked for jobs again, only this time in a fish cannery. And again, no luck. The fall season wasn't prime time for the fishing industry, no matter how willing we were. We kept going west, following the Gulf coast on another stretch of I-90. At least it was nice to look at. There were beautiful white sand beaches all along the way, strung together for miles.

Once out of Mississippi, the next big stop for the day was New Orleans, Louisiana. We changed onto Route 10 West, straight to New Orleans, and that was just what Route 10 was like—straight, a straight, elevated concrete highway going directly across the Louisiana bayou.

Arriving in New Orleans at three thirty, we quickly performed the ritual of tracking down a YMCA. We pulled over to a phone booth, and I found the address of the downtown New Orleans Y on 57 Charles Avenue. After getting directions from a gas station attendant, we got back on our bikes and headed over. Steve and Tom waited by the bikes while I went in to talk with the physical director. I had a couple of objectives. I wanted to find out what the YMCA was really about and also pick up any new ideas from other directors across the country. You see, that was my job—physical director of a YMCA in Framingham, Massachusetts—before quitting to take this trip. After talking for an hour, the physical director, who was my age, said we could use the facilities. I went out to get the guys.

A workout always feels good, but it was just what we needed that day to dispel the tension we'd accumulated during the ride. Then it started raining as soon as we were packing our gear onto our bikes. Of course.

"Now what are we going to do?" said Steve. "It's six, dark out, raining, and we haven't found a place to sleep tonight. We can't stay at the Y; it's too expensive."

"Look, don't get all grumpy," I said. "We'll work something out. We always do."

The YMCA was situated right in the heart of the city amongst all the tall skyscrapers, so we had to drive way out of our way to eat. Since we were right on the coast, it had to be seafood. After dinner, we had planned on doing some partying because it was Friday night, but with the wet roads and being generally uncomfortable, we decided to find a campground and not push our luck.

The only place we could find within the city limits was a trailer park with a small fenced-in, half-dirt, half-grass piece of ground for tents. It really wasn't any good, but it would have to do. The rain had stopped for a bit, but right on cue, it started as soon as we started putting up the tent. It came down lightly at first, but then the sky just ripped open and lashed out at us. We got into the tent, but the wind was blowing so hard that I was worried about it ripping the stakes out.

I looked out the back window. It was going to be a long night, and there was a very good chance that we were going to be lying in a puddle within a couple of hours, no matter what we tried.

The last flashlight was out by eleven. We just laid there listening to the heavy wind and rain. You can really feel a storm when you're in a tent because of the wind pushing and tugging and yanking at the fabric, and the rain pattering on the tarp in a spastic symphony that's only a few inches away from your skin. Later that night, sure enough, I was woken by the feeling of cold water. My hand was in a puddle. I got up and turned on my flashlight. The floor of the tent was covered in water, and as luck would have it, my side had the deepest puddle.

"Hey, wake up, you guys. We're being flooded out. I told you this was a bad spot for a tent." I wasn't happy about being right, but I'd been right.

Steve and Tom just groaned and rolled over onto their other side. Fair weather friends, indeed! Knowing I'd be soaked in another half hour, I couldn't sleep. I rolled up my sleeping bag and doubled up my space pad and then just sat there listening to the downpour outside the tent.

It was still raining at three thirty in the morning. By now there was an inch of water inside the tent. Steve and Tom were sleeping right in it like it was a warm feather bed and not a cold puddle. Because my end of the tent was sloped downwards, I couldn't lie down unless I was in the mood to drown. Biking and backpacking across the country was never going to be easy, but man I felt pitiful that night.

Saturday morning was miserable. After a night of shivering and frustration, I got up and went for a walk at six. It was dark as I walked out of the travel park and down the wide street, looking for a coffee shop where I could warm up and wake up. I passed a lot of closed businesses, a few people standing on a corner waiting for the city bus, an old man sleeping on a roadside bench, and a milkman doing his early deliveries. The roads were wet and shining, and there were big puddles along the sides of the road. Every once in a while a car would come too close to the curb and hit a puddle, sending up a big spray of water, making me jump to get out of the way. At the far end of the road, I passed a small building that was painted purple and black. The door was open and there was a black man standing in the doorway. Inside, I could see a few men sitting at a bar. *Drinking this early?* I thought.

"Hey, boy, what do you want around these parts?" asked the man in the doorway, his hands tucked in his pockets. *Not welcome.* His tone said it even more clearly than his words.

"I'm just looking for a coffee shop."

"Well, there's one down the other end of the street. Why don't you head that way?" He pointed in the direction I'd just come from.

Outnumbered, my best bet was not to say anything and just turn around. On my way back, a little grocery store opened up across the street, so I bought some milk and a package of Twinkies. It was now seven o'clock, and the sun was coming up. Back at the travel park, I sat on a bench near the office to eat and read the newspaper. Then I walked back to the middle of the park where we'd pitched the tent. Steve and Tom were still sleeping so I quietly went to the park laundromat to wash and dry my drenched clothes and sleeping bag. A little while later, I was reading a novel when Steve and Tom walked in with their own soggy stuff.

I looked up from my book. "You guys finally got up, huh? I don't know how you could sleep in that puddle of water."

"My bag still kept me warm," said Tom.

"Where'd you go so early?" asked Steve.

"Just for a walk. I had to get out of that wet tent."

With their laundry finished, they went back to take down the tent.

"Hey, you guys," said Tom, "I'm going to run and get a haircut and do some shopping. I'll be back around one."

"Wait a minute," I said, pulling up a tent stake. "We aren't going to stay here again tonight so we're taking down the tent."

"Why aren't we staying here?" said Tom. "It's—"

"It's too expensive," said Steve.

"Man," said Tom, "you guys are always looking for the cheap way out. Now we're just going to have to spend more time looking for another place. Look, whatever, I'm going to get a haircut. I'll meet you two at the Y at one." He drove off.

The place wasn't great, it was too pricey, and I'd spend the night in a puddle. I didn't care how annoyed Tom was, we weren't staying there again.

Steve broke down the poles, and we hung the tent up to dry. It was noon and wasn't going to take too long, since the sun had finally decided to grace us with its presence again.

We were sitting at a picnic table when Steve said, "It's always you and I who are trying to get things for free, or look for a better deal. If we left it up to Tom, he'd pay whatever the price was, every time, no questions asked. We need to talk to some people and find a place to stay. Save some money."

"I know, I know," I said. "What are you telling me this for? I'm the one who said we should get out and meet people, remember? Tom's just not like that."

Steve and I were willing to put up with a certain level of discomfort until we found what we really wanted. Tom was willing to pay whatever he had to to deal with any minor headache in the moment, rather than enduring something that would sort itself out if given time.

While we were talking, a nice Italian woman came over with some tangerines. "Hi, boys, I see you're from Massachusetts. Are you two brothers? You look Italian."

We looked at each other. "Yes, we are," said Steve. "He's Mark and I'm Steve."

"My name is Mrs. Masacco, and my husband and I are from northern California. That's our trailer over there." She pointed to a big Airstream a few trailers down. "Why don't you boys come over for a bite to eat? My husband would love to meet you."

"We'd love to!" we said in unison.

Mr. Masacco was a short, stocky man with short greyish hair and a mustache. He was sitting and watching TV when we walked up.

"Alfred," said Mrs. Masacco, "look at these two nice Italian boys I found. Doesn't this one remind you of Joey?" she pointed at me. Joey was their son.

"Hello, boys," he said while getting up to greet us. "Can I get you something to drink?" He gave us each a beer and had one himself.

We talked for a while about nothing, and then it was time to go. Before we left, Mrs. Masacco gave us a small bag of canned goods to take with us and also offered us a place to live if we ever came to northern California. We had apparently worked our magic again. All we did was sit down for a chat, and now people were offering us a place to live.

Steve and I decided that the place had been such a crummy mud hole that we were just going to ride out without paying. After the night I'd had, my conscience was fine with that. We met Tom at the Y at one o'clock and headed over to the famous Bourbon Street to see if it lived up to its reputation.

It was unbelievable, honestly. It was one in the afternoon, and there were people everywhere, walking (some of them stumbling) the streets, drinking and being happy. Bourbon Street is a special place, in a special city. It's like a time machine that whisks you back to when Dixieland Jazz was the big thing. And down there in NOLA, it still is. As you walk down the old narrow street, every building you pass is a nightclub, restaurant, or a strip joint. The streets are narrow, and at night, with the gas lamps flickering, the whole thing looks more like a movie set than reality. The buildings were old, and they looked their age. We heard some Tennessee bluegrass coming from an alley and went to check it out. The alley opened up into a little plaza with chairs and tables scattered around. A country and western group was playing up a storm, and everyone was drinking beer. I bought the first round, and it wasn't cheap.

After a few beers, we psyched ourselves up to find a place to stay for the night. Since we were in a big city, it was going to be hard to find a campground nearby, and dinnertime was drawing near. "Let's just find a cheap motel since we're going to be coming back here tonight," said Steve. It was like the conversation we'd just had about money had never happened.

Tom quickly agreed, to no one's surprise.

"We're going to break our record of not using a hotel," I said, "but I don't care. Besides, we might find ourselves some pretty little ladies tonight." If fortune smiled on us, it would be better to have a room to go back to.

We drove around looking for a hotel with a reasonable rate. On Airline Highway in a small suburb called Metairie, we chose a place called the Sweet Home Motel. After washing up, we went back to Bourbon Street for some fun.

The streets were packed with peopleof all kinds—young, old, black, white, gays, bullies, guys, girls, guys who wanted to be girls, anything else you could think of, and maybe a few things that you'd never dream up—although it was obvious that the streets in New Orleans were always going to be packed with people.

"Man, look at this," I said. There were strippers standing right in a doorway, making eyes at us with their hips cocked, trying to lure us and any other customers inside. "That's not something you'd see in Boston."

"Yeah, because it's too cold," said Steve. The thought of anyone in a skimpy outfit

standing outside in the frigid Boston weather while trying to act sexy gave me a chuckle.

Tom saw a topless joint that looked good. "Hey, guys," he said, "let's try this place."

We spent that night hopping from joint to joint, like everyone else. Around eleven thirty, I saw a foxy lady ordering a mixed drink and got ready to approach. We were having a blast, but I wanted some company other than Tom and Steve.

I walked over. She was a petite blonde of maybe twenty-five years, and she looked ready. When Steve saw that I was making progress, he joined in. A few minutes later, Tom came over. She asked us to walk her to a bar three blocks away so she could say bye to the guy she was supposed to be with. When we got to the bar, we waited outside, because it was a gay bar. That wasn't anything to worry about, but we were on the prowl for women. After a few minutes, she didn't come out, so we walked in. It was quite a party, with men dancing everywhere while the music boomed. We looked around and saw the babe sitting in a corner waving bye to us.

"That chick conned us," I said.

"Let's go," said Tom. "We'll definitely have better luck somewhere else."

With that, we drove back to the motel. On our way back, a couple of cops pulled us over at two in the morning. We noticed a few other cars that they'd stopped and wondered what was happening.

"What's the problem, officer?" asked Steve.

"These people are taking a survey," he said in a deep voice.

"Well, what's the survey about?" asked Steve.

"They want to know how many people drink and drive."

We looked at each other and then back at him.

"Don't worry," he said. "We're not out to bust you guys. We're just here to stop the traffic."

We answered a few questions and took a breath test that showed that we'd been drinking before continuing back to the motel. We didn't hit the sack until at least three.

The next day was Sunday—Halloween.

Tom got up, dressed quickly, and raced off to the nearby Catholic church for the one o'clock Mass. I stayed in the motel room, had some cereal for breakfast, and read the paper.

That afternoon around two, Steve and I rode our bikes to Lake Pontchartrain. Tom felt like sleeping, so he stayed behind. The lake wasn't far away, and it was a nice, comfortable drive. For the first time, we didn't have to wear our helmets. When we got to the lake, we followed Lakeshore Drive, a tourist road that took a lazy lap around the water. Lake Pontchartrain is big, and its waters are rough. On the inland side of Lakeshore Drive was a big park filled with picnickers, people playing football, Frisbee, and other games.

The sides of the were road lined with hot rods and motorcycles with young people all over just hanging out, happy to be alive.

We were cruising down the road, feeling free and happy, when two girls passed in a car going the other way. It looked like they were waving at us, which made me even happier. We looked back and saw their car pulling into a parking spot a little way down the road. We immediately pulled over.

"Hey," I said, "what do you think of that? Those girls were waving at us, weren't they? Let's go see what they want."

We turned the bikes around. I pulled up to the driver's side, and Steve parked by their passenger window. Both girls were bubbling with enthusiasm and asked if we'd take them for a ride on our motorcycles. Cathy was a bright-eyed brunette with long hair and a great body. Debbie was the driver. She was blonde, very pretty, and I thought she had a sparkle in her eye that was there for me alone. They got out of the car, and Debbie jumped on my bike behind me. Cathy did the same behind Steve. I have to admit, even with all the chasing and flirting we did, I was in a mild state of shock because we'd just got hustled by these two babes. I mean, I was used to having to work for it a *little* bit. Still, I can't say that being flagged down by gorgeous women on the road was unpleasant.

Cathy pointed down the road. "Let's go that way." We took off and rode side by side. I couldn't have asked for more. We went for a long, gentle ride, laughing in the sun. When we got back to Debbie's car, they asked us to come over for dinner. We talked it over and decided that Tom wouldn't mind. We'd call him from their place.

It didn't take long to get to their place, which was on the west side of town. They lived in a modern apartment complex with a nice pool just below their balcony. We parked near the entrance to their apartment, and the girls led the way up to their door on the second floor.

"Well, come on in. This is our little place," said Debbie.

"Don't mind this pit," said Cathy. "We didn't have a chance to clean it this week." She picked some dirty clothes up off of a couch just before Steve flopped down on it with a thud.

I called Tom and told him where we were, what we were doing, and asked him if he wanted to come over. Tom said he'd just bought a paperback of Marathon Man and wanted to read it, so I told him we'd be back around ten the next morning. I hoped the book was good, because it looked like he was passing up a hell of a nice night with us.

When I hung up, Steve already had his arms wrapped around Cathy as he told her how nice her place was. "What do you guys want to eat?" asked Debbie, now standing in the kitchenette.

"We don't care," I said, answering for us both. Anything we didn't have to scrounge up for ourselves or cook over a fire in the dark might as well have been a ten-course meal back at the Greenbrier Hotel.

Fifteen minutes later, Debbie called everyone to the table to eat. We had a good meal, a few beers, and a lot of laughs.

After dinner, we sat around and watched TV. At nine, John and Pete, Cathy's cousins, came over to have a few beers and talk.

"Hey," said Debbie, "tonight is Halloween! Bourbon Street must be hopping. Why don't we get into my car and drive down? You never know what you'll see." Excited by her own idea, she ran to get her coat without waiting for a reaction.

Everyone got their coats and piled into Debbie's car. It turned out that even the police were in good spirits. On our way to Bourbon Street, we were crossing the Mississippi River bridge when a cruiser pulled up alongside us. The driver glanced over and gave us all a stare. Lo and behold, the cop had on the ugliest mask on you could imagine.

"Holy shit!" yelled Steve.

"Yeah," said Cathy, "the cops are pretty decent around here."

If I had to get arrested, I couldn't decide if I thought being cuffed by a cop would be better or worse if he was wearing a hideous mask.

Traffic was thick and slow, but we finally made it. We'd already seen Bourbon Street, but it was something else entirely on Halloween night.

"Look at this place!" I said. I couldn't help it. The roads were blocked off to traffic, turning a few square blocks into a dedicated party area. There was nothing but people walking and drinking as far as you could see. "Look at that weirdo over there in the monkey suit!" I yelled. I could have yelled things like that all night and never run out of new things to say. There were all types of curbside hot dog stands and little food trucks. That Dixieland magic was everywhere, compounded by more costumed freaks and partygoers than I ever thought you could find in one place. It was impossible not to love.

We walked around, looking at the wildness and listening to the super-happy music. Two big time clubs—the Maison Bourbon Jazz Club and Crazy Shirley's—were right across the street from one another, and both had great bands just blaring away. On the street in between the clubs, little black boys were tap-dancing to the music coming from every which way. Large crowds would gather around to watch and toss coins into the large Burger King cups the kids placed on the ground in front of them.

As we walked, I noticed someone I recognized. "Hey, there's Tom Heinsohn! The coach of the Boston Celtics!" I said, pointing him out.

"Yeah, and that's Johnny Most with him," said Steve. "He's the voice of the Celtics. He helped me out in one of my recreation programs at the YMCA, last summer. Let's go talk to them."

We introduced ourselves and talked for a while. Tom and Johnny said it was good to see and hear someone from Massachusetts. After a while, they said they had to run to catch Al Hirt's last act at eleven, but they told us to come to the basketball game the next night at the Superdome. Steve and I couldn't believe it. We were huge Celtics fans, and now we were going to get to go to one of their games and cheer for them in a hostile crowd at an away game.

We kept walking and drinking until midnight. Then we wanted to go home, but we were so loaded that we couldn't remember which side of the street we'd parked the car on. So up and down we went, looking for the '69 Oldsmobile station wagon. It got so hopeless that we started describing it to people and asking people if they'd seen it. Cathy walked boldly over to a tall policeman standing near Al Hirt's nightclub and tried to explain our problem to him. But being a little under the weather—which is to say, absolutely hammered—she just couldn't get her point across clearly and he couldn't help us. I'd been confident at first, but now I was really beginning to wonder if we'd ever locate the car in our condition. Logic had deserted our addled brains, and we were basically walking in circles.

On one side street, we merry marauders passed by a huge oak tree. Cathy thought she noticed something move in the upper branches. "Everyone stop for a minute!" she said. "I think I saw something up there!" She pointed at the treetop. We watched as she ran across the street to get a better view. She got under the tree and looked up for the shock of her life. It was that nut we'd seen earlier in the monkey suit! He was up in the branches making monkey sounds and shaking the branches. "Come down here!" yelled Cathy. "I want to see if you're a black ape or a white ape!"

The monkey responded with a few grunts and a shake of a branch. Cathy grunted back. He grunted louder and shook the branches he was standing in more vigorously. They matched each other's grunt for grunt until they had everyone on the street laughing. We still hadn't found the car, so Steve finally marched across the street and dragged Cathy away from the grunting contest. After we'd sobered up a little, Pete remembered the name of the side street that the car was on. He'd got it right, and the night finally started wrapping up.

Back at the apartment, John and Pete said goodnight and left right away. Steve put on some soft, soothing music, while Debbie dragged me into the bedroom and shut the door behind us.

The next morning I rolled out of bed at nine, took a refreshing shower, and then walked into the living room to find Steve sleeping on the couch and Cathy sprawled across a big love seat.

"Wake up, you guys," I said. "It's nine thirty. What do you want to do, waste the whole day?"

The girls made breakfast while we hung a plant from the living room ceiling for Cathy.

With the meal over, Steve started talking about jobs. He wanted to go down to the water and look for work on a riverboat. Debbie said she'd drive us around and help. We spent the whole morning checking with riverboat companies trying to get a job as deckhands. The job description sounded great: seven days and nights on board the tug making $40 a day for just being a helper and cook. Each boat had a crew of only three men: the deckhand, first mate, and the captain. At every stop, we filled out applications, and one for Tom since he wasn't there.

Just after noon, we said goodbye to the girls and went to get him. "We should stop at the Superdome in case Tom is there," I said to Steve as we rode towards the city. Our exit came up faster than we'd expected, and we had to bank our Hondas swiftly from the middle lane of the highway right across the right hand lane and down the exit ramp, like we were pilots putting our planes through maneuvers. At the end of the ramp, we heard a loud voice echoing behind us. In my rearview, I saw a big white police car with its lights flashing. We pulled over, quickly checked in with each other, and agreed that we hadn't been speeding. Then we waited for the cop to get out of his car.

He strutted over to us. "License and registration please." He was a heavyset young man with a deep Southern accent and a large, wide-brimmed hat. We quietly reached into our pockets for our wallets. "You boys know you can't race from the middle lane to an exit ramp. First you have to move over to the outside lane then take the exit."

"We didn't know the exit was coming up so soon," said Steve. "When we saw it, we just got over as best we could."

That was the first time we'd heard of that law. Just then, another patrol car pulled up in front of us and stopped, "Come on, Jed, give those Massachusetts boys a break," said the new officer softly over his PA system. Any mild tension that had been there dissolved as we all talked for a while about motorcycles. The first officer, Jed, gave back our licenses and registration and then asked where we were headed.

"The Superdome!" said Steve, with such happiness on his face that Jed laughed.

"Do you know how to get there?" he said.

"No, not really," said Steve.

"Well, tell you what, boys, just follow me and I'll lead you to it," said Jed, getting back in his car.

So the annoyance of getting pulled over resulted in us getting a private a police escort right to the Superdome. We waved at Jed when we pulled into the lot. He answered back with a short wail of his siren.

The Superdome looked like a giant white half moon corning up out of the ground, right in the middle of New Orleans. It's an enclosed arena that can handle just about any sport, college or professional.

Then we hit our first obstacle. The doorman wouldn't let us past the ticket lobby because we weren't with a town group. Steve tried to explain to the doorman that they were looking for a friend, but no dice.

"Let's go back and wait for Tom at the motel," he said after deciding that this guy was a dead end.

"Might as well," I said.

We hadn't been back at the hotel long before Tom returned from his own tour of the Superdome. "Hi guys, the town was great," he said. "You wouldn't believe that place."

We talked for a while, and then decided to go back to the Superdome and get tickets to the Jazz vs. Celtics basketball game the next night.

"I hope there are some decent seats left," said Tom as we got off our bikes outside the dome.

Amen to that. We rushed in and waited in line at the ticket window. When we finally got to the window, there weren't any good seats left. With despair in our souls, we talked to the short lady who sold tickets behind the counter.

"We're from Boston and came a long way to see this game," said Tom, with us looking over his shoulder, as sad as could be. Now, there are worse things than not getting perfect seats at a game, but the lady felt sorry for us. She said that maybe the tall black gentleman standing by the turnstile could help us. "Tell him Zelda sent you," she said. Without hesitating, we hurried across the big lobby to the turnstile area.

"Excuse me, sir," I said, "we're from Boston and are traveling across the country on motorcycles. By coincidence, our home team is playing tomorrow night. Zelda at the ticket office didn't have any good seats left but said that you may be able to help us."

"From Boston, huh? Okay, hang on just a minute. I'll call up to the Jazz ticket office." The gentleman made the call, nodded a few times, and hung up. "Okay, boys, this is what you have to do. I'm going to give you a travel pass to get by the doorman so you can take the elevator up to the fifth floor, Room 526. That's the Jazz ticket office. I told them you were coming up. They'll take care of you."

We thanked him and got the travel pass that let us by the doorman as if it were a skeleton key. Once inside the complex, we were stunned by the sheer size of the place.

"I told you this place was super," said Tom.

"Well, since we're here," I said, "let's take a little tour. You can be the guide, Tom."

"All right. Let's start here and work our way up to the fifth floor."

Tom gave us the royal tour, and then we went into the Jazz ticket office. As we went through the door, a pretty blonde receptionist greeted us. "Gentlemen, you're expected." She left her desk and showed us to a back room where two women and a young man were working hard sorting out tickets.

"You must be the three guys from Boston," said the tall, thin man in his mid-thirties.

"That's us," said Tom.

"Well, guys, I don't have much left, but here are two different sets of tickets. Both sets are good seats." Then he tried to explain where we'd be sitting at game time, but that didn't help us at all. The place was just too big and unfamiliar to be able to picture it. We didn't have a way to choose.

"I'll tell you what, guys, the work crew is setting up the court now for tomorrow's game. Why don"t you go down to courtside and sit in the seats? Then come back and tell me which ones you like better."

"Man, how do you like that?" said Tom when we walked out. "We even get to pick our own seats!"

"It's unbelievable," I said, pressing the down button for the elevator.

We picked out our seats, and then went back up to the office and bought three tickets. We went back to the hotel, showered, and then sat around reading until about eight thirty. Then we decided to go to a movie at nine, at a theater nearby. *Logan's Run* was playing and it was dollar night.

After the show, we decided to walk down a few blocks to Bourbon Street and hang out. Even on a Monday night, the place was wired. As our trio's resident clarinet player, I wanted to catch Mr. Pete Fountain's eleven fifteen show, but it was too expensive for our budget. We finally settled down in Crazy Shirley's for a few beers and listened to the band. The atmosphere was happy, and we jumped right into the swing of things, laughing, joking, and talking to some pretty ladies sitting at the next table.

Two large older men were sitting at a table behind us. They seemed to be a little upset that we were talking to the two ladies next to them. It was possible that I was imagining it, but then one guy got up and walked by Tom, stepping on his foot as he went by. "If you don't want to get stepped on you shouldn't leave your feet in the aisle," he said in a sarcastic tone. It was obvious that the guy was out to start trouble, so we ignored him. He got a couple of beers and went back to his table via another route. I turned around and watched the two guys staring at us while we drank our beers.

"Hey, guys," I said, "I don't think they like us talking to these ladies."

Steve asked the women if they knew them, but they'd never seen those guys before. An hour later, they had to leav, and asked if we'd walk them to their car. The two men were making them uneasy. We agreed, happy to help. It was also late, and we were ready to go. Their car was only two blocks away. "Thanks for the escort!" one of them said before driving away.

When we got back to our bikes, the two men from Crazy Shirley's walked out from behind a parked car. They were carrying pieces of lead pipe as they walked towards us. Things had gotten very serious, very fast. They stopped ten feet away.

"So you boys like stealing other men's girls, huh?" said one of them. "Well, we're going to show you what we do down here to guys like that." He lunged at Steve, who swiftly jumped out of the way. The other man raised his piece of pipe overhead and ran at Tom and me. Tom grabbed his arm and tried to get the pipe out of his hand, while I wrapped my arms around the guy's legs and knocked him down. Meanwhile, Steve was running in between parked cars looking for an opportunity to get the pipe out of his assailant's hand. Tom and I were now both on top of our attacker, pounding away at him with our fists until we'd knocked him unconscious. Adrenaline racing through our bodies, we rushed towards Steve, who was still waging his own little war. When the man saw us running towards him, he turned and tried to escape, but we overtook him at the far end of the parking lot. I grabbed the lead pipe so he couldn't use it. Tom and Steve knocked him down. "We're sick of jerks like you pushing people around," Steve yelled as he kicked the man in the side.

The three of us had similar histories: We'd never been the neighbor-hood bullies, and we were never the kids who went out looking for trouble.

We came from wholesome, happy families that had led to our generally positive outlook on life. But it seemed like we were always running into people who were looking for problems. We'd usually been able to talk our way out of uncomfortable situations, even though later we'd say that we wished we'd just laid a guy out with a right cross from downtown. We could handle ourselves, but fighting had never made any sense to us. It rarely does. Before we'd set out on the trip, we'd even agreed that, whenever possible, we'd back down from aggressive situations. Out on our own, we were always going to be more vulnerable on the road than we'd be back home. But you can only push someone so far before the bill comes due, and these guys had done it.

Tom was choking the guy, Steve was yelling and still kicking him in the side, and I was beating on the dumb ox's legs with the lead pipe. All of a sudden I heard him really scream out because I guess I broke one of his legs. When he stopped struggling, he just passed out and that's when we raced back to our bikes and took off. Luckily, no one was around to see what had happened in that dark parking lot. We got back to our room as fast as we could, racing each other full speed down the last stretch of roadway.

"I'm just sick and tired of being bullied or pushed around," I said from my bed.

"When they come to, they are going to be two sore dudes who wished they never picked up those pieces of lead pipe," said Tom.

"Thanks for jumping in and giving me a hand with the big turkey," said Steve. "I was getting tired of playing ring around the car with him."

"At least none of us are hurt," I said. "Let's go to bed."

Tuesday morning was warm and sunny. We were ready to go by ten thirty. We rode across town to Debbie and Cathy's place to ask if we could stay there one more night after the game. They said that was fine, and to call them once the game was done to let them know when to expect us.

We spent the afternoon in the library, and then had a small supper. We wanted to get to the game early enough to watch the Celtics warm up.

Seven thirty was game time. The crowd roared at the jump ball. I couldn't believe we were there, all the way from Massachusetts, and now I was getting to watch our team play in the Superdome with my two best friends. It was unusual being the only ones in the stands cheering for the Celtics, but no one hassled us about it. Our team lost by five points, but it was a magical night.

When we were done, I called Debbie. She said to come right over, and that they were watching the outcome of the presidential election. Before we headed over, we had to stop at Burger King for free French fries. That night, the announcer at the game said that if the Jazz scored over hundred points, everyone could turn in their ticket stubs for free fries. After the Jazz scored hundred points against the Celtics, we figured that, even if our team was going to lose, you almost have a duty to cheer for free food.

At Debbie and Cathy's apartment, we left our bikes outside and only took in our sleeping bags. About an hour later, Cathy was looking out the window and noticed two small boys trying to steal some gear from our packs. "Hey, you guys! Two little black kids are trying to steal some of your stuff!"

We rushed down the stairs and scared the kids before they could get anything. "I think we should unpack our bikes and bring everything inside," said Steve, panting.

We unloaded the bikes and carried everything upstairs into the girls' apartment. That night, on the late news, it was announced that Jimmy Carter was the new president of the United States ofAmerica. As big a deal as that was, the smile on my face had more to do with the fact that the past few days had involved monkeys, lead pipes, basketball, battleships, a sleepless night in a puddle, and we may have spent more time looking for a car on Halloween night than anyone in the history of the world.

# CHAPTER EIGHT:
# Texas, What a State

We got up at nine thirty in the morning, showered, packed our bikes, and said goodbye to Debbie and Cathy. They were about as fine and fun as you could hope for, but the itch to travel and see new places had come over us again, just like always. They wanted to hop on the backs of our bikes and come with us, but we all knew that was just a fantasy for them.

Unlike us, who then set out on the next leg of our wild jaunt. More than likely, I thought as I waved goodbye, we'd never see them again, just like so many of the people we'd met on the trip. Before we left New Orleans, we got something to eat and hit the post office before setting out around twelve thirty on Route 10.

It was a comfortable day's ride, perfect for thinking, dreaming, hoping, and enjoying the feel of the air and knowing that whatever came next would be brand new for us. The orange sun set, and a bright full moon rose high into the star-studded sky. We'd made good time, only stopping for gas and food. We reached the eastern border of Texas around seven and stopped at a rest area, where we met a guy named John Simmons.

John was a nice middle-aged bachelor who also happened to be the president of the Beaumont Motorcycle Club. We talked for about ten minutes before he said that, if we were going into Beaumont, he'd ride with us.

While we rode with him, we tried to do everything by the book. After all, we were riding with the president of an up-and-up motorcycle club. It felt kind of like being back in school and walking next to the principal—you had to be friendly, but you were always on guard, trying not to lapse into anything like misbehavior. After the day's ride, the final stretch into Beaumont was easy as could be. We stopped for gas and a hot coffee. Steve had his usual cup of tea. The temperature had dropped severely that night, so we were wearing our heavy armor: long johns, knee socks, T-shirts, heavy flannel shirts, denim vests, mountain jackets, and gloves. With all our heavy clothing and helmets, we looked like spacemen. But even though we were bundled up like astronauts, the riding was still damp and cold. All four of us sat in a booth and talked for an hour while the coffee and tea thawed our bones. At nine thirty, John left to visit his girlfriend. We were hoping he would give us a place to stay for the night but he didn't, and that was that.

After John left, we continued west on Route 10 for about ten miles, and then we decided to sleep at the first rest area we saw. You can find some rest areas in this country that look like they'd make great sets for a horror film, but the rest areas in Texas are very well-equipped and maintained. We picked a picnic table under a canopy to sleep on so we wouldn't have to set up the tent. If the thought of sleeping on a picnic table doesn't sound tantalizing to you, that probably gives you an idea of just how much we did *not* want to set up the tent. But we also wanted to be off the cold, wet ground, avoid the morning dew, and stay away from any snakes that might be looking for a warm place to sleep. We flipped a coin to see who would get the wide table and who would sleep on the narrow benches. The Ritz it was not. Steve was the odd man, so he won. Feel free to take my word for it—it's a talent to sleep on a narrow concrete picnic bench in a sleeping bag, and not one that I think everyone needs to develop.

We parked our bikes next to the canopy and rolled out our space pads and sleeping bags.

"We've been sleeping in the oddest places," I said, putting on my stocking cap. What would be next? If the unpredictability of our trip continued, maybe we'd soon wind up sleeping in a treetop, or in the middle of a pigpen, surrounded by squealing hogs.

"Steve," said Tom with a chuckle, "whatever you do, don't roll off that onto me tonight. I'm having a hard enough time lying on this stupid bench."

"Don't worry," said Steve. "I'm not like Mark when he sleeps. I stay in one spot."

Well, he wasn't wrong about that, but I was not about to apologize for not being able to control what happens when I'm unconscious. We fell asleep to the hum of trailer tires and road noise.

The next morning was beautiful. The sun was bright and the air crisp. It all felt like a promise. But we still needed to wear our warmest traveling clothes for the first few hours. We stopped at nine thirty to get a small breakfast at a roadside diner. When we were done, it was much warmer, so we put away our vests and gloves. It was 145 miles to Houston.

Riding into a big city was a challenge for us when it came to finding lodging, especially when we didn't know anyone there. You can't set up a tent in the city park, the trailer parks aid campgrounds are too far from the downtown areas, and we didn't want to spring for motels except as a last resort. Looking back, it was actually one of the greatest parts of the trip: whenever we stopped somewhere, we had to make friends *fast* or we'd have to scramble. On your mark, get set, make friends! So we were almost guaranteed to leave each place having made new pals.

We got to Houston, a big oil town, around eleven. Route 610 is a superhighway that surrounds the city like a large moat. You can actually drive right around the city and see all sides of it from the highway.

Downtown Houston was a complex of streets and tall buildings, just like most other big cities, except that the buildings were relatively new, modern, clean, and there was still a lot of construction going on. People were moving on all the streets like ants around a sugar spill.

When we got to a light on Main Street, I suggested that we ask someone where the YMCA was so we could go do our usual thing. We pulled over to the side of the road and got direction from a short, elderly black man.

"Where you boys from?" he asked, looking at the gear on our bikes.

"Massachusetts," said Steve.

"You boys are a long way from home," he said. "Where you heading after here?"

"We're not sure," said Steve, "but our final destination is California."

The old man leaned closer with a sincere smile on his face, exposing a few lonely teeth. "Well, you boys have fun. I wish I could go along with you."

So many people said that. I empathized with them, but it also made me sad. Anyone *could* do what we were doing, so how come no one did?

We thanked him, looked back to check the traffic, end drove away from the curb. "Everywhere we go, people wish they could do what we are doing," I said at a red light.

"Yeah," said Steve. "But they either don't have the guts to dump what they're doing, or they have too many responsibilities."

But I'm a firm believer that, no matter what someone *says* they want, you learn what they really want by watching what they *do*. Maya Angelou said, "When someone shows you who they are, believe them."

It didn't take long to get to the YMCA. I went in to talk with the physical director, while Tom and Steve waited outside.

"Don't take too long in there!" yelled Tom as I walked up the stairs. "It's hot out here!"

"Keep your pants on!" I yelled back over my shoulder. I couldn't just go in there and get us a free pass. I had to talk a little. People had been happy to help us at the YMCAs, but it wasn't because I walked in with my hand out and said, "Give me whatever I want." It took charm, smarts, some luck, and sincerity.

The physical director wasn't there, so I introduced myself to the fitness director, who was a pleasant, middle-aged, average-sized gentleman. I explained that I was a past physical director in the Northeast and was touring the country and checking out how other Ys were operating. He was very busy, but made time to sit and chat for a few minutes. Then he showed me the entire facility while he went about his job.

That was one of the biggest Ys I'd ever seen. There were fifteen racquetball courts, three weight rooms, indoor and outdoor tracks, two health clubs, a very large and complete cardiovascular fitness testing center, and a large residence hall. The best part of all was that it was always packed with members.

After the tour, he excused himself and rushed off to a meeting. But before going, he told me to come to a fitness seminar they were going to hold on Tuesday, November 9, at ten in the morning.

Steve and Tom were waiting relatively patiently when I reemerged from the building. I came out and said, "No dice, guys, we're not going to be able to get a workout."

"Let's go to Rice University," said Steve, putting his helmet back on. "Maybe we can workout there. Plus, we could meet some college students who will put us up for the night."

Put us up for the night. Or put *up* with us for the night? Same difference, but I liked the idea.

Tom just sat there on his bike, not caring what we did as long as we did it soon. That guy loved to stick to a schedule.

Rice University was on the other side of town. When we got there, we didn't like the setup of the gym. It wouldn't have been worth my effort to try to get us in, so we went to get lunch at a hamburger stand. While we were eating, we decided to try another Y in the area since there were seventeen branches in the Houston area. I'm not sure more time has ever been spent looking for a workout.

At four that afternoon, we pulled into the parking lot of the East End Y, and I went in to talk to another physical director. This time I came back out smiling.

We changed up in the health club, and then went to the gym to play some basketball. There were only three junior high school boys shooting around. Two of them were really cocky. They were as tall as we were but still needed filling out. We asked them if we could play, and they told us we'd have to wait because they were playing a game, which was obnoxious, because they were obviously just shooting. We waited. And waited. "All right," they finally said, "but you've got to take us on." We beat them three out of four games, and I will admit that it gladdened my heart to watch them slink off the court with their heads down and mouths closed. Learning that you can lose is about as valuable a lesson as there is, and we'd been happy to play teacher.

After we showered, took a steam, and dressed, I went downstairs to talk with the physical director, while Tom and Steve sat in the lounge and read. The director was a young guy like me, and we chatted for an hour about the logistical ins and outs of running a facility. More importantly, he said we could sleep in the gym for the night.

After supper, we came back to the Y for some table tennis and TV in the health club. We met Bob Curmings, a big, heavy man who was a petro-mechanical insulator. He overheard us talking about looking for work and offered us a job. He told us to call him early in the morning. Getting a job was great, but learning new skills was going to be even better. That was also the night we met the "Coach." He was a middle-aged man, average build, married with a family, a junior high school physical education teacher, and football coach, and hence the nickname. He was also the assistant physical director at the Y. At ten, when it was closing time, he asked us if we were going to sleep in the gym, and we said we'd rather sleep outside next to our bikes because we heard it was a pretty tough neighborhood for stealing. He then showed us a nice soft grassy section on the side of the Y next to the running track. We thanked him, got our bikes, and parked them on the grass, which was soft, thick, and made a great cushion.

The sky was crystal clear and spotted with thousands of sparkling stars. Provided that we weren't freezing to death, sleeping under the open sky never got old, even though we'd been doing it since September 8.

The next day, Friday, November 5, we were up at seven. We ran into the Y, washed up, and came back to roll up our bags. Steve called Mr. Curmings for us, but it turned out he didn't have work for us after all. Then he told Steve to check with Brown and Root Construction Company. "They're *always* hiring," he said. We'd heard that before. Steve hung up the receiver and looked at us disappointedly. "Well, that was a dead end," he said.

We spent the better part of the morning trying to find Brown and Root, this magical company that was "always" hiring. When we found it, the foreman shook his head. "We're not hiring." Ah, you don't say? We checked with a few other construction companies, and their answers were the same. For our last resort, we followed up an ad in the paper: "Full or part time work available good wages Call 653-7201." One phone call later, we knew where to go for the job, but not what the job was about. For all we knew, it could have been escorting fine ladies to luncheons or working in a slaughterhouse.

We decided that would be our last try for the day because lunch time was coming and the morning had been a waste. The interview was in Pasadena, not far outside of Houston. All we had to go by was a street and number. After stopping for directions three times, we came to a big mall. We parked as close to the stores as we could get. There were days when we just didn't feel like walking, and this was one of them. Since we were going in for an interview, we looked in our rearview mirrors and combed our hair the best we could. Helmets don't do much to help your hairstyle. Then we walked into the mall and found our spot. Our interview was to be held in an unrented store with two plain rooms. One was being used as an office, and the other was a conference room with four rows of long tables and folding chairs. There was a green chalk board at the front of the room behind the head table, which had a small flat suitcase on it.

We walked into the office and the lone receptionist asked what she could do for us. After giving us pencils and applications, she told us to go into the back room and fill out the paperwork. "Someone will be with you in a while."

There we sat with twenty other people, all waiting for our mysterious interviewer. Our curiosity was at its peak when a well-dressed man in his early thirties came in, introduced himself, and took everyone's applications. He glanced at each form, then asked everyone a few questions individually, but most of it was just chit-chat that didn't seem to have anything to do with work. And he still didn't mention what type of job we would be doing. Steve was getting suspicious. He leaned over to us. "Hey, you guys, he wants us to sell stuff door to door. I've seen fast-talkers like this before. Pretty soon we're going to be out on the street with a box of something stupid, trying to con people into buying it."

He was right. About five seconds after learning that we'd be selling cutlery door to door, we politely excused ourselves and got the hell out in an orderly, single-file line, muttering all the way to our bikes. "We just wasted an hour-and-a-half!" said Tom. Why was the universe so opposed to three fine gents like ourselves finding gainful employment?

One thing is always certain, however: when in doubt, eat. We got hamburgers and kept griping like we were being paid by the word.

That afternoon, Steve got a filling replaced with an eight-dollar white cement job, while I dropped off his hiking boots at a cobbler for repairs. Then Tom and I went to a tennis court to play, while we waited for for the dentist to finish digging around in Steve's head.

We were back at the East End Y by six, where I quickly challenged Tom and Steve to some ping pong. I usually won at ping pong. We hung out, talked to a bunch of people that evening, and didn't do much.

Around nine thirty, we'd had enough of lounging and went downtown to look for some night-time excitement, but the city was almost empty. So few people were out walking the streets that it looked like a ghost town. There we were, all three of us walking abreast down the wide main street sidewalk like the Earp brothers heading for the O.K. corral, with no one in our way, or anywhere else, to challenge us. Finally, we saw a young guy walking the other way and Steve stopped him to ask if he knew of any good clubs. The guy said that there really wasn't anything going on in the city. The clubs were along the strips on the outskirts of town. So, we ate, again, because we couldn't drum up anything to do except chew and swallow.

We decided to give up and go back to the Y. Ha! It turns out that Houston might as well have been designed by sadistic scientists who wanted to see how we'd react if they trapped us in a maze for a night. The city is a labyrinth of highways and poor road signs that seem as if they were crafted just to confuse invaders and lead them astray.

But I'm getting ahead of myself. We thought that all we'd have to do would be to turn around and go back the way we had come. Simple, right?

Wrong.

We started our bikes and headed back the way we'd come. Then, for reasons that escape me still, we suddenly got lost. Worse, Tom went one way, and Steve and I went another. Imagine this was happening to you. Now imagine that none of you have cell phones. What would you do? Do you know?

Tom was the lucky one that night. He drove around for a while, lost, but managed to get back to the YMCA by two in the morning.

Steve and I were not to be so fortunate. We spent our night looking for Tom until we couldn't think of anything else to try or anywhere else to go. When that didn't pan out, we tried to get back to the YMCA. Steve led us to one side of town, and we found nothing. Then I took a crack at it, and led us to another side of town, with equally dismal results. As we drove around, maddeningly, we saw different highways elevated over the city but never any on-ramps. In the rare cases where we did find an on-ramp, there were no signs saying which highway it led to. As if that weren't misery enough, sometimes the highway route was posted, but it didn't say whether it was north, south, east, or west.

We drove around forever, neither of us wanting to admit that we were lost. And even if we had admitted it, it wouldn't have given us anything new to do, or to think about.

It was getting *so* late. The stores and gas stations were closed, and the streets were even more deserted than before. How was it possible that a metropolis like Houston was apparently *deserted*? Finally, on a side street, we found a young couple coming out of a bar that was closing for the night. We drove up to the curb and asked for directions out of town, praying that the strangers would take pity on us and save us from the cruel experiment that was Houston. They said that they didn't know how to get to where we were going, but they told us how to get to the police station. With hurried thanks, we drove off in search of our new destination. A left, two stop lights, a right, and two blocks down on the right later, there it was.

Or rather, there it should have been. Because instead of a police station, we had just pulled up to a closed hamburger stand that didn't seem to have anything to do with law enforcement. I immediately wondered whether they'd given us bad directions on purpose. Either way, the quest continued, except now we were looking for another person to get directions from. And now everyone really vanished. It was as if, just because we needed help, the citizens of Houston ran and hid.

After twenty minutes of driving nowhere, we flagged down a black and white patrol car. The cop managed to give us directions to a highway, and you better believe that we followed his directions to the letter. But no, we ended up at a dead end. The highway was there all right, but no on-ramps. Our composure finally broke, and we spent a couple of minutes yelling creative obscenities. With luck, someone might have heard us and come over to see what the problem was, to take pity on we tired bumblers. No such luck. We bumped into a few more people as we drove about the empty roads, which seemed to grow ever more circular and senseless, like we were trapped in some new offshoot of Alice's nonsensical Wonderland. This time, people at least had the decency to say that they had no idea how to get to where we needed to go. "Don't you people live here?" yelled Steve at one point. "It must be tough living in a city and not knowing how to get anywhere!"

His cries did not fall on deaf ears, because they fell on no ears at all.

As we drove on, Steve noticed an on-ramp with a sign saying "Rt. South." We weren't sure if it was what we wanted, but we agreed that it should lead us to Route 610, the loop around the city. So we happily drove up the ramp. After three miles on the dark and empty highway, Steve suggested that we get off at the next exit because he didn't recognize any of the overhanging highway signs. We didn't want to go too far in the wrong direction, especially in the cold. The only place that showed signs of activity was a small, one-room little building across the street from the exit. There were a few cars parked in front of the place, but no people. As we got closer, we saw a light radiating from a side door and heard Mexican music drifting out. Inside, the place was filled with smoke. There were men wearing T-shirts with packs of cigarettes rolled in their sleeves, playing pool just to our right. Straight in front of the doorway was a long bar, where two men and a woman sat drinking. On our left, a few men played cards at a round table. One of the guys had a pretty girl sitting on his lap, whispering sweet somethings in his ear, and he was grinning like the Devil himself.

We cautiously walked over to the bar and asked the bartender if route south would take us to Loop 610 on the east side of town. In broken English, he said we should turn around and go north on Route IE. Once again, not knowing what to do, we got back on the road and gunned our engines. We didn't realize we were going the wrong way until we saw signs that said downtown Houston.

"Damn! We were going the right way before!" I howled as we rode through the cold, endless night. "Now we might as well stay on this road until we hit Route 610, then we'll have to drive all around this stupid city again before we get to the Y."

So that's what we did. We drove thirty miles out of our way around Houston and eventually got back. We shut off our motors and pushed our bikes around the side of the building, onto the grass where Tom was already fast asleep next to his bike. It was three in the morning before we bedded down. What a night. What a freezing, idiotic night.

We didn't wake up until eleven the next morning, when we discovered that we were roasting like hot dogs in their casings. It was close to seventy degrees, and there's no staying asleep in a sleeping bag when it's that hot.

There were some men running on the track nearby, and some others doing exercises on the grass ten feet away. "About time you guys got up," one of them called. All the guys outside working out seemed to get a kick out of us sleeping on the grass next to the Y.

The morning vanished quickly because we got up so late. I decided to do a tune-up on my bike while Steve and Tom were inside watching a college football game in the lounge.

I had the bike apart on the lawn when a tall guy with a fair complexion came over, introduced himself, and sat down on the lawn next to me.

"My name's Dave," he said. "I see you guys are from Massachusetts. You sure came a long way." I introduced myself and apologized for having to keep working while I talked. Dave had a real heavy Southern accent and instantly seemed like a good guy. He was a big man, somewhere around thirty years old, 6'3", and at least 215 pounds.

After some small talk about him living at the Y and his workout schedule, he asked me if we'd like to join him for dinner. Happy to have made a friend, I said sure and that we'd meet him in the lobby at six that evening.

Dave left to go workout, and I finished my tune-up. Just as I put away the last of my tools, a small man came off the track to look over my bike and gear. After saying hi and asking my name, he said, "Call me Tiger." After talking about the trip, we had a conversation about the YMCA. Tiger told me he was seventy years old, and I nearly flipped my lid. He was a great physical specimen, had been coming to the Y since he was young, and it reminded me all over again why I had committed to fitness and strength.

Steve came out to see how I was doing. I introduced him to Tiger, but he had to leave right after that. "Well, are you done?" asked Steve. I was done with the tune-up, but I was going to have to drive my bike to a Honda shop. It was still riding a little rough. Steve said he'd go with me, and went to tell Tom we'd be a while.

It was a short, blessedly uneventful, non-confusing ride down the highway to the Honda dealer. They were closing in a half hour, but the service manager said he would take care of me since I was from out of state. I drove the bike around to the back where a young mechanic came to take the bike into the shop. Steve and I looked at some new bikes while we waited. I had my bike back in short order, and we went to look for something to eat. We saw a beat-up looking restaurant next to a brand new Burger King and decided to try the old place. The place was empty besides an old black man and a young black boy behind the counter. We didn't have much money so we scrutinized the menu hanging on the wall above the counter. We sort of mentioned our money woes, and I guess they felt sorry for us because they said they'd fry us up each a couple of eggs, some home fries, toast, and a drink each for a dollar. It was a lot of food for a single. We thanked them up and down, and then had the usual conversation about our trip. He gave us plenty of food, and the kid gave us large cokes instead of small ones. They both came over and talked with us while we ate. Once we were done, we thanked them and left. It was outside by the bikes that I was overcome with a warm, happy feeling, but it was a familiar feeling by this point. Those people had just been so *nice*. And it wasn't just us; I knew they would have treated anyone well who walked in those doors. We never would have been treated that way in a big flourishing restaurant that was raking in the cash. We would have been invisible, just another way for the big restaurant to make money. Every time I meet someone who's kind, it makes me resolve to do better myself. I rode away from the restaurant feeling hope for the entire world.

At the Y, we worked out and played some basketball. While we were in the health club getting dressed, we met Roland Manzano, a teacher from Dee Dee Junior High School. He was a heavyset guy, the football-player type, twenty-five-years old and single. He wore his jet-black hair medium length and had a thick black mustache. After talking for a while, he asked us if we would come to his school Monday and lecture for his class about our professions and lives. We couldn't pass that up, and Roland was thrilled to hear it. I was looking forward to adding "Guest lecturer" to my list of things we did on the trip.

It was almost six, so we finished dressing and then went down to meet Dave in the lobby, where he was standing looking out the big glass doors. As we passed by, one of the old-timers said, "Where are you taking these boys, Hawk?"

"Just down to the Piccadilly to get some of their good home cooking."

The old man nodded, smiled, and hobbled back inside.

"Where'd you get that nickname?" asked Tom.

"I used to play football in the world football league. Quarterback."

It goes without saying that we were surprised. Here we were, going to dinner with a professional football player, and a quarterback at that. He motioned for us to follow him to his car, and while we were driving to the Piccadilly cafeteria, we bombarded the poor guy with dozens of questions.

The Piccadilly was an old-fashioned Southern-style cafeteria with a laid-back, comfortable atmosphere. The place was packed. Cafeterias seemed to be very popular down south. We found one everywhere we went. It's probably because the food almost feels like it's home-cooked. You have a huge variety to choose from: different main courses, vegetables, desserts, breads, and beverages, and you can pile your tray as sky high as you want. And that's usually what we did because everything looked so deliciously tempting, and the prices were right for our meager budgets.

While we ate, all we could talk about was football. The Hawk was probably sick of hearing and talking football with everyone he met, but he didn't show it. He told us he got injured the beginning of last season and had to leave the game for a few years. He mentioned names such as Csonka, Kick, Warfield, and a bunch of other guys he'd played with. We wanted to believe he was a pro footballer so bad that we believed everything he said without thinking about it. But it's better to trust people until they give you a reason not to.

After dinner, we paid for our meals and went back to the Y, where we watched a dull detective movie until nine thirty. It was so dull that I don't have the slightest clue of what it was or who was in it. The Hawk was even more bored than we were. "Come on, boys, let's go clubbing and rustle us up some foxy women."

I flew out of my recliner like I'd been tossed from a catapult. "Good idea!"

We thought we would see something different in a Texas club, but night clubs must have a code of uniformity from coast to coast. Once inside, just like in any club, we had to strain our eyes because of the poor lighting, and the air was filled with a thick screen of smoke floating about everyone's heads. It was so bad I felt like ducking under it to get to the other side of the club where we saw an empty table in a dark corner. Getting there was like walking through a minefield. We had to be very careful in the dark not to bump into anyone sitting at the tables along our path. I didn't want anyone breaking out a lead pipe to settle a dispute tonight. By the time we reached our table, a voluptuous, middle-aged hostess wearing a revealing black gown was ready to take our order even before we sat.

Steve caught me staring while the band was finishing up a song. "Hey, Mark, what are you looking at? Is it any good?"

I'd been watching two women that were sitting three tables over. "Let's go do our thing," I said.

The Hawk had his eyes on the cashier: a tall, pretty blonde. Tom wasn't in the mood, a little more withdrawn than usual, so Steve and I went over and chatted with the girls. The place turned out to be a dead end for us all, so we headed back, thanked the Hawk, and then rolled out our bags on the grass.

Sunday was another hot and sunny day, so we decided to drive to Galveston because it had been a while since we'd seen the ocean. We gassed up our bikes and headed down Route 610 in the wrong direction. After a few miles, I realized our mistake and brought us to a stop. "We should be headed the other way," I said. I wasn't about to get into a repeat of the other night.

"This is the right way," said Tom. "Let's just keep going." He drove down the road without giving us a chance to say a word. I watched him go and wondered what was going on with him. Perhaps he had solved the riddle of Houston's layout, a mystery as vexing as the riddle of the sphinx.

Steve wasn't feeling as charitable about it as I was. "The hell with him. He wants to be like that, let him go."

We made it to Galveston within an hour. It was the first time it had been warm enough to ride with shorts on, and we lived it up.

That was November 7, and Galveston was pretty empty. It looked like it was mainly a resort town, so the lack of action wasn't surprising. The beach-front was long, but very small, with a narrow sand section backed by giant boulders that were piled against a tall sea wall supporting the main street behind it. It was too cold to go swimming, so we parked the bikes next to the sidewalk and sat on the concrete benches overlooking the Gulf of Mexico. We took off our shirts and lay down.

Tom drove up just as we were getting ready for an extreme bout of relaxation. "How long have you two been here?" He didn't say a word about riding away from us, only that he'd been down the road a ways, watching a Pop Warner football game.

"Half an hour," mumbled Steve, obviously not in a forgiving mood.

When the big yellow sun began its goodnight dip out of the slot, we packed up, put on long pants and our jackets, and discussed the best way to ride back to Houston. As we were talking, an average-sized man in his early forties walked over and asked us what part of the East we were from. "It's great to hear and talk with some Yankees! Oh, by the way, my name is Art." We shook hands. "I'll tell you boys, since I moved down here two years ago from New York, I've gotten used to the slower pace. It's more relaxing."

He seemed to need to talk, and it didn't feel like it was just about chatting with other Yankees, or the pace of life. He told us about Houston, and opportunity, and how he was doing well as a realtor. He seemed like a party-going person with his easy smile and outgoing personality, but it was obvious that something was wrong. He'd been going on for a while when he finally heaved out a big sigh and told us what was weighing him down. Art was divorced, but he still loved his wife. And he needed to talk about it so badly that even three young strangers like us would do in a pinch.

There was no helping him with that, so I said the only thing I knew to be true in that moment. "Art, take it a step at a time and stay happy. Life is too short not to be."

He nodded and swallowed hard. He gave us his card. "You give me a call if you ever need a place to stay." We'd made another friend, but I spent a good deal of the coming ride thinking about Art, his situation, and what I had said. Life *is* short. I knew it even as a twenty-five-year-old. Every second is a choice, and choosing something other than happiness is wrong, even when it feels impossible.

The ride back was dark and cold, and Route 45 N was heavy with traffic. There was nothing to do but endure it.

It was seven before we hit Houston. The Piccadilly closed at eight, so we rushed straight for it. The Hawk was there eating his supper, so we joined him and talked more football. Since the first day we met him, we had begun to doubt whether he'd really been a pro football player. He always came up with an excuse when Steve or I would ask him to throw a football around. Same thing when we invited him to play basketball. Most people I knew with a shred of athletic ability loved to demonstrate it. He even had excuses for not getting the free tickets to see the Houston Oilers game. To this day, we're not sure if we met a real pro quarterback or just someone who wished he was one so badly that he was willing to say it. Ultimately, it didn't matter to me, because the Hawk we met was a great person. Confronting him about it, even if he had been lying, wouldn't have done anyone any good.

The next day, we had another dead end with jobs, phone calls that went nowhere, and I was starting to think I'd never earn another dollar in my life. Since we weren't going to be working, we decided to do some sightseeing. The Astrodome and the San Jacinto battleground were at the top of our list.

There was a stone monument, 195 feet tall, gazing out across the historic site. It looked kind of like the Washington Monument, but with a star on top. Standing at its base, my head tilted as far back as my neck would allow without wrenching my head off, I snapped a picture.

The monument symbolized the countryman of Texas along with fighting men from all over the United States of America. This fight had ended Santa Ana's oppressive hold on Texas. Texas won the land its citizens so dearly loved, and later won its vote to join in the ranks and become the largest state in the Union. Without this fight, Texas's history could have taken a very different course.

Off at the far end of the park, docked in the harbor, was the SS Texas, a 1917 battleship being restored by a Texas youth organization and contributions from visitors who wished to board her for closer observations. There's no downside to learning some history, and it's impossible to travel without encountering the past.

From there, it was back through the larger oil fields and refineries of most of the major oil companies: Shell, Exxons, Standard Sunoco, and the home boys at Texaco. The air was filled with the grayish film of smog produced by the end result of flames rising high into the air as waste, obviously unfit for human consumption. But people are always going to chase massive profits. If there was as much to gain from cleaning up the air as polluting it, the same people who pollute for money would be the first to switch sides.

After that, Tom went off on his own to tour the Astrodome, home of the Houston Astros. Steve and I went back to the Y for much-needed showers. While we were there, we bumped into Roland again. He gave us a little more information on the class we'd be talking to on Monday, and said he'd like us to talk about traveling cross-country, college education and careers, job experiences, and anything else we thought might be interesting for students of the seventh- and eighth-grade level.

On Monday, it was almost noon when we pulled into the Dee Dee Junior High School parking lot. Most of the school kids were outside racing around, oblivious to the world, but there were a few pockets of students who were watching us, taking our measure from head to toe. As we walked across the paved road, a well-built man appeared holding a walkie talkie in one hand raised to his mouth speaking to someone on the other end.

"Ten-four," he said to the person on the other end, before looking at us closely. "Hello, I'm Mr. Taros, head of security. Can I help you gentlemen?"

"Yes," I said, "we're here as guest lecturers by request of a Mr. Roland Manzano, one of your teachers."

His demeanor softened immediately. "Oh yes, follow me and I will help you locate Mr. Manzano."

He led us through the school courtyard, into the front door, and down the school hallways. It was immediately clear that the majority of the students were of Mexican-American descent.

"Excuse me, Mr. Taros," I said. "I'm a bit confused. I've never seen a security guard at a school like this. What's the problem? Why do they need you?"

"Drugs," he said instantly. "We have to watch for pushers selling their dope to the kids. It was a big problem. Now that there are plainclothes guards posted and patrolling, the dealers have stopped trying to sell to the kids, at least on school property. It's only a deterrent, but it has to be done. There's Mr. Manzano now. Mr. Manzano, these gentlemen were looking for you." Roland thanked him and introduced us all.

"I have to run," said Mr. Taros. "Enjoy your stay, gentlemen."

Coming from a guard, it sounded almost like a command. But I was happy to be ordered to have a good time, and I suspected this was going to be a special day.

While he walked us to the classroom, Roland gave us one more briefing on what he wanted from us. "There are going to be more girls than boys in the class," he said. "I want you to talk about traveling, college, courses you had to take, your opinions on school, what you did after college, how you prepared yourself along the way, and . . ." It was a long list, but they were all things we knew. I, for one, had a lot to say about them all. "The kids are going to love you," he said at the end of the speech. "Don't worry. They're great."

Kids love adventure, and I had no doubt that we'd give them something to remember.

As we entered Roland's classroom, the kids started filing in and giving us the once-over as they took their seats. Roland began roll call while everyone got settled, and then introduced us to his class and the topics we would be covering. We had an hour-and-a-half, and Roland didn't care if we took all ninety minutes to talk and field questions. Even the best teachers can use a breather now and then. These kids were going to learn from our experiences, and hopefully that would spur them on to create their own adventures.

We told them how the trip had come about, what had been easy, what had been hard, what had been scary—they loved that boar story!—how cold we were sometimes, how hard it is to navigate Houston, what sleeping in a puddle is like, how we got on TV, the challenges of cooking under a house, how exciting it is to know that we'd be somewhere else by the time the sun set, and on and on. They ate it up, and then came the questions.

"What kind of motorcycle do you ride?"

"What's it like to have a beard? Is it itchy?"

"How often do you take a shower?"

"When are you going home?"

"Do you guys ever fight?"

"How much money do you have to have to travel?"

"Do you have lots of girlfriends? Do they ride on your bike with you?"

It was all music to my ears.

They wanted to keep listening when the bell rang. There was a collective sigh from the group. You know you're onto something when what you're saying is more exciting to a kid than the end of class! The kids thanked us on their way out, but I felt like they'd done us a favor. Everything is new to a kid, and I think that's something they responded to in us as well. They knew that we, even as grownups, could still see surprise in the world, as long as we went out to find it. I think a lot of my joy on the trip came from a similar place of childlike wonder.

Roland tried to buy our lunch, but we refused. Even though I felt grateful for the experience, we did it for him as a favor, no strings attached.

"We had a good rapport with those kids," said Steve.

"We sure did," I said. "I think we speak their language."

Steve laughed. "They sure asked a lot of questions about your love life, Mark."

"Ah, get out of here. I think they were more interested in our beards."

I'm not sure it's wise to go around interpreting everything as a sign, but I believed that it had gone as well as it had because we were living right. We were trying to be good people, and it showed. It was becoming increasingly clear to me that, if I really committed to something, if I put my whole heart into it, whatever it was, I'd have success. God had been dropping subtle hints all along the way, but humans aren't, how shall we say, the most subtle of creatures. When you meet people, or draw them to you, or are drawn to them, you get chances to help each other. And you can't be self-absorbed when you're helping someone else. Compassion and service get you out of your own head. The road—the trip—was becoming something like a college course in humanity. In a short time, we'd experienced so much of what people can offer, and the dangers they can present. If God wanted to show everyone that we all have the potential for evil as well as good, He'd get great results if He just made everyone take a cross-country trip and pay attention to the people they met.

The final bell rang, and we hurried out of there to avoid getting stuck in traffic. We went back to the Y to see if Tom was back from the Astrodome yet. He wasn't, so we played some basketball. While I was staring into my locker, I had a thought. "Hey, Thanksgiving's not far off," I said. "Today's November 8 already. It's only two weeks down the road. I can't believe we've been away almost nine weeks. It doesn't seem that long."

"No, you're right," Steve said. "Only seems like yesterday. It must mean we're having a good time."

"Right, but this year will be the first year we won't be home for Thanksgiving. We're going to miss a lot."

"Yeah," he said. "But who knows? We might just run into a large Mexican family who celebrates like our parents. Let's think hard on just that happening."

We had nothing to lose. I didn't mind the idea of trying to turn Steve's suggestion into a prophecy. Ask and you shall receive; knock and it shall be opened.

"Yeah," Steve continued, "let's think hard on the large, happy Mexican family. It sure will beat hot dogs and beans on the road side."

When Tom got back, he said the Astrodome had been great, but it was no Superdome. I guess not all domes are created equal. "How'd your lecture go?" he asked.

I tried to gauge his reaction as I told him about how well it had gone, but he was tough to read. I couldn't tell if he was miffed that he hadn't gone with us, or pleased.

"I think this trip is the greatest thing we've ever done," I said. "I don't regret it one bit. I wish that every person who's told us they wished they could do it with us had jumped in and we were leading a huge caravan, like a parade from coast to coast."

"I think other people are what's making the trip the most memorable for me," said Steve.

On the way down to play some basketball, we bumped into Roland and invited him to come play a few games.

"I'd love to," he said, "but I have a heavy date later on this evening. Don't want to wear myself out, if you get my meaning. Where are you guys headed next?"

"We have some friends in Dallas we want to see," I said. "Then straight down to Austin, then San Antonio to see the Alamo."

"Then on to Corpus Christi," said Steve.

"Hey, that's my home town," said Roland. "You have to stop in and see my parents. I'll give you their address. I have a younger brother, Mariano. He's twenty-two and quite the ladies' man, so you guys will hit it off. He has his own apartment, too. I'm sure he'd put you guys up. Man, I wish I could take my bike and go with you guys, but I have to teach." Roland didn't have Mariano's address on him, but he said we should just ask his mother when we get there. "Seriously, you make it down there, you look them up. Thanks again for today. The kids and I really loved it. Take care of yourselves and be careful."

One more person who said they wished they could do what we were doing. One more goodbye. One more friend in the rearview mirror.

After dinner at Piccadilly that night, the Hawk retired early because he had work in the morning. To fill the vacuum left in his absence, I called our Yankee business acquaintance, the realtor we met in Galveston. He gave me directions to his pad and invited us over for a few drinks. His place was only seven miles off of the 610 loop surrounding Houston. It was a cool ride, but when we arrived, our Yankee friend had enough bourbon to thaw out a fleet of Arctic explorers. After a few, he started pouring out his life's ailments, all variations on the themes he had brought up in Galveston. We listened. He and Tom talked about brotherly love. And life. And death. Philosophy and pain.

We talked about absolutely nothing. Or maybe it was absolutely everything. We relaxed. Then we relaxed some more. Then we were so relaxed that we forgot to get up to leave and just passed out where we sat.

We were going to rise early the next day to look for a job, but when you party like we had the night before, the next day has to be spent in convalescence. Our bodies were screaming for rest. On the way back to the Y, we checked the post office general delivery to see if anyone loved us today, but walked away empty-handed. Then we split up and took a day apart. I took a cardiovascular fitness test workshop at the main YMCA in Houston and was there all day. Given the amount of bourbon I'd slugged down the night before, I can't say that my powers of concentration were at their peak, but I didn't regret going to the workshop. I finally returned to the Y to catch up on some reading and writing. I wasn't up for anything else. It's easy to forget that booze is a poison until you go so far that you almost feel poisoned.

That evening, Coach told us about a pizza joint where you could get all the pizza you could eat for $1.99. It was pretty close, right off of South Broadway, and we had no trouble finding it, practically guided by the smell of the food. Amazingly, someone also gave us good directions for once. Houston couldn't be bothered to put up signs about anything important or useful, but nearly every sign we passed on the way said "$1.99 Pizza! Beer and wine!" When we got there, we sat down and started eating like we were on death row. A guy came over and asked us all of the usual questions about our bikes and the trip. It made me think we should just get some cards printed up that explained our trip, to get a break from talking about it everywhere we went. Then we kept chewing and wiping our mouths and going back for more, over and over, until Tom cleared his throat and dropped a bomb.

"Guys," he said. "The trip is going to end for me in five weeks. I'm not going to work with you tomorrow. I'll sell my bike and take a plane home. I calculated that, for those five weeks, I'll have enough money. I'm going to devote the rest of my time to working out and touring. When I got ripped off for those forty bucks, it set me back one week." Even as his words sunk in, and I started to think about what they meant, I realized that, more than anything, Tom sounded incredibly lonely. There was a tear in his eye when he finished speaking.

Now the pizza parlor seemed like a place infused with significance. Tom had chosen this spot to draw a line and step across it, leaving us on the other side. Even though we'd just eaten enough to feed a small country, I felt empty and I was sure Steve felt the same. If it had been anyone but Tom, maybe Steve and I could have changed his mind. But I knew Tom too well, not that we didn't try to convince him to stay, to postpone his decision, to give it some time. But we made no progress with him. We had been able to coax him into the trip, but that felt like it had happened in another lifetime.

We didn't know it yet, but there was a man sitting alone in a booth nearby, listening to Tom's farewell speech and our subsequent pleas. He was touched to see three true friends expressing sincere love and care for each other. Tom, Steve, and I talked for a long time at our table, each of us talking about our own various heartbreaks and concerns, and the man listened to it all. We only learned this when the waitress brought our checks and told us that our drinks were paid for.

When we turned to thank him, he had already gone. We never did know who he was, but he made a hard night a little easier.

Joe, our Honda friend and new host, saw that we were finished with our meal and asked us if we were ready to go. He introduced his roommate Jerry to us as we made for the door and out into the cool evening air. The thought of Tom leaving hadn't really hit me yet, not with anything like full impact. I knew it probably wouldn't until the day actually arrived. Five weeks was a long time away. Maybe something would come up to change his mind. Easier said than done, but I knew it wouldn't do any good to worry about it.

The bright floodlights of the Pizza Inn parking lot beamed off our chrome pipes, giving our Hondas a look like you'd see in a showroom window.

Joe and Jerry couldn't believe the excellent condition we were able to keep our bikes in, even though all we'd done was regular care and maintenance. They seemed to think that was an achievement in itself. It was odd to feel admired for basically doing the minimum, as far as bike upkeep is concerned.

We followed them for a short distance to their apartment, where Joe had us park our bikes in front of his car under the carport. We took our sleeping bags, soap, towels, and toothbrushes in, and covered our packs with brown plastic bags. The skies were threatening again.

Joe and Jerry were attending the University of Houston. They were both in their senior year studying to be chemical engineers. Like nearly everyone else we'd met, they too said that they would love to be able to travel with us. They were fascinated by a few of our stories, and they were jealous enough to turn every shade of green you've ever seen.

Since we had to get up early the next morning, it was an early night. The living room floor would be our bed, instead of the Y's grassy lawn.

Joe brought us out an alarm clock, which we set for 5:00 AM. After a few minutes, the dark room filled with a strange quiet. "Tom," said Steve, "don't go. Come to work with us tomorrow. We're your friends."

Tom didn't answer. He was choked up and despondent because his homesickness was overriding everything else for him. Sleep was a long time coming for us all, restless spirits that we were.

Morning came early. With our sleepy eyes half open, Steve and I tried hard to step into our pants without the light, not wanting to disturb Tom. When we stepped out the front door, an unexpected summer breeze tickled us and lifted our moods.

Coach had told us about Peak Load, an temporary agency that paid daily. A day's work load could involve anything from the construction of buildings, roads, to factory labor: hard work at $2.30 per hour. Peak Load's office was next to the post office in Houston. We filled out some forms that asked for our social security numbers and signatures. They wrote up a time ticket and asked us to take a seat, saying they'd call us as soon as the jobs came in. We turned around to sit amongst at least twenty other men who got there before us. They had to have slept there overnight, I thought. We later found out that Peak Load handled the graveyard shifts and operated around the clock. A crew of tired and beaten men walked through the front-door archway, ragged from just finishing a job that had taken the entire night. They were awfully dirty, and most of them were Mexican or African American. They handed in their time cards, and the man behind the counter dealt out $17.30 in cash to each one. Most of the men walked out half asleep, headed (I hoped) for home and a nice soft bed, but a few diehards stayed for a cup of coffee or to place a quarter in a pinball machine and wait for another job assignment. I wasn't sure if they were made of steel or desperation. Maybe some of both. It wasn't a stable arrangement, so it could only draw people who couldn't work steady jobs for whatever reasons. I figured that most of the money would probably go to drugs and booze.

We felt a little uneasy sitting amongst all these shady characters, but just like them, we were there for the money, not the company. We'd done all right, but we needed a little financial cushion.

It was almost eight when we got called up. The man behind the counter said he needed two guys immediately to unload a truck. He gave us directions to Vaughan and Sons Automotive Distributor, just seven miles from Peak Loads. He gave us a carbon copy of our time tickets. "Give it to the man in charge," he said. "Bring it back if you want to get paid for the day."

It took us ten minutes to make it to Vaughan and Sons. We walked into a warehouse and saw a trailer truck being unloaded. Vaughan and Sons sold automotive parts and handled the distribution of car oil and grease to the local gas stations.

The inventory manager, parts worker, and truck driver were unloading the shipment when we entered the scene. The inventory manager's name was

Jack. He yelled to his two coworkers to take a break and come say hi. Jack was a thin man in his mid-thirties. His job was to take orders, see that they were delivered, and make sure that the warehouse was stocked.

After he looked over our time slips, he directed us to the end of the truck. A long track of rollers extended out of the rear end of the twelve-wheeler, loaded to the gills with cases of car oil and twenty barrels of grease at the front of the trailer car.

We had the first trailer emptied by nine thirty. The second truck was loaded with anti-freeze, which didn't arrive until ten forty-five, along with two more temporary workers from Peak Load. One was black, the other white. Both had criminal records, both for drugs. Like a villain in a comic book, the white guy had a slash mark over his right eye and stitches still in his left arm from being stabbed by two guys in retaliation for a girl he beat up.

Their work wasn't any more promising than their appearance, and before long, Jack sent those two dead-end cases back to Peak Load for their money, and then kept us around to clean up and talk. He liked our clean-cut appearance and educated speech even though we'd arrived by motorcycle like vagrant hooligans. After talking to us awhile, the motorcycle-riding, bearded hippy, freak stereotype image dropped away. We only worked six hours, but he put down eight and gave us lunch. He was so impressed with us that he called Peak Load and gave us both a good recommendation, and then he let us go early since the skies were threatening rain. We thanked him for the extra time and drove to the post office to check general delivery for mail. It was still too early to check back to pick up our money. It started to shower, but we got lucky and the rains only lasted a few minutes, just long enough to dampen our jackets and soak our beards.

When we returned to Peak Loads to cash in our time slips, there were still men sitting in chairs drinking coffee or puffing on cigarettes, waiting patiently (or impatiently) for a job call. The man that had sent us out that morning had received a call from Jack commending our work. He dealt each of us $17.30 in cash and told us they had work, twenty-four hours a day, seven days per week. He kept repeating it, and it was so obvious that he wanted us to come back that it was hard not to laugh.

We thanked him and rode back.

Tom had spent the day relaxing and catching up on his letter writing. We had enough energy to play a few basketball games before showering for dinner. But then we were so tired at the dinner table that even eating became a difficult task. When lifting a fork to your mouth feels like a weighty task, you've worked yourself hard. The fatigue of the day had ambushed us all at once. It was hard not to envy Tom's day, which had been discomfort-free, as far as we could see. If we'd had only an eighth of his energy, we'd have been able to finish out the night with something more like vigor and less like lifeless zombies.

We had to get to bed because we were going to be up at five again. We were back at Joe and Jerry's that night, and were entering a veritable coma by nine thirty.

Unfortunately, the next day ended up as a rest day, even though we wanted to work, and even though we did our part. We arrived at six at Peak Loads, like the man said, and were still occupying one of those beat-up chairs at nine fifteen. Exasperated, we turned and walked out, a little disgusted when we realized three hours of good sleeping time had been wasted sitting there for a job that never materialized. Twenty-four hours a day, seven days a week—yeah, right.

Without work, the question of moving on answered itself for us. Besides, Tom was getting restless, even though he was bailing on the trip. We plotted our course, north to Dallas.

That was a Friday morning, gray and chilly. We thanked Joe and Jerry for putting us up and then hit the road. Since the post office was on the way, we stopped off to check out our on-the-go mailbox. We planned on leaving a change of address card for San Antonio, figuring that we'd be there within two weeks. Dallas would be first, and then south to Austin. That would give the mail service just enough time for our mail to catch up with us.

As we drew near San Jacinto Street downtown, great hordes of people were milling around on the sidewalks and street in front of the post office. What in the world was this mob? That's when Steve spotted someone amongst the swarms of people, standing tall and proud. And not just tall and proud, but proud to be black. And not only proud to be black, but having a hell of a lot of fun being black. It was the heavyweight champion of the world, Muhammad Ali! I couldn't believe it!

"Awwwwwright!" Steve shouted and jumped up and down. "That's Ali! Right there!" He kept pointing and screaming as if I couldn't see it for myself. "He must be cutting a scene of his movie right now! Let's park and get over there!"

I was an Ali fan—nearly everyone was—but Steve was on another level of adulation. He had always wanted to meet Ali, and now the man himself was standing there before us. "Not only might you get to meet him," I said, "but we might even appear in his movie."

Steve's eyebrows shot up, and he clenched his jaw as the possibility registered.

Hey, why not? The whole thing had been improbable. We weren't supposed to get on TV at the football game. We weren't supposed to be able to make this trip as easily as we had. We'd beaten the odds at every turn, so why couldn't this happen?

Steve couldn't find a parking space fast enough. I thought he was going to explode with nerves and happiness.

We raced for the front of the crowd to try to get closer to Ali. He was larger than life. Charisma is something you can't buy. He had a presence that you had to be around in order to understand it, and even then, it was impossible to describe. You could have felt it from a block away. He was absolutely hypnotic. There he was, with a clenched fist, holding the shot, knowing all of the eyes were on him, and obviously loving every moment of it. The baddest, fastest-punching, fastest-talking, smoothest man on the planet. But despite his fame, he was deadly serious about civil rights and obviously intended to make a statement with this film.

There was a quick break. Ali signed autographs while the director, Tom Shaw, was getting his camera crew ready to brief them on how to shoot the next scene.

The assistant director, who could have been Yul Brenner's twin brother, was leaning against a studio spot light, dazzled by the onlooking crowd's adoration for Ali. My goodness, what must that feel like? When people treat you like you're a God, do you start to feel like one?

We drew ever closer. This was our prime moment, and he was our prime target. I wanted it worse with every step, and I knew Steve did as well. I had to make this happen. It had to. It just had to. *Stay positive, stay positive*. Soon we were standing in front of the assistant director, jittery with adrenaline.

The assistant director gave us his okay to line up with the other extras when called to be briefed on the next scene. One step closer. It was almost time.

Regardless of the cloudy, cold day, there were a thousand suns shining in our minds. But Tom had backed off, preferring to watch. He volunteered to hold our coats and take some good action shots. The scene was supposed to depict a hot summer day in Houston, and the cast had to remove their warm wrappings to make it look realistic despite the forty-degree weather. But you couldn't have stopped any of them, or us. The dismal weather couldn't dampen the happiness of being in Ali's movie, *The Greatest.*

The scene started off with Ali riding on to San Jacinto Street to park across from the post office. Sitting with Ali in the yellow taxi cab were the actor Paul Winfield, as Ali's lawyer, and his trainer, Drew Bundini. Ali stepped out of his front seat and walked into a telephone booth, a prop, although there had originally been a real booth there. This was where Ali originally called his mother before forging his way through the demonstrators en route to the Houston Post Office to argue against his induction into the ranks of the Armed Services. This is where we came into the picture. The coordinator who'd briefed us earlier instructed us to whoop and holler, to mob Ali as he walked through the crowds of people crossing the street. "Don't throw any punches!" he said. "Just show anger!" I couldn't imagine that anyone would have been dumb enough to throw a punch at the champ, but you never know.

Other extras were supposed to yell on his behalf, shouting about his rights and his privilege to stand up for his religion. Guys in hardhats who represented construction workers screamed at Ali for being a black, yellow-belly chicken. The pro-Ali demonstrators held up signs reading "Fight for your rights Ali. It's not a declared war. It is an illegal War!" *Vietnam.* These people gave him the added courage he needed then to stand by his guns and declare a peaceful war with the US Government.

The scene was set. Director Tom Shaw yelled through the megaphone. "Okay! Send on the taxi! Action! Roll it!" Our excitement doubled with each of Shaw's commands. We decided to wait until after Ali made his call and then started heading for the post office's front archways. There, we'd be closest to the camera when Ali cut his path across the crowded street. The camera rolled on wheels up an inclined metal track, like a train moving slowly on its rails. It would steadily follow Ali and the pressing crowd, accelerating across San Jacinto Street and up the cement steps leading into the Armed Services recruiting branches that were housed in the post office.

Tom Shaw stood high on a platform, watching Ali and the crowd, trying to see everything at once, to feel for anything missing, or anything that might improve the shot. His assistants did the same, trying to see whatever he might not.

After cutting the first scene, Shaw noticed that the crowd had stormed too close, pushing the Houston police back, only six feet from the stairs where Ali argued with Drew Bundini while his lawyer Winfield looked on. They cut the scene as Ali opened the door and walked out, with the trainer and the lawyer trailing in his footsteps.

It was a bad take, but it was just as well. We needed a practice run so we'd know exactly where to stand for the longest coverage. The mind of a schemer can never afford to rest! And beside the excitement of making a movie, we needed to run through it once since we were green horns when it came to this stuff. Because it was only one scene, we had to find a way to stand out with Ali. We weren't going to get another shot at this.

Among the many lessons I'd learned on the trip, one of the most unexpected was this: never underestimate the power of a beard. Beards are the key to glory. The director noticed our facial hair and instructed us to be active pro-Ali demonstrators. Once Ali left the telephone booth, he pushed his way through the crowd right to us. When he was nearing, we moved to each side of him and escorted Ali right to the line of Houston police officers. On our way, we spoke a few words of encouragement and patted him on the back, his lawyer and trainer following behind us.

We made this take from this angle three times, and then Shaw asked for the camera to be shifted off the truck and placed high on a platform for a down-angle shot.

In between takes, Ali relaxed and clowned around with his admirers and slap-fought with anyone who came forth to challenge the champ. He hugged a beautiful black girl who asked him for his autograph and whispered in her ear loud enough for those only in the immediate area could hear. "Come with me. I will make you rich and famous."

She answered, embarrassed, "I already have a man."

"Leave him. What can he do that I can't give you?" Ali then embraced her even tighter, bending her over at the waist and then quickly released her before giving her his autograph while she grinned and blushed. He was the best, but he only boasted in fun, even though we (and he) knew his skills were legendary.

After the last take, on the steps of the post office, someone shouted out. "Hey Ali! Have you lost any speed?"

Ali pointed at him. "I am so fast that, when I turn off the light switch in my bedroom, I'm in bed before the room gets dark. I am so fast—" He stopped to motion to a man, who stepped up and extended his arm out with palm open, in front of him "that I will hit this man's hand with my fist ten times before you finish counting one, two. One, two!"

"One, two!" shouted the crowd." One, two!"

"Do it again!" he said.

We did.

"Again!"

We did.

Then, Ali sized up the man's extended arm and stared at his hand. He was building up the crowd and had them right where he wanted when he came out with the clincher. Everyone was quiet, waiting to see how he was going to accomplish an impossible task.

"Do you want to see it again?" he said with a huge smile.

The crowd roared with laughter.

He stepped down to sign a few more autographs and then rode back to his hotel. The crew was breaking up and packing its equipment into the trailer trucks.

We walked back to join Tom, who had our jackets and an autograph that he'd been able to get from Ali in between scenes.

"I don't believe it. You guys managed to get right into Ali's movie. You were both standing right next to him. If he's on film, so are you." Tom went on as we put on our vests and jackets. "Some drunk started a fight with a black dude and the cops really did a number on him when he tried to resist arrest. I got a picture of that and you standing next to Ali."

Tom didn't seem bothered by the fact that Steve and I had gotten into the movie and he hadn't. But I wondered. He had seemed so bothered, by so much, that maybe I'd lost the ability to recognize it when I saw it.

# CHAPTER NINE

# Dallas

We got up at eight the next morning to rain so heavy that I wondered if I should start building a boat, like Noah. We took one look out the door and got right back in our sleeping bags. An hour later, we woke up, left a sincere thank-you note for Joe and Jerry, and went through our usual routine of packing our bikes and then got on our way.

Something was off. Even before we left, I had an insecure, uncomfortable feeling. It was something nameless, and without an obvious source. I should have been riding high about Ali and the movie, and the trip that still lay ahead, but . . . yes, something was off.

I had a dear friend in Massachusetts who had married recently and then moved to Dallas with her husband. It had been hard to say goodbye to her. Now, three months had gone by, and I wasn't going to let anything stop me from seeing her. But I didn't want Steve and Tom to suffer unnecessarily. Under the present weather conditions, the 250 miles from Houston to Dallas would take a daredevil's courage, and perhaps a daredevil's lack of sense.

I told the guys what I wanted to do, and they didn't argue. We just started to get ready, putting on nearly every item of clothing we had, knowing it wouldn't be enough.

Every mile we rode that day was torture. The cold, driving wind froze our faces, even though we wore face shields. We covered our mouths and noses with our bandanas to help ease the discomfort, looking like three modern bandits riding away from a big bank robbery. We had to keep our fingers and toes moving to prevent them from getting frostbite. It was so cold we couldn't even shiver.

Once outside the Houston county limits, the towns were small, few, and far between. Our slow traveling speed and constant stops—we were always stopping for coffee, food, and to steal a few minutes of warmth in any building or store we could find—hindered our progress. We progressed so slowly that I can barely even say it was slow going. It was a crawl compared to what we'd been doing before.

At one thirty that afternoon, with only a fourth of the ride behind us, Tom signaled us to pull off at the next exit, near a sign that said "New Waverly." We stopped in a grassy area at the end of the exit ramp. "Hey, you guys," he said, "I think we should find a place and camp here for today. I'm too cold and it's going to rain or snow any minute."

On cue, the rains began.

"Oh no," I said. If we got wet or cold—well, colder—we were going to be in real trouble. We'd been inconvenienced by the weather before, but this was the first time I thought we'd be in real danger.

"Come on, let's head for town," cried Tom, starting his bike.

The town was a mile away, and we raced towards it as quickly as we could, given the rain. When we got there, we drove under the canopy of an old, small, dilapidated Texaco station. The town looked empty.

The gas station had two pumps—one ethyl, one regular—under an extension of the roof that kept the attendant out of the rain and sun. The two bays for fixing cars were empty except for some junk parts lying around. The building's exterior was a drab grey.

We walked into the office, dripping wet. Inside, the place was dirty and worn. There were a few cans of motor oil on a shelf, covered in dirt and dust. Behind the counter, a small, elderly black man sat next to a portable electric heater. We said hi and told him we just wanted to stay out of the cold, driving rain. He welcomed us and offered us a spot next to the heater. He was a friendly, interesting guy. His name was Jed and he was sixty-two years old. He smiled easily, and it's his smile I remember the best, because he had only one yellow tooth in the middle of his upper jaw. Just as we crowded shoulder to shoulder for warmth by the heater, the back door opened and in came one of the biggest kids I'd ever seen. He was ten years old, five feet tall, weighed close to 250 pounds, and his name was Terry.

We told Jed and Terry about our trip, and then asked them if they knew of a place we could put up for the night, given the maelstrom outside. Jed thought for a while. "I'll ask a few friends if they come into the station," he said in his thick Southern accent.

There was one extra broken swivel chair in the room, so Steve brought it near the heater and we took turns sitting on it. The heat was a simple, precious thing. If Tom hadn't decided to take that exit, we would still have been out there on the road: stuck, miserable, and in an increasingly dangerous situation. I noticed a small Catholic church across the street with a quaint white house next to it. I decided to check it out in case it was somewhere we could sleep. When I knocked, a middle-aged man came to the door wearing black pants and a white tank top. "Can I help you?" he asked.

"Yes," I said, "my friends and I are traveling across the country on motorcycles and got caught in this awful rain. Would you mind if we slept in the church hall tonight?"

"Oh, I'm sorry," he said meekly, "I'm just visiting here. Father Garland is out of town and I'm not authorized to let anyone sleep in the church. Sorry. God be with you." God *would* have been with us in the church, I thought, but I didn't say so.

Back at the station, Steve had been talking to a small, wiry-looking black man in his late twenties. His name was Tonto, he was Jed's friend, and he said we could sleep in his workshop that night. Tonto was a strange-looking dude, so before we committed, we went to check out his workshop. He was big, weathered, with leathery skin and greasy hair. He twitched constantly, and his eyes never seemed to focus on anything for longer than a second. I also don't think I saw him blink once. He just put out a weird vibe. His workshop was only one street over and five houses down, so we walked that way in what had become, momentarily, a mere drizzle.

The street was lined with small, one-story houses. If they had four rooms inside, they were lucky. Almost every one of the homes was run-down. Dogs and cats ran loose through the junk-cluttered yards, making messes everywhere. We stopped at one house to ask where Tonto's shop was, but no one answered. The house's screens were falling off, some windows were broken, the front door was scratched and splashed with mud, and the roof needed a few shingles.

That was typical of most of the houses on the street. It felt kind of like one of the neighborhoods you see in a movie where characters stumble into after the end of the world, right before the trouble really starts. We finally saw a man in a driveway and asked him if he knew where Tonto's shop was. He pointed to the shack next to his house. No one said anything, but I could tell that Tom and Steve didn't feel any better about the place than I did. The place looked so bad that even a rat would have run from it.

The shack had one room, a tin roof, and a black smokestack jutting out of the rooftop but not giving off any smoke. As we walked around the place, we stumbled over all sorts of junk: auto parts, kitchen sinks, you name it. It was like every peddler in the world had passed through and dropped a couple of things in the knee-deep grass before moving on. The weathered boards on the walls had spaces between them so big that you could see right in.

"There's no way in hell that I'm sleeping in there," said Steve.

"I know," said Tom. "I'd rather sleep outside than in that hole."

"I think I'd *rather* sleep in hell than in there," I said.

Frustrated and anxious, we headed back to the station again, hoping to find another place to stay. But the afternoon was almost over, and Jed started his routine for closing up the shop. "I'd let you guys sleep here," he said, "but my bosses would get real mad."

We understood. He'd tried all day to get us a place to stay, so there was nothing to do but thank him, put on our wet-weather gear, and fire up the bikes. It was colder and wetter than ever. Argh. Darkness was slowly creeping in, which only added to our misery. Instead of taking the highway, we picked a secondary road heading north. That was a stroke of luck, because a few miles up the road was Sam Houston University. Without hesitating, we drove up to a dorm and went inside.

Traveling by motorcycle makes you think. If you don't have the money to burn on motels everywhere you go, you're at the mercy of the weather, which forces you to be creative and aggressive in order to survive. It creates a need for problem-solving in real time with high stakes. It's a good ability to have; it's just not fun to need it.

After deciding to stay at the dorm, we rode back down the street to a Kentucky Fried Chicken and munched out. A lot of the pressure was off now that we knew we'd be okay for the night. It was six o'clock and fully dark before we left the restaurant. Once we got back to the dorm, we parked our bikes in the dirt lot across from the building and went into the lounge.

On the late news we heard that Dallas was getting a freak snow storm. Up to six inches had already fallen on the city. "Driving conditions are treacherous," said the weatherman more than once. Treacherous barely began to describe it. We'd already committed to getting there, though. I knew that I'd see this through, no matter what.

It hadn't been an easy day, but as I was getting ready to sleep that night, I found myself overcome with gratitude. My dream was actually coming true. Despite the challenges, I was *still* traveling all over the country by motorcycle, carrying only essential camping equipment and a meager supply of clothes that would have felt limiting to a hobo. Every day was full of new tests and new experiences. There were always new people, different people, diverse people, and all the good and bad that came with them. I was seeing different states and learning that our country was still wide open, no matter how much we heard about land being lost and developers taking everything they could get. It is a rare thing to have no schedule and, with few exceptions, no definite destination. *Thank you, God,* I thought before falling asleep. *Thank you for my health, and for this opportunity. Help me to continue to be worthy of it.*

The lights went out at one. We each had a couch to sleep on and used our down vests as pillows. Of course, we had to sleep fully clothed, but that was better than sleeping out in the hell of that wet night.

Now, even though I was living my dream—one of them, at least—waking up after sleeping on a couch still isn't anyone's idea of perfection. But it was better to be achy after a night on a couch than dead on the shoulder after a night on the road in a storm.

We'd only made 70 miles the day before and still had 180 miles to go. Steve stuck his nose out the back door, and then shut it abruptly as the winter wind tried to force its way in. He shivered. "Man, it's cold out there," he said, which wasn't news to any of us who had just been violated by the frigid gust of air.

"It's going to be a long day," said Tom, starting to put on his warmest clothes again.

Our bikes had a heavy frost on them and needed longer than usual to warm up. We found our way back onto Route 45 North, where some angry God of the weather cursed us with a temperature of thirty-four degrees. We took breaks every twenty to thirty minutes or miles to warm up. At one exit, the sign said "Streetman, 2 miles." We were hungry and cold so we took it, not knowing how far up the highway we'd have to go before coming to another exit. The road leading to Streetman was a small two-lane stretch with only a few old farm houses along the way. Just before entering the town, there was a big square silver sign with black letters saying, "Welcome to Streetman. Population 286."

As we drove through the town, I tried not to blink, because you could miss the whole thing. It was a ghost town. The population may have been 286, but it looked to us like it was zero. This wasn't the first time we'd seen an empty town, but it never stopped feeling eerie to me.

Steve and I walked into the middle of the street and pretended to have a shootout like we were swaggering cowboys in the old West. But there wasn't much time to fool around. The road beckoned, whether we liked it or not.

But before getting back on the road, we each swallowed a few gulps of Coronet Brandy, which proceeded to warm our insides. Not the smartest prelude to a long stretch on a motorcycle, but it made sense in the moment.

The roads were perilous and the wet spots were beginning to freeze up, but I'm happy to report that we made it to Dallas from that point without a single nightmarish story. It was late in the afternoon and darkness was setting in. The sides of the roads were packed with snow where the snowplows had left their residue. And there we were, tooling along in the aftermath of the storm.

I couldn't wait to call Robyn. I knew she'd be shocked to hear my voice and then more shocked still to learn that we were basically on her doorstep. We pulled off and found a pay phone. Her reaction was everything that I'd imagined. Robyn told us to wait and said that she and Walter, her husband, would come out to meet us, and then lead us back to their place.

When I'd said goodbye to her in Massachusetts, I really hadn't ever expected to see her again. Friends come and go, and we're all slightly poorer for the relationships we lose, no matter how they wrap up. But now, here she was, here I was, and it had all happened in the most improbable way.

After a long hug and kiss, Robyn introduced me and my friends to Walter, a pleasant-looking, tall Texan in his mid-twenties. Robyn was only twenty-one. She was short, had a great figure, and was very pretty. She had worked for me back at the YMCA in Massachusetts.

"You guys must be cold and hungry," she said. "Follow us home, then we'll have something hot to eat so you guys can thaw out. It's incredible that you made it here through all that bad weather."

Robyn and Walter lived in a tidy little second-floor apartment in a nice neighborhood. After eating a good meal, we talked about old times, new times, and our trip. I thought I'd want to talk all night, but it had been such a wearying day that we all called it quits early.

In the morning, Robyn was up making Walter's breakfast before work while we were still lying in our bags in the living room like cocooned cater-pillars awaiting their new lives. I woke up at ten, rubbed my eyes, and crawled out of my bag. After getting dressed, I opened the door leading to the kitchen and there was Robyn, sitting at the kitchen, sewing a pair of Walter's pants. "Good morning," she said. "You don't even look like you're awake yet. You don't have to get up now. Why don't you sleep a little longer?"

"No, I don't want to sleep the whole day away. Besides, I haven't seen you in forever."

She nodded. "Unfortunately, Walter and I have to leave in a couple of days for Massachusetts. He's checking on some jobs back there and then we're spending Thanksgiving with my parents. I haven't seen them for three months so I'm excited about going back. I really wish you guys could stay longer, though."

"We can't stay long anyway with this weather," I said. "You know what? This is why we left Massachusetts, to get away from the winter!" I looked out the window. The sky looked back, seeming to promise that it wasn't done with me yet.

"It's funny seeing snow here this early, but everyone's excited," said Robyn. "The papers said this was the earliest snowstorm that Dallas has had in over seventy years."

"You know what?" I said. "Everywhere we've been so far, we've run into unusually bad weather for that time of year. I wonder if we're causing it somehow? Or like it's *actually* chasing us?"

Robyn laughed. "What do you guys want to do today?"

I hadn't thought about the day ahead beyond taking a shower. There was enough oil in my hair to fry an egg and I hadn't felt clean in at least two days. I got in the shower and the layers of crud began peeling off.

After Tom and Steve rolled out of bed and cleaned up, we enjoyed our breakfast, and then sat around the table and talked. This is one of the best things about real friendships: no matter how much time has passed, you can still pick up right where you left off.

Walter came home for lunch so Robyn could have the car to show us around Dallas. All five of us crammed into their 1975 yellow Celica. Robyn and Walter were in the front, and we were packed shoulder to shoulder in the back seat, which was really only big enough for two people. After dropping Walter off at work, we drove to downtown Dallas to visit the place where President Kennedy had been assassinated. Both Tom and Steve said "I can't believe I'm here," you could feel the excitement in their voices. I had goosebumps.

"This is the first time for me too," said Robyn. "I've been here for three months and just never had time to make it down here."

We were standing in Dealey Plaza on Commercial Avenue, looking up at the sixth-floor corner window of the Texas School Book Depository where Lee Harvey Oswald supposedly took the shot that killed JFK. I tried to recreate the events of that day in my head, putting myself on the street. It must have been absolute pandemonium, between the screams, the shots, and the motorcade racing away. Sightseeing is one of the best parts of traveling, but it's easy to forget that so much of history is grim. America's trajectory had changed on this very spot, with the pull of a trigger.

It looked like it was about to start snowing again at any moment, so we headed back.

Just before supper, Steve ran down to the garage to get some writing paper from his pack and came back upstairs growling and grumbling.

"What's the matter, Steve?" asked Robyn as he came charging through the kitchen door, letting in another frosty gust of pure winter.

"Some damn mouse put two big holes in my pack trying to get into the sugar packets I kept in my side pocket."

"How do you know it was a mouse?" she asked.

"What else could have done it? And anyway, it left its little deposits at the bottom of the packet." He was huffing and puffing like the Big Bad Wolf. From the living room, Tom and I listened to him and laughed. Steve stomped in and sat on a big red bean bag chair that was in the corner of the room next to the couch.

"Don't laugh," he said. "It could have been your packets."

"What do you mean?" I said. I couldn't stop laughing. "Are you forgetting the little mouse that got into my pack and ate my crackerjacks in the Great Smokies?"

At least the rogue boar hadn't followed us all the way to Texas to get into Steve's gear.

It was another evening of warmth, a soft couch, and good friends. Even the fact that the floor had a rug on it was a heavenly comfort. It was weird, but part of me just kept feeling cold. You can get so chilled that, even though your body thaws, you can't quite convince yourself that you're warm. Ever since, whenever I've felt cold, I think about that drive and I know that I've got nothing to complain about. At least I'm not back on that drive, on that road.

Ten full weeks on the road had passed. For seventy days, everywhere behind us, people had carried on like usual with their jobs, families, obligations, and struggles. We'd been out here.

We said bye to Robyn and left their apartment early without a specific goal in mind for the day. It was one of the rare occasions when the old YMCA gambit didn't work, but we happened to pass by a big old college, SMU, while we were wandering aimlessly, so it looked like we'd have a place to stay in that evening. For sixty-nine nights, we'd always found a place to sleep. Today wasn't going to be the day when we broke our streak.

SMU was a very religious school with a student body of ten thousand. The campus had a picturesque, Southern-style architecture that exemplified a plantation owner's large mansion, all tall pillars and buildings shaped like they'd been made to host lavish balls. The main entrance was wide and lined with large shaded elm trees that blotted out the sun's rays, leaving the paved roads in shadow. Its yesteryear appearance recalled the era of slaving and cotton, and harvesting done by hand and suffering instead of by today's modern machinery. There were a couple of well-kept fraternity and sorority houses, but there wasn't a lot of movement on campus when we got there.

Fatigue was setting in on us as the earth tilted towards darkness. It was then that Steve got the idea.

"We should be able to stay at a fraternity for the night. That was one of the deals when I joined Phi Mu Delta." But there was no guarantee that Phi Mu Delta had a frat on that campus, as we immediately found out when we started checking out the Greek letters on the houses. But we still felt like someone would take us in, so we kept walking down the fraternity row, on the prowl for sleeping quarters.

The landscaping around each frat house was impeccable, and the buildings were just as nice—their outsides, at least. We peered in through the half-drawn curtains of one building and laughed. The decor was a bit undernourished compared to the immaculate presentation outside. Furniture has a short life expectancy in a frat, and the house was barer than you might expect.

When we walked into the Pi Kappa Alpha house, a few brothers in jeans were feverishly twisting the knobs of a foosball game. There was also a pool table, two long couches, and a bunch of soft chairs. The adjacent room had a decent-sized couch and a TV with sound, but no picture. Otherwise, the house was fairly neat in appearance, given that twenty-two college-age guys were living there.

As we were introducing ourselves and giving a crash course version of our story, the two guys quit playing their game to listen. They quickly offered their couches for the night. We didn't even have to mention the fraternity policy for fellow brothers in need of lodging. I doubt many people ever actually need to take advantage of it, but it was nice to know that it was an option.

We woke up at nine to the *thwack* of a cue ball sending fifteen billiard balls in all directions at the other end of the pool table. I opened my eyes and looked up into three smiling faces. "Well, it's about time you woke up, sleeping beauty," said one of the frat brothers.

"Can't a guy get some sleep around here?" I said. "You guys play pool day and night. When the hell do you study?"

Tom and Steve woke up, and we got ready for the day. We tightened our drive chains, which we had to do every five hundred miles, checked over the bikes for loose parts, and packed our few belongings back in the packs. We thanked the guys for letting us crash in their building and then off for a fast lunch at the downtown Y's cafeteria, then we went and looked for Route 35 South. However, while looking for the road, we managed to lose Steve. It was like a trap door had opened in the earth and swallowed him up. "What do you think happened?" asked Tom.

"Ah, he probably dropped something, stopped to pick it up, and lost us in the city traffic," I said. "Let's head up the road a little ways and wait. I'm sure he has enough sense to find the highway."

Five minutes later, we were sitting on the grassy bank, about to give up and go looking for Steve, when he came cruising down the highway and stopped in the breakdown lane behind our bikes.

"Where the hell were you?" we yelled. "I've been on and off this road looking for you two dummies! Why did you leave me back in the city?"

"We thought you were right with us," I said. "But when we looked back, you were gone. Then we couldn't find you so we got on the highway and waited."

He shook his head and I couldn't tell if he thought I was lying or what. "Let's go," he said in a huff. "We lost enough time."

We drove as far as the outskirts of Austin before a light drizzle began. We decided to try our luck at the University of Texas. Easier said than done. The campus was huge, and it was almost impossible to find our way around without asking for directions.

It was past six, dark, and the rain was coming down harder every minute.

Once we got oriented, we went straight to the McDonald's in the student center. With our bellies full once more, we walked around trying to find a good place to sit down and watch TV.

The student center was a big complex, a maze of hallways and rooms. Wherever we went, there were students making use of the facilities. It looked like just about every ethnicity in the world was represented. Education is an amazing thing and a monumental global project. People from all over the world were here in Texas studying whatever had caught their fancy.

Steve and Tom plopped down in one of the lounges, while I went around the corner to an old-fashioned wooden phone booth to give my family a call. It made me feel good to hear the voices of brother Gary and my parents on that cold and uncomfortable night.

When I finished, I left the booth and resumed the endless search for a place to sleep. At times, even though we'd made the choice to come on the trip, it felt like we were the subjects in some sadistic sleep-deprivation study.

Eventually, we found a dorm where a bunch of guys were watching TV, so we sat down and blended in. Around midnight, we each fell asleep on one of the well-worn couches. Then, each of us were separately awakened by a small, young man with shoulder-length hair.

"Sorry to wake you guys, but you can't sleep in the dorm. It's against the rules. Who are you visiting anyway?"

Because Steve was the only one of us awake enough to come up with a straight answer, he responded. I was groaning inside, sure that we were about to get tossed out. I prayed that this kid wasn't out to flex on us, wielding his authority and tossing us out.

"Well, you see, I'm the second-floor resident assistant. By rights I should kick you three out of here. But I know what it's like to travel and have to look for a place to sleep. Two of you are welcome to sleep in my room and I'm sure my friend will put one of you up in his. Oh, by the way, my name is Roy." We thanked Roy in a grateful, weary chorus, and then followed him upstairs. Steve slept in Roy's friend's room, and Tom and I crashed with Roy. With a sigh of relief and a prayer of thanks, I dozed off for the night.

Heaven, at least in part, has got to feel something like this, when you wake up nice and comfortable and a bed has never felt better. The next morning was like that. I've rarely felt so content and happy, and if everyone could start every day feeling like that, we'd probably have a better world.

We showered, gathered all our dirty clothes from our packs, and went down to the basement to do our laundry in the dorm's laundromat. After we put our stuff in the machines, Steve said he was going up to the lounge to read while we waited for our clothes.

He had just walked out the laundry room when a tall lady—the dorm mother—stopped him and asked him what he was doing here. Her tall, frizzy hair only made her look more towering. "I'm just visiting friends," he said, looking up at her. He looked like a little boy caught stealing the cookie jar with his mother standing over him during a scolding. "I need to see some identification, please," she said. Steve reluctantly handed over his license. She took his name down, gave him back the license, and let him go up to the lounge.

"Do you think she saw us?" I asked.

"I'm not sure, but she's gone, anyways."

"Let's run up to Roy's room. Maybe he's back from class," I said. We ran up the two flights of stairs. I didn't want that lady coming back to investigate. Roy wasn't back yet, but we saw that his name was on a daily schedule of his classes, pinned to his door, which was convenient: we needed his last name in case anyone asked us who we were visiting.

Tom headed to the lounge to read. I stayed behind to write in my journal. After a while, I went back downstairs to check on our laundry, and wound up writing a little in there as well. There was only one other guy in the laundry room, and he was sitting at the table reading a magazine. After a bit, I happened to look up from my writing in time to see a police officer walk by and look in. I couldn't shake the feeling that he was there checking us out. The next time I looked up, a moment later, there were two of the men in blue, standing directly in front on me.

"Okay, son, stand up. What are you doing here? Do you go to school here?"

They never gave me a chance to answer their questions separately, but went on and on with the rapid-fire interrogation. When they finally took a breath, I calmly told them that I was visiting a friend and doing his laundry. They searched my jacket and toiletry bag, which was sitting on a table next to my helmet. Their suspicions about my very non-suspicious behavior were escalating for no reason whatsoever.

"Let me see your license."

As I took my wallet from my back pocket, they stood at the ready, as if I was about to try something wild. I was anxious. Cops can make a lot of trouble for you if they're in the wrong mood. I hadn't done anything wrong, but the cold sweat running down the back of my neck didn't agree. When a cop pressures you, you feel *pressured*. All I could do was keep my story straight. The truth was always best.

"I'm traveling across the country with two friends," I said calmly. "They're in the lounge reading." I half-expected them to bellow "READING WHAT?" before handcuffing me, but they just thought for a moment.

"Watch him, Pete," said one. "Let him sit on the stairs, and make sure he doesn't move." Then the other one went up to the lounge to apprehend the hideous book-reading outlaws known as Tom and Steve.

I was glad that we'd found Roy's last name, and I hoped that Tom and Steve would tell the same story I had. The cop who'd stayed behind watched me with cold, petrifying eyes, like a wolf over its prey.

Steve and Tom would tell me later that when the pudgy officer stepped into the lounge, they both got a jittery feeling in their stomachs. He quickly picked them out of the crowd and quietly asked them to follow him out to the lobby. "Is that your buddy over there?" he asked.

"Yes."

I looked at Tom and Steve, trying to develop some immediate telepathy and let them know what I'd done and said so far. They separated Steve and Tom and interrogated them, not giving us a chance to get our stories straight. The moments passed by slowly. Students who walked by would ask one of us what the cops were there for, and we were all tense. It was absurd that this was the result of three desperados who were just doing some damned laundry.

It turned out that there was a little more to it. We finally learned that the coin machine in the laundry room had been broken into and $40 worth of quarters had been stolen late the night before. We were the prime suspects. Well, that made a little more sense, given that there had been an actual crime, but we weren't the quarter bandits they were looking for.

Luckily, Roy came back from his class early and saw us being hassled in the lobby. When Steve told him what was going on, he abruptly told the pudgy cop that we were sleeping in his room the whole night as his guests. The dorm mother, who was standing by watching the whole scene, came over and told the officers that Roy's word was good.

"Stay put," one of the cops told us, and then they huddled for a conference. When the two Gestapos were through conferring, they reluctantly gave us back our licenses. "Get your clothes and get off the campus in thirty minutes." Just as they finished their ultimatum, another officer ran in from the rain, dressed in his yellow plastic rain suit and blue police cap.

"Hey, I found them! I found their bikes!" He sounded like a little kid who had just tied his shoes on his own for the first time. "Here's their tickets; they were illegally parked."

The cops looked at us as if they thought that, in light of this new evidence, they might be able to pin every unsolved murder in the past thirty years on us.

We took our tickets and went down to get our clothes. Then we thanked Roy, said goodbye, and got the hell out of there, heading towards San Antonio. The whole way out of town, I looked in my rearview mirror. I couldn't figure if those cops had been bored, malicious, incompetent, or what. Maybe all of the above. *Hey! I found them!* I kept hearing it over and over in my head. Soon the anxiety passed, and I couldn't stop laughing about how excited he'd been. I guess we all take our little joys where we can find them. But his next joy probably lay in something inane. Mine was ahead of me on the open road.

# CHAPTER TEN:
# Splitting up

The sun showed all its splendor and warmth in San Antonio, Texas, like it was trying to win some sort of celestial contest. We wanted to wear shorts but chose not to because the weather could change rapidly and we didn't want to have to change quickly on the fly.

Every day, I felt like I became more of a bona-fide traveler, not someone who was just taking a trip. As such, I was doing a lot more thinking about travelers as a breed. There are certain characteristics that I think we all tend to share. In general, we're kind, courteous, generous, and eager to help. Travelers also know how to pay attention. When you're in new places, it's almost impossible not to look around and *notice* things. Not only that, it can also make you feel afraid to let something pass by, so you pay attention harder than you would if you were somewhere where you already knew what was around you. When you pay attention, you can see beauty, love, and happiness in just about anything, because it's harder to get settled and comfortable. You expect things to be unexpected. I have every reason to think that this makes (or keeps) travelers happy. When we're tired of a place, we just move on and find another.

We were eating our breakfast in the sun, having this very discussion. I thought it might be possible that Americans are simply a restless species, a mobile, nomadic people, never satisfied for long where they are. The immigrants who settled the colonies were the unquiet ones in Europe. The steady people, the people with roots, are still there. But everyone else here, except for the Indians and the African Americans who were forced to be here or come as slaves, are descended from those restless people who couldn't stay put. All I knew for sure was that travel was a need for me, and the deeper and more ancient the urge, the more impossible it is to resist.

We made our way to the world-famous Alamo late that morning. As we rode into San Antonio, we were surprised to see that the shrine that was the Alamo was housed smack dab in the middle of tall city buildings and roads. I'd imagined that the city would have maintained something of the original surroundings for such a monument, but I couldn't have been more wrong. We had pictured the Alamo in a large dirt field, not plotted in the middle of a city district.

There was a story there. In fact, the Alamo had only survived at all with a bit of luck. A patriotic woman—Mrs. Driscoll—had paid cash for it to make sure that it was preserved. Otherwise, it would have been torn down and replaced with a hotel. The state of Texas would later buy the Alamo from Mrs. Driscoll, and then the Daughters of Texas had maintained the shrine ever since.

The courtyards were decked with flower gardens and beautiful shade trees, but inside the walls of the Alamo, those tall trees on the outer perimeter failed to shut out the sights and sounds of the city. It made it hard to recapture the grandeur of the place when we could hear honking horns nearby and see the utterly normal city right on the other side of the windows. Davey Crockett and James Bowie were the last to die inside those walls as they were bombarded from outside, but the current state of the place failed to capture any of the gravity of the past. I have to say that it really bummed me out to see something so original made to feel so . . . unoriginal.

We wandered the city streets nearby, getting a feel for the place, and trying to picture a battle that took place over 130 years before. The San Antonio riverways were similar to the canals of Venice, although overall the setting wasn't as dramatic. But there was a very romantic atmosphere. It would have been a grand place for two honeymooners. There were military personnel everywhere, taking pictures and sightseeing, which surprised us until we learned that there was an Air Force base nearby. We sat at a table at one of the riverway's more active sidewalk restaurants to put down a pitcher of beer.

It was ten when we started making our way out along the fabricated canal to the real-world streets of San Antonio. Two pretty girls overheard us talking and commented on our Boston accents. They asked us to sit and have a drink with them. They were both from Austin and were staying at a friend's apartment nearby for the weekend. Happily, they were also both anxious to continue our little get-together in a more private setting. We suggested they give us a ride to our bikes and then we could head back together. That turned into a long, fun night of wine and laugher.

Sunday morning, we were excited to go out for breakfast, but when we went outside, San Antonio looked like a ghost town. Most of the stores were closed for the day, which discouraged people from shopping, not to mention that it was cold and windy. Just the night before, those streets had swarmed with traffic and people, and now they were barren and lifeless. There was nothing going on but the hum of the streetlights. It was easy to think of ourselves as the last human beings on earth, or intrepid explorers who had landed on a foreign planet and were now waiting to see what the new life forms we might encounter would look like.

We stumbled onto an all-night Mexican restaurant. After we deciphered the menu, which was in Spanish, and placed our orders, our Mexican waitress was back in no time with our breakfast.

After breakfast, the girls had to return to Austin. We spent the day resting at a KOA campground where we had stayed, seven miles away on the outskirts of town. The night before was long so the rest was welcomed. Steve sewed the holes in the bottom of his backpack where the garage mouse at Rob's back in Dallas had chewed through the nylon bag. We sat and watched the New England Patriots beat the New York Jets. Every Sunday, I said that the Patriots were going to win it all just because we weren't there.

We were relaxing when three guys and a girl, who were sitting at a picnic table nearby, invited us over to their campsite. They were all wearing stylish leather jackets. They handed us each a beer when we sat down.

Our hosts were brothers. One was married to the girl that traveled with them. The third guy was a close friend. The single brother had been having some trouble with his old Triumph 650 Bonneville. They'd traveled eighty miles out of their way to the nearest Triumph dealer, only to learn that the part they needed was going to take five days to arrive, so they were stuck for a while. It made us glad that we owned Hondas. There were more Honda dealers in the country than any other dealership going. And the Honda parts were almost always in stock, so we just weren't ever going to be stuck in a similar situation.

It turned out that they were taking a trip similar to ours, although they were only touring the South of the country. But they'd only given themselves two months. This meant they were nearly always in a hurry and hadn't been able to stop and see a lot of places that they would have if they'd had more leisurely schedules. But they were loving the experience, and I totally understood that.

Monday morning, Tom was more taciturn than usual. He pulled out a bottle of wax, as if he were about to wax his bike. He noticed that we were watching him inquisitively and looked at us both with a sad expression. It just about broke my heart. He looked like he was about to lose his two good friends forever. A small, disturbing twinge of fear crept along the base of my neck. What if there was more to the story than homesickness? What if something worse was wrong, and we didn't know it?

At first, when he tried to start talking, the words just wouldn't come out. His mouth moved and he took some deep breaths, but then he had to start over. "Guys, I'm leaving for California tomorrow. I checked at a travel agency to ask about the cost of a plane ticket back to Boston and they said they'd better reserve me a seat before December 15, or my chances of getting home by Christmas were almost zero. Plus, I'm going to need that extra time to try and sell my bike. I should get at least five hundred for it and that should be enough money to finish our trip, book a flight back to Boston, and have some time and money to buy Christmas gifts. I want you guys to keep going to Corpus Christi and do all the things you want to do and take your time. I want to make it alone. I figure I can be in Phoenix by Thanksgiving, and San Diego before the first."

"You want to make that trip by yourself, Tom?" I asked, because it was the *last* thing the old Tom would have wanted. "That's a long way to ride alone." It would also mean going through the most barren stretches of road we'd encountered so far, on his own.

"Yeah, I know. But if I can make it to Phoenix in three days, I'll just have to endure it. I think I'll enjoy the challenge. I guess I'll find out how much of a loner I might actually be. Maybe I'll find out that I can't stand to be lonely. Who knows? But I want to find out. I hope you guys understand."

"Tom," said Steve, "you said that we were all going to make it together to the West Coast and make it work, and then find jobs and all that. Now you're going back on the oath. I guess you knew all along you were going to go home. That's why you discouraged Mark's idea of making a written oath and writing down all of our goals for the trip. That way, we each would have known where we stood and it would have been harder for you to back out."

"I did try, Steve. I left my job, same as you, and thought maybe we could pick it up again in California, but you guys want different things out of life than I do. What I want is back home. This trip has made me more aware of that. I'm not knocking you guys. I think it's great that you have high ideals and you believe strongly in them, but they aren't for me. I still want to be friends and I hope you don't think any less of me because I'm choosing to leave." He put out his hand.

That he actually believed we might stop being his friend just because of his choice made me even sadder than him leaving. We both took his hand

and shook hard. This friendship was a treasure, and it would be stronger than this temporary split. If he wasn't happy traveling, then he wasn't happy traveling. Trying to force him to stay when he was miserable was just going to make all three of us feel like crap.

Tom had more to say. He said that people were always asking me and Steve, "What's your third friend's name?" and he often felt left out when it happened. "I tried it for seventy-six days," he said. "It's not like it was just a trial run; I really tried. And now I just need to go home and pick up my life again." Tom wanted to finish school and get his associate of arts degree in business, and then find a good job. He was feeling his love for the slopes and the call of winter skiing. As he talked, I could see that he was actually getting excited about being home soon, and there was no way to argue with that. You should only want friends who want the best for you, and this is what was best for Tom. That excitement was also giving him the courage he'd need to take the toughest part of the trip alone. He knew that the road ahead was barren and cold, but there was no stopping him. I could respect that.

My bike had taken ill yet again, so we headed to a Honda dealer for help. Tom stayed behind to wash his bike and make some final preparation for the next leg of his journey. But when we got there, a beautiful girl behind the counter told us that the place was closed, but she referred us to a good mechanic who worked nearby. She even called him up to make sure he could see us.

The guy took my bike for a test drive, and told me that he thought I'd taken in some bad gas. That wasn't a surprise to me, since so much of the gas you can buy is absolute junk. He recommended that I check the screen in the set cock and clean it if it was dirty, and then went into the shop while I got to work.

I got my tools and quickly had the set cock off with a few good turns of my little wrench. He'd been right. The screen was filled partly with the sludgy residue of cheap gas. I took my spark plugs and screen into the mechanic's shop so that he could sand blast them clean, which he did for free. After a couple more minor tweaks, the bike was good as new.

At lunch, Steve and I discussed Tom's departure and decided to take him out to dinner that night. Then we'd grab a six-pack and party back at camp. Might as well enjoy our last night as the Bachelors Three, since by the next afternoon, we'd be down to a duo. We drove to the San Antonio post office, which was across the street from the Alamo. We each had mail waiting for us. Then I went to a few stores to shop for something small for my mother and father and my brother Gary.

After a good part of an hour, I returned with a few gifts I planned on mailing out in fond appreciation: one for Gary, one for my mother and father, and the last to my aunts in Clinton, Massachusetts, for all the help and concern they'd given us while on our trip.

Steve was thinking of sending out the ten rolls of film we'd taken and mailing them back so our folks could see what we'd done so far.

"Good idea," I said. "And sending them now instead of carrying them will be safer. There are a million ways they could get lost. And it'll give them a better idea of what we're actually up to, and they can kind of follow along with us, better than with just the letters." As Steve opened his letters, I asked, "What does your mom and Debbie have to say?" Debbie was his sister.

He snorted. "She puts in a dig about Thanksgiving. She thinks that we're going to be out here settling for hot dogs and baked beans on the road-side while they all feast."

"Well," I said, "they're going to be in for a surprise, because we're going to be sitting down to a big turkey dinner with a large Mexican family who are going to treat us like family and make us feel right at home." I knew it was just a dream at that point, but I couldn't help but feel that we were going to find a way to make it happen, or that somehow the opportunity would just appear.

That evening, we took Tom to a Cantonese restaurant on the outskirts of town. He never could get enough oriental food, so we wanted him to have one more chance while he was with us. It was Monday night, and out of two large dining rooms, there were only three tables that were busy. It was a special time, even though we were sad. While waiting for our special dishes to be prepared, Tom produced an itemized list of equipment he thought we might need to finish out the trip. He read down the exhaustive list, Mr. Organized, mentioning the tent, stove, tire irons, candle lanterns, a Honda manual, and more. He said there was no need to pay him until we got our feet under us and had some money.

He was showing some signs of happiness. The hardest part for Tom was over, and the pressure he'd been feeling for who knows how long was relenting. The burden of wanting to tell us that he had changed his mind had been weighing him down for quite a while. Now he'd done it, and the worst hadn't happened. It rarely does.

It still made me sad, though. I wished it were different for him. Tom was sacrificing many new experiences that were coming, because he was going to rush through the best part of the country and do it without any companionship. There were stories he could have had, that we could have had together, that would remain untold. He was going to have some long, lonely evenings, and if he encountered anything like that horrible drive to Dallas while he was alone, he was going to be more vulnerable than we'd been as a trio.

After dinner, we bought three six-packs of beer and went back to the camp. I was up and down emotionally, torn between wanting to ask him to stay and wanting to wish him well. Hell, I don't know everything I was feeling. I could tell that if I tried to say too much I was just going to break down crying like a baby. We were all feeling it. I knew I loved Tom, but it took the thought of him leaving to really make me understand just how much he meant to me. Sometimes we don't know exactly what we have until we're faced with the prospect of losing it.

Overall, though, it wasn't a sad night, and long before we finished the third six-pack, we were killing each other with funny stories. Luckily there weren't any other campers there, not at that time of year, so no one else had to deal with us as we got louder, and louder, and, at least in our minds, funnier and more clever. That might be the only time I actually laughed myself to sleep, leaning against a big old tree with my friends, eventually snoring away like three chainsaws.

Steve would tell me later that, before he dozed off, he looked up at the heavens and said, "I'll miss Tom." Then he asked God to watch over our friend as the creatures of the nighttime forest replaced our noises with their own music. In the morning, we woke to a cool breeze, and Tom got into the first aid kit and dug up some painkillers to take the edge off of our unsurprising hangovers.

By late morning, the air mass rose as high as fifty degrees and the ugly gray sky accentuated the mood that we were all feeling but trying not to show. Now that we had divvied up the gear, the new arrangement of our furnishings had grown to a preposterous height on our bike racks.

Tom flashed a few candid shots of us standing by our Hondas with his trusty instamatic camera. We forced a smile when Tom gave the command, and I hoped that it didn't look like it took as much effort as it felt like it did.

Before pulling out, I gave my bike its regular inspection and noticed that everyone's rear tires were wearing thin.

"Tom, your tires aren't as bad as ours, but keep an eye on it anyway." I couldn't believe we were talking about such minor things. I couldn't believe we were actually splitting up.

"We're going to need drive chains soon also," said Steve. "Tightening them lately doesn't seem to work." Another entry in a mundane conversation, just so we could avoid talking about the fact that Tom was about to head his own way.

We rode out together, heading for San Antonio for one last breakfast together. Sitting down to beacon, eggs, and refried beans, we tried to figure out a way for Tom to let us know if he made it to San Diego.

"Maybe I'll drop a note in the general delivery mail at a point where you guys'll be stopping in eight or maybe ten days," he said. "That should be about the time I want to hit San Diego." He pulled out a map, and we chose Dryden, Texas, for the mail drop. Then breakfast was over, and it was time. I tried to think of a way to stall, to prolong the moment, but there was nothing to do but fill up our gas tanks. I guess I could have slashed his tires. That would have slowed him down. But I didn't. He was going to need them.

I didn't know how to say goodbye. I'd known Tom for twelve long years, and Steve had known him for three. We all had our differences, but none of them mattered in that moment. It seemed crazy that we'd ever fought about anything.

I took off my glove and started in with the goodbye handshake, figuring that might be a good way to start. Then Tom looked us both in the eye and was obviously fighting back tears. We each lowered our hands and then embraced in a group huddle, reminding ourselves one last time of our bond.

Then he was gone. He was really gone.

CHAPTER ELEVEN:

# A Dream Thanksgiving

It was hard not seeing Tom in his usual position as Steve and I headed down the road. There was nothing but air in the space he had filled, and it left me feeling empty and hollowed out. I kept looking in my rearview mirror, just in case Tom had changed his mind, and I think Steve did as well. But wishing wasn't going to make Tom change his mind. After about ten miles of false hope, we pulled over to talk. We reassured ourselves that we were going to finish the trip no matter what, and that feeling guilty over Tom leaving wasn't going to help anything or anyone. That talk cleared my mind a little. We turned our attention to Corpus Christi and the dream of sitting down to a turkey dinner with a large Mexican family. That's when I started thinking about Roland's clan. Maybe they'd be the fulfillment of the prophecy we'd made six weeks earlier.

The road to Corpus Christi was straight and narrow. Roland had told us that we'd see a bunch of ranches on the way, and he hadn't lied. Ranch land, fenced in on both sides of Route 181, stretched south as far as I could see. It was like that part of the country had never heard of the color green. You couldn't find a green plant to save your life, but if you ever wanted to see an ocean of dirty brown sagebrush, this was your place.

We stopped at a few of the ranches to look for work, if anyone was interested in hiring novice ranch hands, that is. We'd even decided that we would be willing to work for only room and board, just to have the experience of learning a new set of skills. No luck. Our dreams of rounding up cows died as quickly as the brief dream of working a shrimping boat.

The skies were gray and heavy when we rode into Corpus, late in the afternoon, ravenous with hunger. The beachfront, desolate in the dismal weather, was lined with hotels and palm trees. There were tons of beautiful houses, but no restaurants that looked promising, so we kept going, finally finding an Italian restaurant that served us up two incredibly mediocre sandwiches that we could barely finish.

Hungry or not, braindead or not, it was five o'clock and time to find a place to sleep.

A guy named Stanley was sitting at the bar, listening to our conversation. We told him about our trip, and he asked the waitress to bring us two beers. After telling him a few adventure stories, he bought more beer. We could have kept going all night, if he'd have kept buying beer, but we had to think about our sleeping situation. Stanley said that he would have let us pitch a tent in his backyard, but it had been storming and the ground was sopping wet, with another storm on the way.

We left, mildly annoyed and fairly tipsy. As I saw it, we had two options. We could take our chances on the beach, fighting the strong winds coming off the ocean and being battered by the downpour of rain, or we could call Roland's family, the Manzanos. Honestly, we could have dealt with the weather on the shore, but there was a big, forbidding sign that said, "CAMPING PROHIBITED ON THE BEACH. VIOLATORS CAN BE PROSECUTED AND LEVIED WITH A FAT FINE." It wasn't worth the potential hassle.

Thanksgiving was only two days away. If we were going to make it happen with Roland's family, now was the time. The thought of a warm house, the smell of turkey, and a laughing family were more than enough motivation to get us to a telephone booth.

I'm not sure how to explain it better than this, but I felt an energy moving through me as Steve got ready to make the call. I believed that we could actually make this happen. So far, all of my dreams on the trip had come true, except for my dream of us finishing the trip as a trio, and it really felt like I was the one making it happen, as if I had some influence over events. I couldn't prove it was true, but no one could have proved that it *wasn't* true, either.

"Hello, Mrs. Manzano," said Steve into the phone, after introducing himself. "We met Roland in Houston and he told us to look you up when we arrived in Corpus Christi. We're from Boston, Massachusetts. My friend and I are traveling across the country by motorcycle to California."

Even though I wasn't the one on the phone, I could hear the noise of children in the background, making it hard for Mrs. Manzano to hear everything Steve was saying. When it was quiet again, he gave her the full rundown on our story and said that Roland had mentioned that Mariano, his brother, might be able to put us up for a night.

It turned out that they lived only a few miles away. Steve gave her the number from the pay phone, and she said she'd have Mariano call us right back.

While waiting for his call, a street beggar approached us, trying to hustle us for our spare change so he could buy booze. "Please guys, just a little. Please."

I turned to him. "You don't need that, sir. You just don't need it. You're stronger than you think and you can fight the bottle. I don't want you to give in."

Steve joined me. "He's right. I don't want you to give in either."

He flinched. He was obviously used to being dismissed, or pitied, or having people hand him money so he'd go away. He wasn't used to people caring about him.

"I beg so I can drink, and I drink so I can feel confident," he said, looking at the ground. "I can't remember the last time I heard anything encouraging. You're good men. I want to do better, but it's hard. And then, when I can't do better, I drink to forget."

"You're as important as anyone else," I said. "You don't need to forget. You need to be in your life and stare right at it."

"It's true," said Steve.

The man was quiet for a moment, and then he looked up and smiled. Something had sunk in and warmed him up better than a belt of Jack Daniels ever could have. His whole appearance had changed right before our very eyes. He began to glow with happiness, knowing he'd made two good friends. We kept on talking with him, telling him what he was worth and that there were many good and kind people in this world, people willing to help, if he was willing to seek them out, because good people aren't hiding. "But you've got to be willing to help yourself," I said, "or this feeling will pass."

He stood up straight and put his shoulders back. "The craving I had for a drink five minutes ago is gone. Bless you boys," he said. "You have to be angels sent down from heaven to help me in my hour of need." He walked away, head held high.

Steve whistled. "Mark," he said, "that man feels one hundred percent better. Wow. Did we do that?"

I smiled. "Yeah," I said. "We did, but it feels more to me like we were just here to witness it. And something came through us. I don't know who feels better . . . him, or the two of us, and that's the truth."

The phone rang. Mrs. Manzano was on the line. She said that Mariano was at work, but gave us directions to her place and invited us over.

We made it there just before the rain started.

The front porch light was on, and two of their small children were on lookout duty, watching for us. Whatever Mrs. Manzano had told them about us had them all excited. They were bouncing from foot to foot and peppering us with questions about our bikes. It was immediately obvious that any friends of Roland were good friends of theirs, and I felt at home within seconds.

Mr. and Mrs. Manzano both came out to greet us. They were warm and friendly, and I was feeling so good I wondered if I was glowing.

There were lots of Manzanos in that house. Terry was six, and the smartest little tyke you could ever imagine. She warmed up to us fast, which Mr. Manzano took as a good sign. Kids can be excellent judges of character. Paul was nine, tall for his age, and semi-quiet until he met us. Belinda was sixteen and pretty, with long, brown hair and a pleasant personality and smile. Their next oldest son, Robert, was not home yet from his varsity basketball practice. While we met everyone, Mrs. Manzano warmed up a special delight for us. It was called Menudo, a Mexican specialty. Well, the meat that made the soup famous was from the lining of cow intestines. That thought alone was enough to make my stomach rock like a ship at sea, but chewing the meat, which is more like a gummy paste, was enough to make me gag after a few bites. I tried to hide my reaction with bread, swallowing big bites of menudo without chewing it.

"We were hoping that Roland would be here for Thanksgiving. He is coming down from Houston, isn't he?" I asked.

"Yes, he'll be here," said Mrs. Manzano. "We'll call him when we get back. I think he'll be surprised that you're here. We're so happy that you're visiting!" She went out to the car, where her husband was waiting to go to the market, while we settled into our new, temporary home.

It was a one-story house with two bedrooms. It had been built with cinder blocks underneath that raised the house and kept it off the damp ground. Besides the two bedrooms, there was a kitchen and a combination living room/dining room. There were a bunch of trophies proudly displayed on the tops of the bookshelves, bureaus, and nearly every other available space. Apparently the Manzano brothers were an athletic force to be reckoned with: basketball, football, and baseball. The house was small and there was little beyond the basic necessities, but the Manzanos were obviously proud of what they had and they worked hard to get it.

When the Manzanos returned from the market, Mr. Manzano led us outside to the back room where we would stay. It was a very small separate building. There were a few old cars parked on the wet grass on the way. The room had two single beds, a color TV, and a couch. We couldn't have been happier to see the results of our dreaming.

We unloaded our stuff and went back to the main house, where Mrs. Manzano was on the phone with Roland. "That's incredible! That's incredible!" I heard him shouting. Steve and I each took a few minutes to talk to him. He said he was definitely trying to come for Thanksgiving, but it depended on whether he could get a ride with a frat brother who wasn't sure of his own plans yet. But, worst case scenario, he said he'd take a bus.

I was surprised to find that I was wishing he could just drop everything, come with us on the trip, and make us a threesome again.

A few hours later, after relaxing by the TV and talking more with the family, I said a prayer for Tom and went to sleep.

Late the next morning, Mariano Junior, one of Roland's brothers, poked his head in and invited us to a cafeteria with him, since it was nearly lunchtime. On the way, we stopped at the Memorial Medical Center to pick up his check, where he worked as a guard. Mrs. Manzano also worked there as a nurse, which was no surprise, given how much she liked helping people.

At the hospital, Mariano introduced us to a few nurses. "These are my cousins from back East," he said, which made them laugh. As usual, they asked if we were brothers, and, as usual, we played our roles and went through our *shtick*. Mariano arranged for us all to meet that night at a place called "The White Rabbit."

Then Mariano led us to the hospital cafeteria to see his mother. The tables were filled with interns and nurses with wandering eyes. They stared at us so hard that we could practically feel the force of their looks piercing our bodies. It was Mariano's job to guard all of these beautiful, staring nurses? Sign me up.

Mrs. Manzano looked up from her lunch, and her eyes widened. She waved us over and then introduced us excitedly to everyone at her table. "Have you eaten yet? Have you eaten yet?" she asked over and over until Mariano assured her that we were on the way to eat and were not going to starve to death. She told her friends all about us and their Thanksgiving plans, and it was hard not to feel flattered by having someone absolutely gush with excitement about our mere existence.

Later that night, we all went to the market for Thanksgiving supplies. After picking out a turkey, we happened to come by a chest of menudo: cooked, frozen in a package, and sold by the pound. In another bin was a bunch of frozen pig heads that could be used in soups. It wasn't the kind of market we were used to, I must say, but it was inexpensive and seemed to have everything that Mrs. Manzano wanted.

"Hey," said Steve, "it sure would have been nice if we could have afforded to foot the food bill."

"Maybe someday we won't have to worry about money," I said. "But you're right."

Rain was in the forecast for Thanksgiving, but we didn't even care as long as it wasn't raining on Tom. We were exploding with happiness, and the bad weather wasn't about to spoil the mood.

Mrs. Manzano made her family chicken tacos and reheated the leftover menudo, which we politely passed up this time. Robbie and Paul knew we weren't big fans. "You should try some," they kept saying, trying not to laugh. Not in on the joke, Mr. Manzano jumped in, too. "Menudo will clean you up. It's good for whatever ails you. A bowl of menudo in the stomach after drinking too much beer or liquor and you'll feel much better the following day." He listed so many benefits that he started sounding like an old-time snake oil salesman. Nothing, including manna from Heaven, could have accomplished as much as he said menudo could.

Mariano called at nine and invited us down to the hospital. Apparently a few girls were anxious to meet us, which sounded spectacular. Mariano also asked his dad if he could use the car. Mr. Manzano gave us the keys, not in the least worried about us taking it. It was like the Manzanos couldn't stop giving. What was theirs was ours, even though they'd only known us—and known of us—for barely twenty-four hours.

When we got to the hospital parking lot, Mariano came out to the security door to meet us. He led us through a few of the halls and introduced us to a few girls who would also be going to the White Rabbit after their shifts.

Mariano walked tall and proud, built like a horse. With his badge and his swagger, you could tell he made everyone feel safe. He was also a good talker and an even better actor. I could tell that he'd know how to look and sound mean in a hurry if he needed to defuse a situation.

Next he showed us his TV security monitors, which he used to zoom in on the parking lots entrances, the lobby, and the corridors on each floor. After a while, we each went out to a lonely corridor and put on a Three Stooges style comedy show for Mariano and his partner to watch. It was a short-lived show since they were supposed to be monitoring the area with a close eye and couldn't let themselves be distracted for long.

The man working the midnight shift came in early, allowing Mariano to escape ahead of schedule. Mariano drove us back to his apartment and changed out of his uniform and into his man-about-town outfit. He enjoyed looking and being cool, but he wasn't conceited, although there were some girls who might have said otherwise.

After a few quick brews with Mariano's roommate Oscar, we all got back into Mr. Manzano's car and headed for the hottest Chicano spot in town,

The White Rabbit. When we got there, a line had just started to form at the front door. The doorman was waiting for someone to leave before admitting anyone new. Through the door, I could see two uniformed policemen with flashlights checking IDs. We only had to wait about ten minutes before we got in. The place was packed, and mostly Mexican. It always felt strange being in the minority, again, which we hadn't experienced since cheering on the Celtics in the home team's arena.

The dim dance floor was crowded with bodies in motion. A revolving silver globe hung from the ceiling, shooting out beams of light that could hypnotize you if you stared for too long.

We followed Mariano, whose watchful eye had spotted a table of girls from the hospital. We made our way through the horde and let them pull us onto the dance floor.

When Steve returned to the table after a dance, Mariano motioned him closer. "Hey, Steve, you have a secret admirer at the next table. She was putting holes in your pants with her eyes while you were dancing your tail off. She's gorgeous. Go talk with her. She already told three guys no because she was watching you. I know Mexican women, and you're already in with her."

Steve took his advice, went over, introduced himself, and sat down. The mysterious girl with long blonde hair never once took her brown eyes off him. She stared so constantly that it made him uneasy. For once, in the company of an admiring woman, he wasn't sure what to do next.

Tired of watching Steve squirm, I stepped in and asked her if she liked to dance. Her friend immediately said that the woman—her name was Debbie—who'd been watching Steve was from Mexico and didn't speak a word of English except to say, "Thank you," "I'm sorry, but no speak English."

Steve regained his wits in an instant and asked the friend to tell Debbie that he thought she was beautiful. He was right, too, and although she had to have known how attractive she was, she blushed. Her hair ended in a small curl on each side of her face, she had long, painted fingernails, and when she got on the dance floor, she moved like a goddess. It was a master class in body language. They didn't have the words to communicate, but the chemistry came through loud and clear.

At the end of the night, Debbie told her friend to relay a message: she wanted to see Steve the next night at the White Rabbit. She kissed Steve softly on the lips without ever closing her mysterious eyes. She had fallen in love with Steve the moment she laid eyes on him and Steve could feel it, although he couldn't figure out why. He wasn't dressed up in nice clothes. He did look Mexican, but it wasn't that. Her friend said that Debbie was actually pretty shy, but something about Steve had just turned that off.

Steve knew that any type of relationship was out of the picture since we were moving constantly. Steve told her that if, he could get back soon, he'd try to see her but that we were about to head to Laredo and weren't sure if it would be possible.

"You could have had her if you wanted, Steve," said Mariano as we left. Then he took us to a late party that was full of yet more nurses. We ended up leaving the party at five in the morning. It was a great time, but we were done. It had been a long day, a longer night, and we were tired and hungry. The sun would be up in an hour, and all we wanted to do was get into our beds. Thanksgivings Eve had burned us out well enough to last until Christmas.

Turkey Day officially started for us at about eleven thirty. We got up, saw that it was raining, and quickly moved our bikes into the extra open space in the garage before making our grand entrance into the house, where Mrs. Manzano was basting the nineteen-pound bird we would all be devouring that afternoon. It was wild to look at that family and felt like they were both real and a dream. There they were, right in front of us, but it was like we had put something out into the universe that had brought us all together.

As we all bustled around trying to get things ready, it was happy and comfortable and perfect. There's nothing like preparing to sit down to a feast that only comes once a year. But before we sat down, Mrs. Manzano insisted that we call our parents and tell them we were okay and that we were about to enjoy a turkey dinner for the ages.

Steve called first and wished his family a happy Thanksgiving. I heard him laugh as he told them the story, and that it was a far cry from the hot dogs and beans at a roadside rest stop as his family had predicted. I got close to the phone and listened and talked as best as I could. They were proud of us. They couldn't stop saying it. They even made an Italian Thanksgiving toast in our honor. "Salute! To our sons!" Then they all started crying over the phone, and I got emotional as well. I did feel like Steve's brother, and their son, and as I looked around the room, it felt like there were new relatives everywhere my eyes came to rest.

Mrs. Manzano got on the phone with them. "You have a beautiful son and we are so glad he is here with us."

"God sent our boys to your home," said Steve's mother. "He works in strange ways."

I called my folks thirty minutes later, and luckily, everyone was still at home. They reacted just like Steve's family had, with pride and excitement. They kept saying that they always knew big things were going to happen for me, and the evidence was everywhere I looked.

I'd had an idea of something I wanted to do for Christmas, and I told my mother about it over the phone. I wanted to give my car to my brother and father as a gift. It was just sitting in the garage, collecting dust and taking up unnecessary space, and I knew they could use a second car. I was going to write to a good friend named John, who is a great mechanic, and ask him to get it all ready for them. "I want you to put a big red bow on the car with a note telling them that they can do whatever they want with it," I said. She started to cry, and it's hard not to cry when your mother is crying, so we wrapped up the call and I headed to the table, where I had been given the honor of carving the bird.

There were thirteen people at that big table, and as I carved, they started passing the plates, which included a wide variety of vegetables, four different kinds of potatoes, stuffing, gravy, three different flavored Jello fruit salads, candied yams, and a big green salad. There was beer, wine, milk, juice, soda, and just plain iced water. There were nuts and apples and probably a million other things that I'll never remember.

We ate and ate and didn't stop until much later on that rainy afternoon. The only thing that could have made it better would have been if Roland had been there. But then his brother Robert had an idea. He put a metal-framed picture of Roland in the middle of the table. "We're all here now," he said, and we all laughed and toasted Roland.

The weather cleared up and, despite the fact that we were each weighed down with fifty pounds of food, we decided to play a few games of basketball on a court at Rickie's, a friend of Mariano, apartment. But before we left, it was picture time. Everyone who had a camera snapped photos and adjusted flashes and commanded everyone to smile, not that any of us needed much encouragement.

After basketball, we went out to a club with Rickie, his wife, Mariano, and his fiancée. We stayed for a few dances, and then beat it. The last few days had been jammed with so much excitement and late nights that we were spent. We managed to get in bed by one, which had become a rare occurrence for us.

In our cozy room, we talked about God.

"Maybe He's telling us something, Steve," I said. "Like He wants us to learn as much as we can and then use any good fortune that comes to us to help others. He might be showing us that you don't need a ton of money to be happy. But maybe He'll give it to us if it means that we can create a business that could help other people, like giving jobs to our friends who might be struggling."

"I don't know, Mark. But I do think this is supposed to teach us to learn everything we can and stay humble. I think God's going to show us as much as we show Him that we're ready to experience. I think we're going to do great things."

One of the simplest lessons a child learns is that everyone wants to feel important. All along the trip, we'd found ways to help people feel important. It wasn't because we threw parades for them or fell at their feet in worship. We never needed to flatter people or lie. It was just because we treated them decently and that we obviously liked to help people out. People respond to that. It had always been this way for us, but being on the road had shown me that it wasn't just a geographical reality. People are the same everywhere.

"You know what else, Steve, before leaving we didn't think this way," I said. "At least, I didn't." The truth was, I had left Massachusetts thinking that people were basically rotten. "Remember that lady back home who thought we should bring a gun to protect ourselves from all the nuts we'd meet out here?"

Steve laughed. "Yeah. You'd think we'd have met more of those lunatics she was imagining."

We hadn't met a single truly bad person. Even Luke, in the depths of that drug house, had treated us kindly. I was starting to think that I should write a book about the trip when it was over. We talked about it for half an hour before falling asleep. It was like we were part of a large puzzle and the most important piece had just been snapped into place.

The next morning we had planned on heading to the beach, but we wanted to help find a way to repay the Manzanos. Luckily, there was a bunch of work to do. Mr. Manzano had two piles of dirt that he wanted to move around the sides of the house. Once we built it up, it would prevent rainwater from seeping under and forming a large pool. He'd hired a neighbor named Mondo to do the work. Mondo was a very thoughtful, friendly man in about his early forties. He lived next door to the Manzanos with his elderly mother. He had black hair with grey highlights and usually wore dark green work pants with a white T-shirt. Because he was a little slow, he couldn't work or drive a vehicle. We never learned where he got his money from or how he lived, but that was none of our business. Mr. Manzano would pay Mondo sometimes for doing odd jobs around the house, but it couldn't have been much. But we immediately saw that Mondo was part of the family, just like we were. He was generous and kind, and that's all that really mattered.

So before we started on the jobs, we went and talked to Mondo, asked if he would help, and told him he could keep the money. "It'll be a good workout for us," I said. He was more than happy to let us pitch in. In fact, he rode to the store on his bike and returned with a six-pack of tall root beer sodas. As we worked, Belinda kept reappearing with food and iced tea, making sure we had the fuel to keep going.

It wasn't until early that afternoon when those two dirt mounds were finally leveled and built up in a helpful way. We also fixed somethings around the property that were broken. Boy did that make us feel good. Then we spent some time trying to get Roland's car working, but didn't have any luck. When Mr. Manzano got home, he saw that we'd done the work.

"That's a big help, boys," he said. "But you didn't have to sacrifice a day to help me."

It hadn't felt like a sacrifice. It had just felt like the right thing to do.

Just then Robert's car pulled into the yard, and Roland stepped out. Little Terry tore out of the house like it was on fire, just to be the first to give her big brother a hug and kiss. Roland walked over to us, put down his brown leather suitcase, and shook our hands.

"Hello, boys, how's the family been treating you guys? And how's my car running?"

"Your family has been excellent," said Steve.

"That's an understatement," I said.

"And we missed you yesterday," said Steve.

"Yeah, my ride canceled out at the last minute, but here I am. And here you are."

"Unfortunately," I said, "your car's a different story. She won't work. I think the engine has frozen up."

"I'll call Jerry tomorrow and have him tow it," he said. "I can deal without having a car for a while longer." Roland went inside, said hello to everyone, and then was instantly on the phone with a girl he knew, making clubbing arrangements for later that evening. He was truly a man after my own heart. "All right," he said, hanging up the phone, "we're meeting a bunch of girls at the Saville Club at the Holiday Inn at nine thirty." We went to the Y, played some basketball, worked out, showered, and then headed to the club, where we quickly made the acquaintance of two tables full of beautiful girls. One of them worked for Channel 3 TV as a reporter. She was twenty-seven, had never married, and was quite a looker. At the end of the night, we drove her and her cousin home. I had asked a ton of questions about her job, so she asked us if we'd like to come down to the Channel 3 TV station and watch them report the news live at ten. Then we'd go out for drinks.

We met two other girls who wanted to party, but we still hadn't gotten enough sleep and just weren't in the mood. We made it home by three thirty in the morning and collapsed into our beds like dead men.

It was raining hard the next day, so we felt good about staying in bed and not showing our faces until early afternoon. Belinda made us some

French toast, and then we relaxed in front of the tube and watched Navy beat Army and USC destroy Notre Dame. Getting up late made the day fly by. It felt like it was time for dinner as soon as we finished lunch. After we ate, it was time to start getting ready to go to the studio. Roland insisted on trying to upgrade our wardrobes before taking us out. Mariano's build was the closest to ours, so we raided his closet, and then waited for our turns at the one shower in the Manzano house.

When we stepped out the door to head to the studio, a sheet of rain disrupted our view, but we were about to get there safely around nine thirty. Our reporter friend and her cousin were waiting for us at the back entrance.

The TV studio consisted of a bunch of small rooms, nothing fancy. The reporters sat up on a desk platform that was raised two feet above floor level, with two TV cameras pointed at them. Each camera was operated by a technician who told the reporters which camera they were shooting from, how much time they had before going live, and then doing the countdown.

After her thirty-minute news broadcast, she gave us a breakdown of all the tricks and illusions that technicians use to make a TV show look like TV. It was all fairly interesting, but I kept wishing that there was some way she could interview *us*. It might have happened if we'd planned on being there longer, and if the weather would cooperate, but neither of those were the case.

We took the girls out for a few drinks, and called it an early night again since none of us had totally recovered from all of the recent partying.

The next afternoon, we crawled out of our bags at one to find that it was hailing and very cold. Our little, converted garage room wasn't heated, but we hadn't realized it was so cold because our bags were so warm. Shivering, we put on our clothes, ran across the backyard, and into the house, where Mrs. Manzano had all the stove's gas burners on to help with a little extra heat. Way down in Corpus Christi, they weren't really prepared for really cold weather, because they had it so rarely.

Roland spent the day making calls, trying to find a ride back to Houston. Late in the afternoon, he got a hit and told us it was time to say goodbye. He wished us luck in our travels and walked outside, suitcase in hand, to where a car was waiting. Steve and I felt like we were saying goodbye to a brother, again, like with so many of our other new friends, whom we might never see him again.

But just because someone left didn't mean the home felt the difference. The Manzanos' house was like Grand Central Station, always full of people, family, and friends. I said to Mrs. Manzano, who was sitting in an easy rocker, "Boy, you wouldn't know what to do if you were here by yourself."

She laughed, nodded, and went back to watching TV with everyone talking and yelling, a rare skill set.

Later that night, when Steve went out to get a book from our little room, he noticed that Belinda's rabbits were loose, running around the yard. He rushed back in. "Hey, Belinda, your rabbits got out of their cage!" Paul, Belinda, and I ran outside to help. If we didn't catch them and get them back in their cages, they could freeze to death during the night.

"Man, it's cold out here," said Steve as I was crawling around, looking under the porch for a little white rabbit.

"This is unbelievable," I said, getting to my feet. "Everywhere we go this crazy cold follows us, even way the hell down here!"

We looked all around the yard and finally chased down two of the rabbits, but the third one was missing in action. While we hunted, we noticed a small puppy hiding under a pile of junk in a neighbor's garage and decided to take it in for the night so it wouldn't die from the cold. It was the cutest little brown and black pup you'd ever seen.

We felt bad about not finding the third rabbit, but there was nothing else we could do. That night, Steve took the pooch into his sleeping bag with him to keep him warm. It was the beginning of a beautiful friendship.

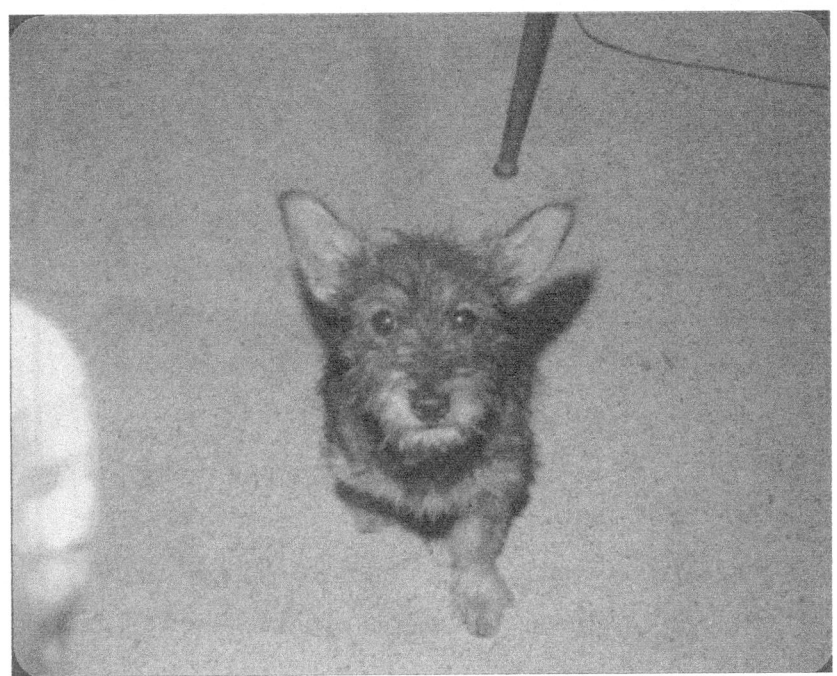

Monday morning was freezing, but the skies were clear. We got up at ten and decided to make it a day for cleaning and repairs. After a small pancake breakfast, Steve started cleaning the room where we slept, while I went with Robert, Paul, and Lewis to a store for some hardware to fix the back and front doors of the house so that they would stay shut when they were closed.

Back at the house, I was eager to get to work and repair whatever I could. I liked to help people, but I also got a crazy amount of satisfaction out of fixing things. By noon, the latches on both doors were fixed and working fine. The next item on the agenda was to readjust the carburetor or on Robert's red 1969 Opel Kadett; the engine was idling too fast. It was an easy job since I'd had to do the same thing with my own 1970 Opel.

When I finished, Steve had cleaned up the back room and was tidying up the house, which was a job and a half. With the kids being home on vacation, and both parents working full time, things had gotten topsy-turvy in a hurry.

Late that afternoon, we washed, waxed, and tightened up our bikes, getting them ready for the race against time, straight out to the West Coast.

That night's supper was Spanish rice, stewed hamburger, salad, and chili. Living with the Manzanos gave us our first real experience eating Mexican food, and we were starting to get a real craving for spicy meals. The Manzanos put red peppers on nearly everything they ate, and so did the kids. Even though a mere taste on the tongue would burn like fire, they dumped it on like it was candy. By the time we'd leave, we'd be doing it as well.

After dinner, Mrs. Manzano went to stay with a sick neighbor. While we watched TV, Mr. Manzano said, "This has been the coldest weather we've had in many years."

"Of course it is," said Steve. "Everywhere we've gone so far, we've run into unusually cold weather." He almost sounded like he wanted to apologize for it.

I was sitting at the kitchen table with a five-hundred-page novel, trying to reach the halfway mark. But fatigue overtook me, and I went out through the back door, across the yard to our room. The cold nylon lining of the sleeping bag warmed up quickly, and I was out within minutes.

The next day was a Tuesday, and our eighty-fourth day on the road. Everyone was back to school or work, but Mr. Manzano left us his car to use because he knew it was too cold to ride our bikes.

We had four important things to do: buy the Manzanos a gift for their hospitality, try to get Anthony's (Belinda's boyfriend) old beat-up motorcycle running for him, change the oil in our bikes, and pack up the bikes for the long ride tomorrow. Boom. It hit me. We were about to get back out on the road for the home stretch. I was excited, but also a little sad, a feeling that I pushed away quickly. It had been wonderful to have a home base for a while.

We headed down Padre Island Drive with Steve at the wheel. Anthony told us to check at Continental Cycles about his bike, where the owner had asked us to bring it in so he could take a look. Then we drove to a big mall down the road and walked around, looking for something to buy for the Manzanos. The Christmas decorations were out.

"Steve, do you remember last year's Christmas season?" I said. "We're so far away from home. I'm just not feeling anything like the Christmas spirit."

"Yeah, I know," he said. "I'm usually starting to get excited by now and I'm really just not. It doesn't really feel like Christmas."

We kept walking and looking. It was tough to know what to get when we were buying for so many and had such limited funds. We finally agreed on a five-pound box of chocolates from a Fanny Farmer's candy store. Then we picked up a card, grabbed our motorcycle oil, a tick collar for the dog, and headed back.

Shortly after we got there, Anthony came by to check on our progress with his bike. While Steve gave him the update, I went in and filled out a thank-you card for the Manzanos and left it with the gift on the table. Anthony was thrilled that we'd followed through on our promise to help him get his bike running. In fact, he was so excited that he wanted to take it to the shop that instant. So I helped him get it into the van he'd arrived in, and we went and dropped it off together.

When Mr. Manzano came home from work around seven thirty, he asked if I was ready to go and get a haircut at Billie's Barber shop, which was only four blocks away. I didn't really want to, but it was a little long and I couldn't say no to him. Billie's was one of those old-time shops with a spiraling barber's pole on the outside, the big white porcelain chairs with black, cracked leather padding, and a barber who looked like he only knew how to cut hair one way: short.

We parked the car out front and walked in. Mr. Manzano introduced me, said a few words to the barber in Spanish, and then said he'd be back in half an hour to get me. The barber's eyes looked hungry: he couldn't wait to get at that mess on top of my head. My hair wasn't even that long, but according to this old-timer's standards, there was much work to be done.

"Just a trim, please," I said as I sat in the chair.

I watched my curly brown hair fall to the floor in clumps. Whatever was happening up there, it was not a trim. It was torture sitting there, watching my hair being hacked away, but I didn't want to be disrespectful. Mr. Manzano had gone out of his way to take me there, so the least I could do was not fuss too much. He came back just as the barber finished. "How do you like it?" asked Mr. Manzano with a smile that showed a gold-capped tooth.

I was now standing in front of a big mirror. "It looks good. I like it real short like this."

"Of course," said Mr. Manzano. "Billie has been my barber for thirty years. He always does a good job."

I was reaching into my pocket to pay Billie for the haircut when Mr. Manzano told me to forget it, that it was all taken care of. On the way back, I kept thinking about Steve. He was going to take one look at me and laugh his head off. He'd know instantly that something had gone terribly wrong. Oh well. It was only hair, and it would grow back.

It was almost six when we got back to the house. Paul was getting ready for his Pop Warner football game that would kick off half an hour later. We helped him put on his armor for his battle ahead. Then we all got in the car and drove to the football field. It was dark and cold when Paul jumped out of the car and joined his team, which had already started warm-ups. We stayed in the car with Mr. Manzano because it was too cold out to stand and watch the game.

After dinner that night, we wrote in our journals, making sure we were up to date. As I wrote, I noticed that Mrs. Manzano was putting together a small bag of first-aid supplies for us.

"You don't have to do that," I said, and Steve echoed me.

"I don't want you boys to spend your money. This is your home now. Anytime you want it."

Mariano called at ten and told us to meet him at work just before he got off. He said he had some hot chicks waiting for us. We begged off because we had to get up early the next morning to ride out for California. It's one thing to stay up late partying when you don't have anything to do the next day. It's another when you have a long stretch of road on a motorcycle waiting on the other side of the night. Mariano understood and said he'd come see us off in the morning.

Around eleven, Steve was taking a shower when a girl he had gone out with one night during our stay called. I answered the phone and the girl thought I was Steve.

"I'd like to see you tonight," she said.

I asked her to give me a second and went to ask Steve, but he said to give her an excuse.

"I'm too tired to go out," I said, doing my best to sound like Steve. "And I've got to get up early tomorrow to leave for California." I said goodbye and hung up. It wasn't the first or last time that someone would confuse one of us for the other, even with my new haircut.

# CHAPTER TWELVE:
# Big Ben National Park
# - The Banditos

Today was the big day. We got up early, packed up our gear, and looked around the yard for something we could carry our new partner in. Schnapps was going to take the remainder of the journey with us and seemed as excited about it as we were. "Steve, what about this four gallon milk case?" I said, holding up the plastic container.

"Yeah, that should do it, but we'll want to insulate it to keep the cold out."

The plastic milk crate's four sides had triangular holes on the top half and the bottom half was solid walls. We cut some heavy-duty cardboard to fit inside the case as to cover up the holes on three of the walls, the back, and two sides. We did this to keep out the cold wind. We left the fourth wall facing backwards open so the pup could enjoy the fresh air. Then I cut a piece of quarter-inch woodpaneling I found in the garage to make a top cover to keep rain out and also allow me to stack my gear on top of it. We lined each wall and the floor with thick pieces of foam for insulation and padding and to help keep our new buddy warm while traveling. There it was, a comfortable home that protected Schnapps from the chilling winds of the ride west. I daresay she was going to be traveling more comfortably than we were. I mounted her new mobile home on my luggage rack, and then packed my gear around it. It took some ingenuity to pack everything I had around the milk case, but I managed.

Taking Schnapps meant we each had to carry extra gear, plus having the responsibility of taking care of a puppy. But hey, at least we were a threesome again. And if nothing else, she was going to make a great conversation piece.

Before we finished packing the bikes, Mondo rode to the store on his old one-speed bicycle and came back with a big bag of groceries. He said, "Here, this is for you. This is food for you and Schnapps. You will need it to give you energy to travel on your long journey. May God go with you."

By eleven, we were ready to go, so we said goodbye to the Manzanos, including all the kids who stayed home from school to see us off, said goodbye to Mondo, and then drove away knowing that we'd had an experience we would remember for the rest of our lives.

The skies looked threatening as we drove out of Corpus on Route 358 West. Ten miles down the road, down came the rain, so we pulled over and put our rain suits on. I'd never wanted to see the sunshine of California so badly, but there was still a long way to go. We drove through Freer, Texas, and on through to Laredo. It was early afternoon when we reached the bustling border town. It was dusty and dirty, and only the main roads were paved. The population was largely Mexican. Nearly everyone seemed to drive a truck, and nearly every truck had a rifle racked in the back window. We stopped at a market for some canned food, and then began our perennial quest for lodging. After checking out the school playground, an empty lot between two factories, and a small thicket near Route 59, we finally stopped at a small, unkempt ranch, where a long muddy driveway led to the back door of an old one-story house. After we fought our way through the chickens and junk, we knocked on the front door. A tall young man came to the door, and we asked him through the broken screen if we could sleep in his field for the night. He said he just worked there, but that he'd ask the lady who owned the place. He came back and said it was fine, and then led us to an old horse field filled with big lumps and coarse sagebrush. We drove our bikes through the gate and onto the field. It was very hard driving a motorcycle with a full load over the field's rough terrain, so we didn't go too far. We parked the bikes, let Schnapps out, and swiftly set up the tent. The sun had called it quits, so we had to resort to our flashlights and the moon. "Mark, get the stove out so we can start supper," called Steve the second we got off our bikes.

After I got the stove ready and started cooking, we had to tie Schnapps up because she was getting too close to the supper table. That dog had no manners, but we happily shared our dinner with her. After our moonlight dinner under the stars, we cleaned up and went into the tent to play a game of cribbage and do some reading by flashlight. Around nine, we climbed into our sleeping bags and said goodnight. Schnapps abruptly woke us up shortly after by squatting near Steve's head. "You little mutt! What the hell did you do that for?" yelled Steve. "Go on, out you go!" He shooed her outside. "Then you can come back in."

But she'd already done her business, right in his corner of the tent. Grumbling, he let her back in, and the three of us slept.

When we left the Manzanos in Corpus Christi, I knew that each day of our race for the West Coast would be long and taxing. But when I woke up at seven and felt a warm bundle of fur down by my feet, it felt like things couldn't go that badly. I don't know how that dog managed to crawl all the way down into my bag without waking me up. I got up, got dressed, went outside, and chased Schnapps around for a while to give her some exercise.

When Steve woke up, we worked together to fold up the tent and take the poles apart. Since Tom was no longer with us, we'd had to devise a new working system to pitching and breaking down the tent. What had taken five minutes with the three of us now took eight, since Schnapps was no help.

We left the place looking like we'd never been there and headed out, excited to get back to Laredo to see the Rio Grande River and Mexico. It was the first time for both of us. We were huge Western fans and had seen the Rio Grande a million times in films.

But first, we got breakfast, and then checked the post office to see if we'd gotten any mail from Tom. Not a thing, but we trusted that he was okay, wherever he was.

Laredo looked the same as it had the day before. Mexican men were peddling three-wheeled vehicles all through the streets, collecting flattened cardboard boxes. They drove up and down the streets like ice cream men peddling their wares. We never found out what they did with the cardboard, but I imagine they sold it to recycling plants.

The American customs station was the busiest place of all. There were hordes of people walking or driving through their checking stations back and forth each day. It was hard to imagine it ever stopping, or even slowing down. We saw tons of Mexicans carrying shopping bags filled with booze that they were taking back to Mexico to sell for a profit. Evidently whiskey is cheaper in America. Then there were the many tourists driving to Mexico for a vacation or a quick party weekend.

We wanted to see Mexico, but we'd heard too many stories about the Mexican Federales stopping Americans for doing nothing wrong and making them pay a big fine or, if they couldn't pay, throwing them in jail and then tossing away the key.

We weren't scared of that, but we still had too much to do to take a chance. We had too many adventures ahead of us to risk getting derailed. Besides, with our beards, blue jeans, motorcycles, camping gear, and a dog, we figured that we might have actually looked suspicious to them.

We were content to stand on the US bank of the river and snap a few pictures of the other side.

"There's Mexico," I said.

Steve laughed. "Yes, sir. There it is."

We drove up one of the dirt side streets in order to avoid the waiting traffic. The side roads were awful to drive on, dusty and riddled with potholes. I'd never appreciated paves roads so much.

It was noon when we gassed up at a Mobile station and left Laredo on Route 83, heading north to Carrizo Springs. Once you left a town in West Texas, there was nothing but open land. You were lucky to come across even a home, let alone a gas station. Along the road we saw real cowboys herding cattle, just like the Old West. We stopped and took a few pictures and noticed that the cattle stampeded. The men wheeled their mounts about quickly and gave chase to the runaway steers. When they finally had them rounded up again, one of the cowpokes rode over towards us, and we felt like we were in some John Wayne movie. "Please move on, boys. You're spooking the cattle," he said in a calm voice. He was dressed in a plaid shirt, blue jean jacket, old scuffed-up cowboy boots, and a ten-gallon hat. His face and hands were a dark weather-beaten brown, and he looked tough. His horse's sides were heaving from its efforts, and its flanks were shimmering with sweat.

We apologized and left. At Carrizo Springs, we switched to Route 277 north and picked Del Rio, another hustling border town, as our destination for the day. It helped to have a destination to reach; otherwise we may have been tempted to quit driving too soon.

When we got to Del Rio, it was six thirty and already dark. We bought some food at a supermarket and continued on what we thought was Route 277. It ended up in a dead end at the customs station, where everyone crosses the border to visit the famous Boy's Town in Mexico, just a mile from the border. Desperately, we looked for a little clearing where we could camp for the night. Nothing. We turned around and drove an eighth of a mile back down the road, and then up to a small white one-room shack with a sign reading "Taxi Service." The shack was situated in the front middle portion of a big gravel parking lot, illuminated by two big flood lights. A few Mexican men were standing in front of the shack next to their green cabs. When we asked them if they knew of a place for us to bed down, one of them said we could use the upper corner of the lot, which was a huge relief. We thanked him and drove over the loose gravel to the spot.

I got off my bike first and looked around. It looked like the opposite of a comfortable place to spend the night, but I was too tired to complain. Not far from where we were going to lay our heads was a big pile of junk and a graveyard of broken-down cars.

Schnapps was now running around, exploring. She kept looking up at Steve, either for approval, or to say, "What's this? Another new place?"

We sat down to a flashlight dinner of hamburger and corn, which we shared with the pup. We had to eat fast because an intense, dry cold was forcing its way through our clothes. Within minutes, I couldn't locate a single part of my body that wasn't frigid.

"Steve," I said quietly, a few minutes into dinner, "don't look now, but there's a big white horse standing right behind you, watching your every move."

Steve slowly turned around. The horse was in a pasture about ten feet away, standing behind a barbed wire fence. I might be wrong, but I swear that horse looked at us like we were crazy. Maybe he was right.

We decided to leave the dishes for the morning and headed into the taxi office to get warm.

I got my writing materials and walked across the lot to the so-called office. Both doors were falling off their hinges and would not close snugly. There was also an old brown desk, a broken convertible couch, and a worn-out armchair, the type grandpa would sit in. Aside from that, there was a Coke machine, and everything was filthy. There men were standing around a portable electric heater. We were desperate, so we walked in, made friends, and started talking. We learned that their main business came from hustling customers—almost entirely males—for taxi rides to Boy's Town. It was $2 per car load, whether there was one person or eight guys all trying to pile into one cab. Boy's Town was famous for its cheap prostitutes. Every night, many American men were parking their cars in the lot and then taking the joy ride across the border for some fun.

One of the taxi drivers was named Manny. He was so fat, he had trouble squeezing behind the wheel of his cab. His head looked like it had been set on his shoulders and someone had forgotten to give him a neck. His bright white eyes shone like stars in his round olive-skinned face. Manny was a native of Mexico, but he worked under the table in the United States, which he spoke openly about.

He paced back and forth in the office while he talked, always looking out the window for cars. Whenever he saw the headlights of an oncoming car or truck, he would crash through the front door—probably why it was broken—and run out to the street waving his hand. "Taxi! Taxi! Taxi!"

We talked Manny into taking us over one at a time, so one of us could stay behind and watch our belongings. Steve went first and took Schnapps with him. "Have a good time, Schnapps!" I yelled as they got in the cab. On his way back through customs, the US officers saw the dog and told Steve that he couldn't bring animals into this country. Steve and Manny explained that they had taken the dog into Mexico for the ride and were now on their way back. Recognizing Steve's Northern accent, they figured he was telling the truth and let him back through.

Then it was my turn, but I had to wait until Manny hustled up more customers. I finally got my ride over, but it was no big thing. It was just a dirty, sad little town. Behind one club, there was a long, grubby building with about twenty single rooms. The girls would stand outside a room, and you'd just go and pick the one you want, pay the money, and you were all set, if that's the way you wanted it. No thanks.

We headed back by eleven, but Manny said he'd be hustling until at least twelve thirty. Manny said we could sleep in the "office," so we rolled our bikes next to the shack, locked them up, and brought in our sleeping bags. When Manny finally called it quits, we opened up the couch, which was only six feet long and five feet wide, and then rolled out our sleeping bags. We slept side by side. It was just as cold as it would have been outside, but there was no one to complain to, and it wouldn't have done any good anyway.

The next morning, Manny woke us up bright and early. After a quick breakfast, we decided to fix the front door so it would open and close properly, hoping to repay everyone there for treating us kindly. We used what crude tools we could find to rehang the chipped and peeling door. We collected a few odd-sized screws, and, with a hammer and a screwdriver, we got the job done. My carpentry and mechanical skills had proved to be a big help all along our trip. Manny thanked us and asked us to stick around, but we had to go. We rode out with a shout of "Adios, amigo," and I watched him waving at us in my rearview mirror.

We didn't drive very far before we stopped to fill up with gas. We decided to fill up our spare quart-sized containers with gas as well. The roads out there were so long and empty, I couldn't shake the idea of running out of gas out in the desert and not having any clue how close we were to another station. After the bikes were filled, we made sure Schnapps was comfortable, checked our loads and tires once more, and kept going.

The roads were mostly empty except for an occasional pickup truck. Eventually, we saw some motor homes towing a jeep for off-road use, traveling south.

The blue-green Pecos River, deep within its gorge, looked like a glittering treasure from atop a high overlook. It was a different sensation seeing a river sunken deep within the earth when all around it was flat. It reminded me of the old Western fable "Pecos Pete" that I had endlessly watched on TV. From our lofty perch, we could also see where the Pecos branched into the mighty Rio Grande River before continuing on into the mountains of Mexico.

We left the overlook and crossed one of the tallest bridges in the country to cross the river, and then continued our trek northwest, hopefully for warmer climate.

From the time we left Laredo to Marathon, we had noticed the gradual change in geography. Flat lands eventually gave ways to low plateaus, that then became small, rounded hills that in turn grew slowly into tall, rounded hills. They eventually began to form box canyons here and there, and then finally there were jagged, rocky mountain in the distance. But that was all the horizon. Back where we were, the road was flat, and the dry grassless land stretched for miles.

"Hey," said Steve at a rest stop, "that sign back there said it was twenty miles to Langtry. Do you remember that movie 'Judge Roy Bean' with Paul Newman? That's where they made it. Let's stop there." He was so excited that I couldn't have raised an objection even if I'd had one, which I did not.

We got to Langtry at 1:00 PM. It was a small, very touristy place. It was basically a few shacks for houses, a general store combined with a post office, and a couple of gas stations. The Judge Roy Bean historical site was surrounded by a nice wall and preserved by the state. There was no admission charge, so we went into the lobby and listened to the history of the real man named Judge Roy Bean on prerecorded tapes that corresponded to pictures hung along the wall.

We took pictures of each other posing like Paul Newman on the porch of the old saloon.

After we'd seen enough, we went back to the bikes and let Schnapps out to stretch her legs and christen some unspoiled ground. When all three of us were ready to ride again, we got on our way. Dryden was our next stop. Just like all the other desert towns, you could see it for miles before you got there because of the flat treeless land and straight endless roads. The town was tiny and rundown. Many of the stone and stucco buildings were deserted. We located a big white store with the American flag waving proudly overhead, so we knew the post office must be connected to it, and we were right. The general store carried everything from candy to guns and ammunition. We were expecting mail, and were happy when the lady behind the counter handed each of us a package and some letters. We thanked her and left a change-of-address card to forward any late-coming mail to our next big stop. We couldn't get out the door fast enough to sit on the cement steps and open our letters. We finally heard from Tom! It was a brief letter, saying only that he'd made it to Phoenix, Arizona, and was doing pretty well. We were both relieved to know he was okay and still heading to California. I was also happy to get a package of Armenian pastry and a letter from my mother. Steve got a letter and package of cookies for both of us. While we were enthusiastically reading our mail, a miracle happened: I told Schnapps to sit and she did. Now if only she could master "Don't pee in the tent," we'd be set.

It was only three thirty. We still had good traveling time left, so we decided to go down to Sanderson and spend the night. When we got there, we looked everywhere for a place to take a shower. We'd gotten so oily and dirty, we wouldn't have appealed to a female grizzly, even as food.

Sanderson was another small town with a small population of two thousand. It was set in a valley of mountains. There were an extraordinary number of motels for such a small town, and every one was nearly full. There were no public showers, so we stopped at a few motels, hoping they'd let us use a shower for a couple of bucks. No luck: it was either against policy or they were full. Personally, I think our grubby appearance just scared off the clerks. Like we were so dirty that even their showers couldn't recover from having to deal with us. We would have settled for a cold bath in a river, but there were no streams around. So, stinking and oily as all get-out, we bought some food in a small market and got into a conversation with an old man who had lived in Sanderson all his life. He said that every fall the place was packed with hunters coming down from the mountains and staying in the motels. The town had a small school system and a few businesses.

He said the hunting was enough to make the town self-sufficient. Food and supplies were expensive because they had to be trucked in from a great distance. I still had questions. For instance, everyone that lived there couldn't possibly be working. There were only so many hotel jobs. So how did they survive? Where did they get their money? How did they live? I never got any answers, because the old guy suddenly walked off to his truck, and that was that.

We drove west out of town, hoping for a rest stop, but didn't find one. The sun was racing down the sky when we passed a dirt road branching off from the highway. It led to a dry riverbed beneath an overpass. We got off our bikes and looked around for a good spot to lie down for the night, but all we found was animal shit, graffiti, and picked-clean skeletons of various animals.

"Mark, why don't we sleep up there tonight?" Steve said pointing to a plateau off to the right.

"That land's fenced off. We could get picked up for trespassing." As we were planning our trip back home I expected that when we were in the west, we could drive anywhere off the road and camp, but to my disappointment, there was barbed wire everywhere. Sure wasn't like in the cowboy movies I watched.

"Well look, there's a cave on the side of that ledge. I'm gonna check it out. Wait here." Steve jumped the barbed wire fence and worked his way through the prairie brush almost up to the cave.

While he did that, I searched the area again and found too many bad signs that some sort of wild animal or crazy man was using this area for a dining hall, so I decided it was time to leave before the sun went completely out of sight. For all I knew, some maniac lived in the cave that Steve was approaching. I didn't want anyone gnawing on our bones, so that did it. I hollered for Steve to come back. He did, and we made tracks. Back on the road, we soon came to a small ranch house. We drove down the long dirt driveway and stopped in front of the building. Steve knocked on the door and asked the young black man who answered if we could camp on his land for the night. He said it was his boss's land, but it was alright for us to stay one night.

We drove off into the prairie a ways, parked our bikes, and set up a small camp. We didn't build a fireplace or set up our tent. Better to keep things simple.

The night closed in fast and we ended up eating in the dark, like usual, but we managed, like usual. The setting took us back to the days of the cowboy roaming the Great Plains with his horse. So much of Texas did. Here we were, lying on the ground, propped up on one elbow around a small stove that gave off an orange-blue flame, eating stew before the backdrop of rolling hills and stars. Since we didn't bother to set up our tent, the cold began to creep in, so we got into our bags. We fell asleep to the lonely call of a coyote off in the distant hills and the hiss of the burning stove.

We were in for a surprise in the morning. I was the first one up. When I untied the drawstrings to my bag and popped my ski-hat-covered head out to check the beginning of a new day, our bags were white, covered with frost! Heavy frost! I squirmed out of my bag and tiptoed for the camera in Steve's pack. There I stood in my long johns, shaking like a leaf. I wanted to be quiet, but I was also on tiptoes because the ground was so cold it was like I wasn't even wearing socks. But I had to get the picture or I thought no one would believe this. *Click.* The shutter opened and closed. I got a good shot of Steve balled up inside his completely sealed bag with a heavy layer of frost on it, lying next to the cold stove and his bike, with the rising sun and hills as background.

It was too early, only seven, so I jumped back into the bag to keep warm until the sun restored some sanity to the land.

An hour later, I got up to water a bush. While I was concentrating on my task, Steve quietly got up and caught me in the act with the camera. When I saw the picture later, my head down, facing a bush, there in my long johns, I looked like old Festus on the TV show "Gunsmoke."

We broke camp, packed up the bikes, and policed the area to make sure we hadn't left any rubbish. We also roughed up the ground we had flattened to make it look as natural as before. The day was warming up, and the sun felt good. We road back a short way down the dirt road to thank the man for letting us camp for the night.

A short way down the straight and open road, we stopped to check the map to know what to look for on the road ahead. There it was: **Big Ben National Park.**

"Steve, what do you think about taking a small detour and go to Big Ben? It's only about one hundred miles out of our way and we're due for some recreation."

"Yeah, okay, but we can only stop a couple of days."

"That's good, as long as we go there. By the looks of the map, when we get to Marathon, we switch to Route 385 due south, which goes right into the park."

We gassed up in Marathon, another small town, and drove the lonely but beautiful road to Big Ben. Occasionally a herd of deer would gracefully leap across the narrow two-lane roadway.

It seemed like an hour-long ride from the first sign saying "Welcome to Big Ben National Park" to the ranger station. We got to the park station at 2:00 PM and stopped at the small, deserted ranger station. Before going in, we took off our helmets and tried to comb our shiny, greasy hair, but it was no use; we just needed a hot shower. Inside, we picked up an information sheet, pressed a button on the wall, and then sat on a wooden bench to listen to a prerecorded message about the park's attractions. It sounded great, but the idea of a shower had invaded my mind and expanded into every nook and cranny. I felt like an addict whose mind knows only one craving.

We drove a mile to the main ranger station. From there, it was another mile's ride up into the mountains to find out about renting a horse for the next day. A cowboy told us that the only way we could rent a horse was by going on a tour, and we didn't want to do that. At the main station, we asked the ranger about using the campground and facilities. He told us that the campground was closed for the season. He told us we could camp at the end of this long dirt rode next to the Rio Grande river, so we bought some food in the camp store and drove down the road that ended in a cul-de-sac by the famous river. It seemed like it took us an hour riding our bikes in the dark. As we drove around the loop, we saw a canopied picnic table and decided to make camp. We unpacked and got ready to eat when I noticed that I had lost my handy Swiss Army knife. We made dinner quickly, planning to look for it afterwards, but when dinner was over, we cleaned up the mess and started writing in our diaries. We never set up our tent; we planned to sleep under the bright full moon.

It was eight when we saw a car drive down the road and stop near the bank of the river. Next, we heard the door open and close. Next, we heard hoofbeats coming up the bank of the river. We sat still, straining with our ears.

"Hey, amigo," said the man on the horse, speaking with a Mexican accent. Then he said something we couldn't understand. At that moment, the man in the car opened his door, got out, and said in an angry voice, "Hey man, my boss don't operate that way." It sounded like a conversation from a TV show, right before a deal goes wrong in a storm of double-crosses.

They talked for a while, but we couldn't hear everything. Then the man in the car got in and slammed the door shut, and then drove right past us spinning out his rear tires. We weren't sure if he saw us or not because we were hidden behind some tumbleweed. We figured it might be a narcotics drop. The car was gone, but we could still hear the horse's hooves on the gravel road, and so could Schnapps. Her ears were standing straight up. She stood bravely facing the direction where we thought the mysterious horse and rider were, and growled. We both looked at each other, and then at Schnapps who was now facing in another direction, but was still growling. Cattle could be heard crossing the river and also a few more men. A twinge of fear stroked us, and we started imagining all kinds of wild things. Back at the store, there had been five Mexican cowboys with a case of beer. Maybe they were now out for some fun at our expense. Who knows? We got ready for action, just in case. I had brought along my hatchet and a bowie knife which I kept packed on my bike. Steve grabbed the hatchet, and I had the bowie knife in one hand and a spade shovel in the other. We both sat quietly in the shadows trying to keep Schnapps from making any noise. After a while, our legs were getting tired from squatting quietly behind the tumbleweed. We stayed still another minute or so, and then heard the horse and the rider move out of the area. At that point, we decided it was best to pack up our gear onto our bikes, get

Schnopps back into her crate on my bike, and get ready to leave. The moon was full and illuminated the ground with soft white light.

The white smooth sand glistened in the moonlight. Nothing but a grove of bushes and trees separated us from the unknown. I stalked off to the right like an Indian in a movie, while Steve made his way down the road. The moon was too bright to go very far without being seen, so we came back to the picnic table in the shadow of its canopy.

"Steve," I whispered, "whatever happens, stay back to back and don't quit fighting."

We were both pretty scared because that's what uncertainty and waiting do to you. But after sitting for a half hour, I wanted to make a move. Apparently, I was more willing to run the risk of moving than to just stay put and deal with the boredom and fidgets.

"Come on," I said, "let's pack up and get out of here. If someone is over there, they will either make their move or not, but I'm tired of sitting here like this."

"Mark, are you sure it's a good idea?"

"Sure, we could sit here all night tensed up like coiled springs and there might not even be anyone out there," I said. Steve nodded. We were packing up as quietly as we could when—*crash.* I stepped on the garbage can cover that was on the concrete slab under the table.

"Hey! What the hell are you doing?" Steve whispered loudly.

"Sorry, I didn't see the stupid thing in the dark."

We finished packing and were ready to go when I got brave, or maybe crazy. Sometimes, I'm not sure there's a difference. "Wait a minute, Steve. We can't just run away from all this adventure. Remember, if Clint Eastwood was here, he wouldn't back down. He'd go check it out. What do you say?"

Steve had been just about to get on his bike. Was he thinking, *I say we're not Clint Eastwood?* He pondered for a minute, looking at the ground, and then nodded yes. "Okay, let's do it," he said. We heard more horses and men down by the river. With our weapons concealed under our jackets, we walked side by side down the moonlit road towards the river.

At the edge of the road, we stopped and looked down to the river, and all of a sudden a dark figure stepped out from behind a tree. As fast as he showed himself, I dove off into a bush to my right. It was too late for Steve to move, so he just stood there, trying to be cool.

"Hey man, what's happening?" called the shadow in a heavy Mexican accent.

Steve didn't move.

The dude was wearing a big sombrero, two gun belts crossed over his chest, and a side arm, just like someone out of a Western movie. Only this was real. When Steve didn't answer him, he started whistling, and then he turned and disappeared into the shadows and yelled to his friends. What sounded like at least seven or eight horses came charging across the shallow river. That was our cue to exit.

"Come on, Mark, let's get out of here!"

I crawled out of the bush, and we both ran up the road for our bikes, jumped on, and kicked them over. Steve had some trouble with his.

"Come on, Steve!"

Steve gave one more kick and the deep, throaty sound of the engine emerged. We both raced up the gravel road in the dark without our headlights on. As we drove, I looked back once and saw six to seven riders all with guns and gun belts chasing us. The lead guy was on a light tan horse. They were clearly after us!

This area of the park was a one-hour ride from the ranger station, so we figured we wouldn't get any help. We also thought we didn't want to keep riding in the dark in case we made a wrong turn and ended up in a box canyon (dead end). As we drove, we saw a campfire to the left in the campground that was supposed to be closed. "Steve!" I yelled over. "Let's dump the bikes off the road on the right in the brush and run over to the campsite." We did just that.

As we got close to the campfire, we could see about five guys sitting there, so we slowed down and walked in. Just as we got real close, I said, "Hey, guys, you mind if we join you?" Strangely enough, they said, "Sure, come on in." No questions asked. I mean really, if you were camping and all of a sudden two guys come in from the dark from nowhere with no camping gear, nothing, wouldn't that raise a question? We sat by the fire and introduced ourselves. Just then, the group of riders came galloping up the road, their horses' hooves echoing like thunder. They stopped near the entrance of the campground and talked in Spanish. We could just barely see them through the brush and trees. Again, we could see that the lead guy wore a round, wide-brimmed hat and rode a tan horse. That's about all we could make out. The men only stayed there for a short time and then headed back for the river. We left our bikes hidden where they were, hoping to make friends and stay where we were for the night. Safety in numbers. We didn't tell the guys at the campfire our problem, just that we would like to join them, which they agreed to. The guys told us they were veterans from the Vietnam war and were doing some camping and smoking some pot. Around midnight, they all decided to hit the sack, so they said goodnight and went into their camper. As the last guy went in, I asked if it would be okay to sleep under the camper, and he said yes. Remember we had no gear with us. Around 1:00 AM, we heard what we thought was machine gun fire off in the distance. The guys came running out of the camper one by one, so I asked what was wrong as Steve and I stilled lay under the camper. One fellow said, "Did you hear that?" I said it must have been heat lightning. "Heat lightning my ass," he said. "That was machine gun fire, M16." The second time we heard the sound, it convinced us all. That night everyone slept with one eye open.

CHAPTER THIRTEEN:

# The Drive to El Paso

W e were up at sunrise, which seemed to come later than usual, given that the tall mountain peaks delayed the sun's rays. A park ranger driving a Jeep Cherokee came to the site and told us all to get out of the park right away. With sleep still in our eyes, we said thank you and buy to the five vets, funny they never asked where we came from or what we were doing there. Then we quietly went and got our bikes and let Schnapps out for a pee. Once we made sure our bike and gear were okay, we rolled our bikes back onto the gravel road and started heading out the park and then westward on towards California.

We'd learned the previous evening of some hot springs not far away, located near the Rio Grande river, so we headed towards them. At the road's end, a flat gravel-filled parking lot was occupied by a lonely beat-up jeep. A long-haired man with a curly beard was in the driver's seat. The only other vehicle was a light-green truck that had a sign on its door: "PARK RANGER PATROL." Two rangers sat inside, and it looked like they were watching the drifter with the beard. All of a sudden, they fired up the engine and peeled out, leaving the lot in a cloud of dust.

We were getting a weird vibe from the guy, so we decided to take turns bathing so one of us could watch our gear.

Hot springs have had a long reputation as healing pools. In Hot Spring, Virginia, Ulysses S. Grant and his wife used to strap themselves to a large, heavy wooden chair and be lowered into the spring. This supposedly cured her arthritic pains with one thirty-minute dip. Well, whether this one healed our aches or not, I can tell you one difference between the hot spring on the Rio Grande and Grant's getaway in Virginia: privacy. Grant constructed an octagon-shaped building enclosing the pool, but we were as exposed as could be.

But it was still pretty wonderful. A strong flow of clean, hot water bubbled from the depths of the earth, up into a large outdoor man-made tub. Like the settlers had over a century before, we washed our dirty hair, beards, and bodies.

It took us about a mile to walk back to our stuff. When we were both done, the shady character from the jeep started a conversation with us, inquiring about our trip. He was calm, genuine, and nice, through and through. I felt a bit bad that I'd judged him on his appearance alone. It's not like we looked like clean-shaven, pristine men on their way to church.

We started riding to Presidio later that afternoon. It was a picturesque, comfortable drive. We stopped at most of the rest stops to get pictures of the mountain views of Texas and the expanses of the distant Mexico sands. All along the Rio Grande river, we stopped to see a few ghost towns. Everywhere it was the same: adobe huts and the utter absence of people.

Continuing west, the road climbed the mountain ridges ever higher, which gave us a view of the other side of Mexico.

Except for taking pictures or filling up the bikes, the only other time we stopped was at a ranch. We still wanted to try our hands at being cowpokes, at least for a day or two. When we stopped, a twelve-year-old boy came out, very cautiously. We asked him about the possibility of a job. The gate was closed, and our engines had been far louder than a knock on the front door. He was the only one in his family that could speak some English. No one else stirred, but we could feel their eyes watching us. The boy couldn't give us much information with his limited English, but he did give us directions to the next gas station. Apparently, playing cowboy wasn't in our future, one dream I hadn't been able to bring into being.

The gas station was also the multipurpose general store for its small town. Across the street was a small elementary school. There were a few kids in the school yard playing basketball. Once we passed the school, we were already leaving town; it was that small. Back on the road to Presidio, the land on either side grew barren again. Every so often, we would see an arroyo when we passed over a bridge, far below, filled with dust and rocks, mere suggestions of the former streams that had once run through.

We passed by another ranch house. There were four men outside, sitting around and shooting the breeze. This time the gate was open, so we drove right up. One was sitting in the front seat of an old pickup truck carving a piece of wood with a sharp knife. When we cut our engines to talk, he ceased his whittling. The others were sitting down, fiddling with straw stems in their hands.

After a few simple questions, we all knew that communication was going to be impossible. English just wasn't their lingo, and Spanish certainly wasn't ours. Before they could get the wrong idea, we waved, said "Goodbye, amigos," and rode on out.

We hit Presidio around one o'clock and started looking for a decent restaurant. Any enthusiasm we might have felt about cooking had vanished during the tiresome ride after the hot springs. After a relaxing dinner, we bundled up and started looking for a place to stay. Our faces had been exposed all day, and our foreheads felt overheated, almost like we had fevers. When we walked out into the cool evening, the contrast between the chill of the air and the heat of our bodies made me feel a little nauseated. And at the same time, like they knew they were about to start losing heat, our back muscles tightened up in protest.

The days were getting shorter as the first day of winter approached. It was dark when we pulled off the road into a thicket of tall sagebrush. We hadn't traveled very far from Presidio when we found that perfect spot. It was far enough off the road that no one could spot us, and the sagebrush hid our bikes. We covered our mirrors so the headlights and full moon wouldn't toss off any reflections that might give away our hiding place.

We laid a large piece of plastic down on the packed flat sand to keep the bottoms of our bedrolls clean. Schnapps was running and playing with the plastic, having all sorts of mischievous fun. A full moon rose, and there, with just us and the sky, it felt like we could have been on the frontier in another age. I couldn't have been happier. I didn't even want to sleep.

It was really cold by seven thirty, and Schnapps wanted to be in the warmth of our bags. She picked Steve as the lucky winner, crawled down into his bag, and snuggled herself into a small ball close to his chest. In a matter of minutes, Steve found Schnapps three sheets to the wind. The long day's up-and-down ride, followed by a hot dinner of pork chop bone, bread, and milk, did her in like the rest of us.

We were up at eight, our breath puffing out before us in misty reminders of the cold. Even Schnapps was shivering as she shuffled around, looking for a place to do her morning duty.

After a quick ride, we had a hot breakfast, and then went into a discount department store to look for some Christmas cards. If we wanted them to get to our families in time for Christmas, they had to go out that day. We bought a few, and then went to the library to fill them out. When we were done, we headed towards a rest area where we planned on staying. We were in Marfa, Texas.

It was an unbearably cold two-mile ride from the store to the rest area, which was pretty desolate. There were two concrete picnic tables that didn't look very inviting. Off to the left of the tables was a lonely stone fireplace that would soon come in handy. I went to check back at a farm house we had seen to ask them for some of their fire wood. Ten minutes later, I carried back a full load of excellent timber.

After warming up our vegetable soup on the miniature gas stove, the sun dipped down behind the mountains to the west as the magnificent full moon began to rise.

After we pitched the tent, Steve built a fire and I made two cups of hot cocoa, which seemed like a pitiful defense against the wind chill. It wasn't even blowing that hard, but it had a different quality to it than any of the wind we'd encountered so far. It could cut through anything. We weren't dressed as warmly as possible, but we could have been bundled up like Eskimos and still have felt it. The only way to fight it was to keep moving. Schnapps kept running around to combat the chill, and Steve and I did what we could. Sleeping lowers the body temperature, but we had to try anyway. Steve scooped Schnapps up and put her in the chest of his coat, probably to warm himself up as much as her.

The firewood was running low by ten o'clock when a car pulled into the small rest area and parked about ten yards away. We could make out two people sitting in the front seat. We figured they were drinking, since one tossed a bottle out the window, which landed unbroken in the grass nearby.

We watched carefully. We were alone in an unfamiliar, barren land. The nearest person was two miles down the road at a farm house. The flames of our fire were small by that point, but the full moon revealed our bikes and our tent. They had to know we were there.

We watched for about ten minutes before two guys got out of the car. We could see the glow of the cigarettes they smoked. Happily, our anxiety came to nothing. They walked over without a care in the world and asked if they could share the fire for a while. They had a little booze in their veins—hard to blame them on a night like that—but they were friendly. They offered us a cold beer, but we couldn't stand the thought of anything else that was cold that night. We asked if they wouldn't mind running one of us into town to pick up a couple of bottles of Blackberry brandy at a liquor store. They offered to pick it up for us and be right back.

When they came back, we tried to pay, again, but they refused. So we made them sit with us and forced hot cocoa and Graham crackers on them. By eleven, the alcohol in our blood was beginning to wear thin and the cold was seeping back into our bones. The two guys left, and I couldn't blame them.

I couldn't stand that cold. Neither of us could. The fire was doing so little that there wasn't even any point in sitting by it, so we got in our bags.

The misery reached its peak at three that morning. It was like an alarm clock made of ice had gone off inside of us. If you've never woken up because you're suddenly shivering so hard you think your bones will break, you're not missing out. It was a shuddering, deathly chill that ripped through everything in its path. The inner walls of the tent felt like a meat freezer. Looked like one too, with heavy frost on the inside walls from our breath. We both sat up in our bags, but were afraid to leave them. My first thought was, *We should run*, because the fast movements we were trying to make in our bags weren't helping. Then we remembered that Steve had brought the stove into the tent. We could use it for some heat, provided we didn't burn the tent down. We put it in a mess-kit dish as a precaution. The thought of going up in flames didn't seem as dangerous as the thought of trying to get through the rest of the night without heat.

Steve raced to get the gas, stove, and wooden matches, while I rearranged the bags. After Steve filled the stove with gas and tightened the lid, we just had to strike a match and turn up the stove for some good-old modern heat. Between a couple of good belts of brandy and the hot flames, we managed to chase the cold out of our bones. We munched on some Graham crackers while we thawed out. Well, we thought we were thawing out!

We didn't dare fall asleep before the stove ran out of fuel, in fear of knocking it over while we snoozed. But finally it was warm enough for us to put out the flame.

In the morning, Steve was up first. He took a picture of me in the tent with the stove propped in the middle of the floor, sitting in the mess-kit tray as Schnapps jumped on my head, trying to get me moving.

The sun was up, but it didn't feel like it. Frost covered the seats and handlebars of our bikes. It took quite a while for the frost on the inside of the tent to start melting. We waited until eleven thirty, letting the sun do its thing for a while, before once again heading towards El Paso, now 190 miles distant. The road ahead was wide open. Grazing land extended back as far as the foothills of the mountain range, which was silhouetted against the horizon.

We made it to El Paso just after three. It had taken us four-and-a-half hours to go the 190 miles, which is just the about the right amount of time for that distance. It was warmer than the day before, but with the previous night in mind, we knew we had to find a place to stay, and fast. Also, we were desperate to feel clean. The last time we'd had a hot bath was back in the Big Ben National Park. We were creatures made of grease and grime who also happened to look like men. Our clothes weren't doing any better, either. If there'd been a room to stand in, we wouldn't have been able to abide the smell of each other. We stopped at the first campground we saw. It had hot showers, a laundry room, and sandy, soft ground to pitch our tent in. After we registered, we parked our bikes at our site, let Schnapps out, and headed straight for the showers. We must have stayed in the showers a long time, because they began to run low on hot water. Showers out of the way, laundry was the next item on the agenda. I looked at Steve's red cheeks and knew I was just as sunburnt as he was. This is what happens when you spend all day riding towards the sun.

We sat in the small, heated office and watched the six o'clock news and weather. The meteorologist confirmed that last night's temperatures had dropped to the low teens. It had been as cold as it had felt.

On the way in, we'd noticed a truck stop. The office manager said the food wasn't bad there, so off we went. It was within walking distance, which was a good thing, as the air was already filling with a new round of menacing cold. But we were too tired to walk. We put Schnapps in her pen and rode our bikes over the bridge to the restaurant on the other side of the freeway. There were trucks of all kinds parked all over the place, almost like a family reunion of semis. The surroundings were neat and clean.

In the restaurant, without realizing it, we took a booth in the section for truckers who needed fast service. But since we looked like two husky truckers with beards, no one looked at us twice.

After dinner, we browsed through the clothing store and tried on $25 ten-gallon cowboy hats with enormous brims and $50 cowboy boots with big pointy toes and high heels. Gazing into the mirror with our new outfits and full stomachs, it was hard not to feel like the scales had been balanced. We were happy and warm again. The lady behind the counter saw us fooling around and chuckled. We tried on nearly every hat in the place and didn't quite act our ages, but it was hard to care. We put on a real show for her, and she enjoyed it as much as we did. "I wish you didn't have to go so soon," she said when we started to leave. "Try something else on. Entertain me until closing." It was too bad we had already paid for our tent spot because I'm sure she would have let us stay over with her, but the owner of the campsite had taken pity on us and said we could sack out in his heated office for the night.

We tipped our hats to her, put them back on the shelves, and left. But before going to the campsite we stopped at a bar. We generally did this as we traveled and ended up in cities with no campground nearby. The reason was, we hoped to meet up with someone that would let us sleep in their house or backyard. We were sitting at the bar stretching out the one beer we could afford when, on the eleven o'clock news, the news reporter said that, "Three days ago in Big Ben National Park down by the Rio Grande river, there was burning and looting on the Mexican side and three federal agents were shot and killed by machine gunfire during a raid to stop a big drug ring". Right then, I was more scared than when we were being chased, because first I realized it was real and we could have been killed. Even worse, I thought that, if they had killed us and dragged our bodies over the border, our parents would have never known what happened to us. We left the bar without an offer to stay, and drove to the campground and slept in the office: not too comfortable but better than freezing again. The owner of the campground came into the office early morning and woke us up with the sunrise. The early morning sky was a bit hazy, but the sun made its way out eventually. We moved back outside and started cooking hot cereal. Before going, we checked and found a small bit of waste Schnapps was going to leave behind without telling us. Every day we had to teach Schnapps a new lesson on where not to relieve herself. She was, how shall I say it . . . learning resistant.

The day before, Steve's rear tire and chain had both turned over the fifteen-thousand-mile mark. He'd need to replace them before another day's ride. I had another thousand miles to go before it was my turn. So we found a Honda dealer. At the dealer, we tied Schnapps to a bar post and went to work changing the tire. Having our own tire irons made that job a snap. The mechanic helped us put on Steve's bike chain, which was very nice of him. The chain was even easier than the tire. With some time to spare, I started cleaning my carburetor jets to see if that might get me the same gas mileage that Steve was getting.

By the time Steve was finished with his packing, I had tightened the last screw and we still had a couple of hours of daylight left when we headed for the New Mexico state border, which we knew was within fifteen miles.

We landed at a rest area in Antony, New Mexico. It was like the Hilton of rest areas. There were tons of concrete picnic tables enclosed by three walls and a roof to block out the bad weather. Each little bungalow had its own fireplace with a grill for cooking. Plus, a night light in the roof lit up each picnic area with enough light for reading, writing, or playing a game. We went to check out the building where the rest rooms were housed, and found a well-lit, heated lobby. There was an empty information counter on one side of the room and showcase shelves opposite the information counter, which had no glass doors and was wide open. We thought they must take all the brochures and fliers out each night and replace them the next morning.

This looked like a good, warm place to lay out our space pads and sit on the floor, kick off our boots, and enjoy the sandwiches we'd picked up on the way. We kept Schnapps quiet with a few bites of our subs. The people passing in and out didn't bother her, or us. When we finished eating, we read for a while as the hours passed by slowly. That was the first night of our trip that had felt that way to me.

Schnapps was the main attraction for all the people who passed through. Nothing will stop a roomful of adults in their tracks like a cute dog. By ten, no one had stopped by to close up the rest room, so we assumed it stayed open all night. We made our beds in the confines of the information booth. I took a picture of Steve and Schnapps snuggled into the information booth, ready to snooze the night away.

We were all three sheets to the wind when we were roused by a man wearing a badge. "No sleeping permitted inside this building, boys. You'll have to move outside."

He could have carted us off to jail in violation of this ordinance, but we were polite and he felt sorry he had to wake us and boot us out of there. It was eleven when we made our new beds on top of two concrete picnic tables. The cold woke us up again around two fifteen. But it was nothing like the night in that meat locker of a tent, and a few slugs of brandy warmed us up and got us back to sleep in no time.

CHAPTER FOURTEEN:

# On to Phoenix, the Proud
# Lady of the Theater, NYC

I was up early the next morning and got to talking with an old Army veteran who traveled year round through the country on a monthly veteran's
stipend of $1400. He stacked all his worldly possessions into his 1964 white
Ford Fairlane. "There's nothing I enjoy as much as experiencing this country," he said. "There is so much beauty in the places and the people. You just
don't know until you see it for yourself. I'm seventy-two years old and I'm
healthy and sharp enough to do it. I'm happy as a lark. An old lark," he said
with a laugh.

I realized that I had almost never regretted striking up a conversation
with someone. I truly think we can all learn something from anyone we
encounter, if we're open to listening.

While waiting for the sun to bring the earth to life, we caught up on
our journaling, fed Schnapps, who was now infested with worms, washed the
few breakfast dishes, and had all our gear loaded back on the luggage rack,
ready by ten o'clock to knock off a few more miles. A couple of days earlier,
Schnapps had started dragging her butt on the ground at every chance,
obviously itching like crazy. We were planning on getting her some meds at
the first opportunity.

Phoenix, Arizona, was our destination—Sun City, or so we had
been told.

We couldn't wait to lay out in that hot desert sun. The last time we were able to sit in the warm sun with nothing to do had been back in September at Virginia Beach. The only other time was picking golden delicious apples in Singer's Glen.

The weather in the past ninety-four days hadn't been the typical Miami-Beach, light, short-sleeve-shirt kind. It had been cold and cloudy like New England most of the time. Only the sand and people were different. The people were different because of their environment. For instance, the waitress in a roadside stand said good morning before we had a chance to discuss breakfast. It was as though she *liked* the idea of meeting every single person who walked up. She was enthusiastic as she asked about our trip. In the middle of the country, strangers talked freely to one another without caution. It was beautiful. Most of the people who lived on the East and West Coasts had forgotten how rich and lovely the countryside is, the deep topsoil and wealth of great trees, the beauty of its many national parks, the forest country of Tennessee, handsome as a well-made woman, dressed and jeweled. Out here, the earth was generous and outgoing in the heartland, and perhaps the people took a cue from it.

The road we took into New Mexico gradually sloped upward for eighty miles. When we cruised into Lordbury, the gradient of the road didn't take a downward track until thirty miles into Arizona.

The countryside in New Mexico was cultivated, with dairy farms, windmills, and miles of green alfalfa fields that were being cut and packed into bails. I know that I'll most likely remember New Mexico by the essence our nostrils had to endure on our hurried ride in and out of the high altitudes. I'm positive that we had to have driven through the worst of the state. We passed through in four hours. Back at the rest area in Antony, we had come across a tourist magazine at the information counter. According to the magazine, New Mexico was indeed a beautiful state and had much to offer to the adventurous person; we just hadn't seen it. Well, I had to take the magazine at its word, because nothing else had convinced me. But we had to move quickly to warmer climate. Old Man Winter was still on our tails as we traveled to Phoenix, although we thought that, if we could lose him anywhere, surely it would be there.

Route 10 was a heavy travel route that was in pretty poor condition. Legions of Yucca trees spread out across the prairies. The windmills grew more frequent, although they would never rival the density of the oil derricks we'd seen in Texas.

It was midday when we crossed the Arizona border. Suddenly, there were cacti everywhere, some as tall as fifteen feet. They stood erect like statues on one leg, being robbed at gunpoint, one hand in the air. *Freeze.*

The mountains gradually shifted in size. Those near the roadway were small rolling hills, but as we went, they became mountain ridges with high peaks and jagged shapes. The road finally started to descend, and the air lost its winter chill for the time being. We stopped to buy a small supply of food in case it got too cold to travel on to the next town. We only had a few hours of daylight left. Phoenix would have to wait until the next day's ride. Globe was the next big town that was within our reach. We could be there in an hour and still have some daylight to set up the tent in a rest area and eat.

Now the road was bordered with white dotted fields of cotton. The tractors were out in the fields harvesting the crop with a special tractor that only picked the white cotton balls off a small brown shrub bush that was eighteen inches when full grown.

Our prediction on arrival time into Globe was only off by fifteen minutes, but the sun disappeared behind a large mountain ridge and nightfall was on us before we could set up camp and eat dinner.

We thought being up that high was going to put the old cold chill back into our bodies, but it fooled us. The death-defying chill we experienced sleeping in the desert of Texas wasn't present that night way up there in Globe. It was now early to mid-December.

We found a rest area three miles from the west end of the town where we pitched our tent and settled in. I decided to call it a night, while Steve walked across the six-lane highway to a Kentucky Fried Chicken to read and catch some heat until closing time. He'd tell me later that, besides him, there was only a trucker occupying another booth. It was quiet and relaxing to read and listen to the piped-in music. All the workers appeared to be high school age except the manager, who didn't look any older than a recent college graduate.

One of the girls who was out wiping the table clean was outgoing and amiable. She picked up on Steve's accent, just like everyone did. Most people guessed New York, but she got it right and was very proud of herself. "Boston, right?" she said. Steve confirmed. Caught up on their work and with no customers to wait on, the other workers drifted over to Steve's table, intrigued by his cross-country trip. Even the manager got into it, and gave Steve a free Coke as he talked.

An employee who had the night off stopped by with six homemade tamales that his mother had just finished preparing for his fellow workers. He gave Steve a tamale, which Steve liked so much that he asked the boy to write the recipe on a napkin.

Finally, Steve said his goodbyes to all his newfound friends and re-crossed the highway to his temporary home. I was in dreamland, and Schnapps was resting comfortably, curled up next to my bag. Just before Steve was going to crawl into his bag for the night and let my rhythmic snoring sing him to sleep, car headlights lit up the inside of the tent and than flashed outside. Steve could hear voices, and some people jumped out of the car. They walked over and a voice called out, "Hello, Steve, are you there?" He recognized the voice of his female friend! He opened the tent door and stuck out his head.

They had stopped by to get Steve's address so they could write to him, which made Steve's night, even better than the tamales. The next morning when he told me the story, he said, "We're all Americans. We all want the same things, no matter how different our backgrounds are. It sounds kind of corny, but they went out of theirt way to reach out to me, and it gave me hope."

We were up at seven thirty. We had hot cereal and half a cinnamon coffee cake each. While we were cleaning the area before breaking camp, an older woman drifted over with a curious eye. We expected the same old questions, but she was quickly overbearing. "How in the world do you manage to carry a dog on a motorcycle?" She kept up the barrage of questions, rapid-fire, and even though it was tiresome, her face simply seemed sick with loneliness. She was old and wrinkled and dry, and I figured that anyone would look the same after a few decades in this climate. She wore a long woolen coat, stained and spotted, topped with a black-and-red stocking cap, a gift perhaps from the Salvation Army. I wondered how long it had been since she'd had someone to talk to.

"That beat-up Plymouth over there has been my home for the last two years," she said. The Plymouth was full of animals, a veritable litter. I could see that any dog or cat seeking refuge would be taken in under her wing, mothered, fed, and spoiled. There was even a Saint Bernard in there! The animals were obviously her solace, and probably some form of therapy. She trusted them over humans. She glanced at the leftover cinnamon coffee cake we couldn't finish eating at breakfast.

"Bless you," she said when we offered it to her. There was a heartbreaking air of desperation around her. But she sounded highly educated, was very proper in her manner of speech, and civil almost to the point of parody. She told us she was once the "Proud Lady of the theatre" in New York City but had not been able to return. She vaguely mentioned an ill fate that had scarred her appearance, which had led to the constant downward spiral in which she still found herself. Her aspirations and dreams had been replaced with a car full of animals and the kindness of strangers when it came time for her next meal.

I'd heard and read statistics on people starving right here in one of the richest and most powerful nations in the world and people having to resort to begging in order to survive. Here, now, standing before us, stood one of those statistics. There are things that don't seem like they could possibly be real until you see them for yourself. She took her coffee cake back to her car, probably to share it with her dogs and cats.

Then there was a wild coincidence. The jet pilot we'd met at the hot springs in Big Ben saw our bright orange tent from the road, the gear on our bikes, and pulled in to make sure it was us. People who wander seem to find each other again and again, even without specific destinations in mind. It was a happy, if brief, reunion. We talked for a while again, and then continued on our separate ways.

We pounded on to Phoenix. The road led downward, twisted along the sides of small ridges. The pressure that had built up in our ears as we had climbed slowly started to equalize. We helped it along by swallowing constantly. An army of giant cacti marched across the desert landscape. The land was barren between one town and another, and you could start to feel like you were the last people in the world until you saw a car. Soon we were in Mesa, which was beautiful. A few places in town were very green, which was almost shocking in the middle of the dust bowl. You could forget that there were things that were still vividly *alive*. The road was flat and bordered on both sides by commercial businesses. Trailer homes and vehicle parts distributors lined both sides of the street extending miles from town to town, all the way from Mesa to Phoenix. We stopped at a McDonald's to quiet our howling stomachs.

As soon as we stopped, we peeled off the extra clothing and stacked it with the rest of the gear. Schnapps started hollering for her freedom at once. Now it really was getting hot for her in her traveling house. A few onlookers smiled at her, like always. She'd been worth her weight in gold as a conversation starter. "Oh, look, it's a puppy dog. How cute!" It never failed. She especially attracted cute girls!

Schnapps started right into her familiar new dance step, the "worm dance." She would sit on her bum, extend her hind legs in the air out in front of her two front legs, and start walking forward with only the push and pull of her two forward legs, dragging her rear end on the ground, relieving the itching caused by the worms. Right after lunch, we checked into the nearest phone booth for a look into the yellow pages, hoping to find a Humane Society. We needed a free clinic, if possible. A veterinarian would be out of our price range. There were two full pages of vets and pet groomers, but no free rescue leagues or animal clinics listed in the immediate area. And many said in their ads that they were closed on Saturday, or only open Saturday until noon. It was twelve thirty. We next inquired at a gas station on the whereabouts of a college veterinarian clinic we had spotted in the fine print of an ad. A man at a self-service pump overheard our conversation with the station attendant and offered an economical solution. "Worm pills at your local drug store. A box will run you a buck fifty, tops." He said they worked wonders when his own dog was doing the worm dance. Well, we got to the college veterinarian clinic sixty minutes too late and had no choice but to try out the suggested worm pill from a store

We rode to the next town, Tempe, where a druggist willingly volunteered what sounded like all the knowledge humanity had ever accrued about worms and dogs: symptoms, cures, how to administer pills, and on and on. He recommended a brand, and we took it. The information he gave us would have cost us at least $25 at a vet.

Walking out in the hot desert sun reminded us that we were mortals with skin, roaming about the brutal landscape of Arizona. We returned to the store quickly for a bottle of suntan lotion, our first on the trip.

After buying the lotion, we were standing by our bikes when a girl named Tammy walked over with a few questions in mind.

Our loaded bikes reminded her of a three-week cross-country trip she had taken with her boyfriend the past June. Her experience was far behind, but when she saw us, she knew we needed a place to stay, not to mention a good shower, by the look of our greasy hair. The simple act of having traveled across the country had put her in tune with exactly what a fellow traveler would need.

We followed her to her apartment complex, which wasn't far from the drug store. Her abode consisted of a bedroom, living room, kitchen, and bath. Right outside their front door was an irregular-shaped swimming pool, which we both sampled with all due haste. But first, off went the heavy clothes, and on went our gym shorts and suntan lotion. Our hostess made us a nice cold pitcher of lemonade, while we swam and then basked in the desert sun. After we showered, and just before dinner, we met Tammy's boyfriend, a guy named Albert. He was from Newton, Massachusetts, and was in his last year at Arizona State University.

After dinner, we learned that Tammy had finished school, had majored in physical education like ourselves, and was without a job. She was currently a substitute teacher, while Albert was finishing his degree in aerodynamics engineering. Tammy then called their good friend Hank and asked him if we could stay at his house for a night or two. Hank's accommodations were much larger, thought Tammy, and we'd be comfortable sleeping on a couch instead of a floor.

Hank dropped by to do his laundry at their apartment since it was cheaper, which also gave him a chance to meet his two new (potential) house guests. Hank was twenty-eight years old and was also in his last year of an aerodynamics engineering degree. He couldn't stay long, but he told us to meet him at his place at ten that night. I don't think buying a bottle of suntan lotion had ever had such a great result.

We relaxed for the rest of the evening, and then rode our bikes to Hank's house. Hank had his own waterbed, two baths, and a large living room and kitchen. We told them all a few of our adventure stories, which brought us up to eleven. Hank excused himself because he had to get up early the next morning. As had become our habit, we thanked **God** for good people before turning in and closing our eyes.

Sunday morning was bright and sunny. At nine thirty, it was already seventy-five degrees—yowza.

Tammy rode her bicycle over at ten thirty and found us washing our breakfast pans. She invited us over to her apartment to lay out in the sun again. We put Schnapps in her box and headed over, after giving Schnapps her second dose of worm pills, which she disliked having coaxed down her throat. It was obviously something she wasn't going to get used to, or start loving. A pretty girl sitting on the other side of the pool helped us down her second pill with a technique that worked like magic. She rubbed Schnapp's throat once the pill was in her mouth, which allowed it to pass down effortlessly, and without gagging. The sun felt as fantastic as it had the day before.

However, at three, it started to cool off fast, so we decided to try our luck at tennis. We went to the drug store to buy a can of tennis balls, and then treated ourselves to a whopper at Burger King.

After three hours of tennis, we decided to get in ten quick wind sprints. After that, there we were, two physical education majors from the University of Massachusetts, huffing and puffing like we were going to faint after a mere ten sprints. We laughed, but it was sad. Since we were in warmer weather now, we vowed to work out at least every other day, especially while we had a place to shower.

We asked Tammy and Albert if they wanted to join us for dinner. They didn't feel like going, but suggested the Golden Coin, which had all the Chinese food you could eat for $2.25. We were really hungry and Chinese food was light and healthy, or at least we thought it was, which sounded great after facing down those rather pitiful wind sprints. An older couple sat in the booth adjacent to ours. Of course, they noticed our New England accents and then asked if we were brothers.

We talked for three quarters of an hour about travelers and the many good people we met during our trip. The stories seemed to give them a boost. You can't have too many reminders that people are mostly good. It can be the only thing that keeps you from getting too cynical.

They tried to pay for our meal, but we told them that getting to talk with them and putting them on the list of great people we'd met on our trip was reward enough. Then they gave us their son's address and phone number in San Diego and asked us to look him up. They thought he'd love to meet us. He was thirty years old and a bachelor again. Having just finished up a divorce, he could use some company. We thanked them for their kind gesture and returned to Tammy's apartment. On arrival, we talked with another young couple who noticed our Massachusetts plates. They were from Maine. They had just returned from visiting Mexico with a few bottles of Mexican booze and a hand-woven blanket. They invited us to have a few shots of the booze and a couple of games of cribbage. We took their offer and played a few games. They also offered us the use of their couch cushions to sleep on for the night, which was perfect, since we didn't want to impose on Tammy and Albert again.

Monday morning the sky was no different than it had been on Sunday: deep blue, and not a cloud could be seen. We were up early. The janitor at the apartment informed us that they were serving free orange juice and donuts at the poolside clubhouse. After eating, we rode to a motorcycle dealer shop in East Princess without our helmets on; Arizona law doesn't require them. Now we could hear each other much better when we talked, riding side by side. Our hair flew high and blew straight back, which made Steve look somewhat like Clint Eastwood, only on a horse made of metal.

A mechanic helped me pick out a new tire and chain. He also helped us cut the old chain and attach my new one, which was self-lubricating. It could go for twenty thousand miles and never need a lube job.

Ten dollars more expensive, but I'd never need to spend money for lube or get my rear rim dirty from excessive grease flying off my chain. Sold. It took two hours to complete, which gave us all afternoon to play. But first, we wanted to mail a dozen roses to our mothers for Christmas. Even though money was running low, our mothers would be happy to know we were thinking of them. This was the first time we'd ever bought a dozen long stem red roses in our lives, and what better time to send them than the day before Christmas? We both wished we could have seen the expression on their faces when the mailman would walk up, white snow covering the steps, and say, "Merry Christmas, Ma!" Tears would run down their faces. Our fathers would walk in and know who they were from and understand the tears. They might even want to cry, but would hold back, since it would make it worse. Their son's absence had affected the entire families. But then the roses would be placed in a lovely vase, and Christmas spirit would fill the air.

Back in Tempe, we met Tammy back at the pool again and took another dip. No one was more excited about it than Schnapps. You should have seen her go!

That evening, we did some washing before going out with the couple we played tennis that afternoon. The next day, we'd be heading for San Diego. It seemed sort of funny that the trip was coming to an end. Sort of sad, sort of exciting. A lot of things. A lot of feelings. Our destination point was now only a few days away after being on the road for nearly hundred days. A strange quiet came over us as we thought of the people we'd met and the experiences we had had. And yet, we were still excited to leave again, looking forward to the next day's ride. How would we feel when it was over? Would we remember everything that happened, what we had learned? I was so grateful that we had written in our journals every day.

*California*, I thought, *here we come. I hope you're ready for us, because we're ready for you.*

# CHAPTER FIFTEEN

# California, Here We Come

Steve got up early and tried to pack quietly, but still managed to make a fair amount of noise. The door, in particular, squeaked like crazy. In Phoenix, we stopped at the main post office where we both had some mail waiting for us in general delivery. So far the general delivery system had been working well for us and Tom. Then I wanted to get a new Swiss Army knife, so we started looking for a store. We stood on the sidewalk in front of the post office and looked up and down the street. Phoenix is really spread out. Nothing feels like it's close to anything else.

We managed to go into two stores and not come out with a simple knife. No one stocked this simple item!

Tired of looking, we drove out. Six miles down the road, we stopped at an A&W root beer stand for barbecued beef sandwiches and frosty root beers while Schnapps relaxed with us at the outdoor table as we read our mail.

We got back on the road thinking, *California, California!* We were getting close. The highway was straight with barren desert on either side. Being from the Northeast, we, like many other people who had never seen a desert, drove by much of it without realizing we were *in* a desert. We expected to see white sands and rolling dunes, deserts straight out of the movie "Lawrence of Arabia." But about ninety-five of our Western deserts are covered with low-growing thorny plants with small gray and green leaves. The mountains were just as harsh: rocky and bare.

As we continued our tiring ride on the two-lane roadway to California, every once in a while, a trailer truck would roar by and shake us up a bit, keeping us awake. But aside from that, it was all pretty dull that morning. I broke the monotony of driving by pulling alongside Steve and yelling over the bikes and the rushing wind. "Hey, Steve! Only twenty more miles to go to reach Yuma!"

"I know! But it seems like so much more!"

While riding motorcycles, conversations must be short and sweet. You can scream yourself hoarse in a hurry. It's a luxury today that so many bikers can hook up radios through their helmets and talk to each other. But back then, most of the time it was best (and safer) to stop and talk rather than struggle on the bike.

The city of Yuma appeared, starting out as a little dot, and then getting bigger and bigger with every mile we drove. Then we were right on the edge of the arid city.

We stopped at an Exxon station and hung out for a while after gassing up. I let Schnapps out of her little house and laughed while she ran around and played and looked for a spot to do her business. She sniffed everything, and every bumper in the lot, with such interest that I almost felt jealous. What must it be like to think everything is as captivating as a dog?

"Wow," I said when she finally got down to it. "How can a little dog like that hold so much liquid?"

"I don't know," said Steve, "but that is one hell of a puddle." He wasn't kidding. It was an impressive defiance of the physics of volume and bladders.

With Schnapps back in her travel house and the gas paid for, we drove out of Yuma and headed for the California state line.

While we were waiting for a red light, a guy in a pickup truck pulled up alongside and asked us the same old question. "Did you guys ride those things all the way from Massachusetts?" It must be what it's like for tall guys when they get asked if they play basketball, or what their height is, every time they talk to someone. Then the light turned green, and we were on our way.

It wasn't long before Steve noticed a big green sign up ahead. "There it is! There it is!" he yelled at the top of his lungs while he pointed at the sign. "There's the California state line!"

Within minutes, we were crossing the border blowing our horns and both yelling, "We made it! We made it!" That's when the desert finally showed up: white sand dunes, everywhere we looked. I could picture a caravan going across the horizon, with camels and sultans heading off to some foreign war.

We stopped, took a few pictures, put on our vests—it was late afternoon and the temperature was falling fast—and we drove on. At about six, we stopped in the small town of El Centro, just off the highway. We had a good Italian meal and got engaged in a conversation with an Italian man and his family sitting in the adjacent booth. Speaking of the same questions over and over, the man asked us if we were brothers. We said yes, which seemed to tickle him to death. After we ate, we said our goodbyes and got back on our bikes, even though we were tired, cold, and sleepy. We got back on the highway and headed for San Diego. At the first rest area we came to, we stopped to see if it would work for sleeping. As we walked around, checking the area out for a place to roll out our bags, we came upon a sign: "NO OVERNIGHT CAMPING IN STATE AREAS."

We looked at each other. The West Coast was going to be very similar to the East Coast. You just didn't find signs like that in the middle of the country. One reason could be that the population are greater on the coasts than inland, but when you're as tired as we were, those signs felt as inhospitable as could be, like they had been written just to torment us. Well, it was too late for us to obey a stupid sign. We found a good spot in the shadows of the streetlight and hit the sack.

The last big day of our journey seemed like a test, like someone was probing at us just to see how determined we were to get there. As we started to climb into the Coyote Mountains, rain channels had cut grooves into the road, which gave our motorcycles a wobbly feeling as we drove. The strong gusts of wind began when we hit three thousand feet. Sometimes it would hit us from the side and abruptly shove us over two entire lanes. We even had to lean our bikes at specific angles to the wind just to keep from being blown over. It was fun riding behind Steve and seeing his bike angle over so far without falling—a miracle of physics. In Greek mythology, Anemoi is the god of the winds. I pictured him glowering at us from on high, determined to throw up any obstacle he could.

But we persevered, managed to stay upright, and made it to the city limits of San Diego around one that afternoon. Our psychic powers suddenly took hold, pulling us together for a spontaneous high-five before we drove up through the Mission Hill area. Without a shred of deliberation, we headed for the Pacific Ocean. We'd been excited the entire way, but now it felt like everything had been building to this moment. I wondered if the gold miners had felt like this at the height of the westward expansion during the Gold Rush.

We parked our bikes in the mostly empty lot. It was a Wednesday at midday. I took Schnapps out of her house to let her run around on this surface she had never seen.

"I'm going to change into my shorts and take a dip in the big blue," said Steve.

"I think I will, too. And we'll give Schnapps a bath."

Steve started picking through his pack, and soon its entire contents were strewn all about.

"Look at this," he said, "and all just for a pair of gym shorts. I have to take the entire thing apart every time. How do you keep your pack so accessible?"

It was a funny question to be asking, here at the very end of the trip. "It's just a gift, I guess," I said. "You can call me the patron saint of orderly packing."

Steve, Schnapps, and I went into the men's room and reemerged, dressed for swimming. We'd been hearing about this ocean for years. Finally stepping into it was a thrill, but we didn't stay in too long. Schnapps fussed at the water's edge. She didn't like being there alone.

We were drying off our bikes when a big, jolly-looking guy riding a pearly white chopper drove by, noticed our plates, turned around, and came back. "Boy, that must have been a long ride on those bikes!" he said as he got off his bike. "My name is Tony," he said when he got to us and extended his hand.

We talked about bikes for a while, and then a young guy who was working on his MG came over and joined the conversation.

"Hey," said Tony, "do you guys drink beer?"

"Sure. Why?" said Steve.

"I'll go get a six-pack," said Tony. With that, he hopped on his chopper, pressed the electric starter, and off he went with a roar. A few minutes later, he was back with a bunch of Coors. We thanked him and popped the tabs.

A couple of hours later, we began our usual quest for sleeping quarters. There was nothing around the beach, and of course, we weren't looking for motels either. We drove downtown to the heart of San Diego. First place we went to was the post office to see if we had any mail. We expected something from Tom, but the only mail we got was a letter from my godparents in Florida. While I read my letter on the steps of the post office, Steve kept Schnapps company. A smiling heavyset man in his late thirties approached him, and they began talking.

I walked over a few minutes later and joined in. The guy's name was Jerry. He and Steve had been discussing philosophy before I stepped in, and our discussion led us right to the second floor of a two-story building two blocks away. Jerry had invited us to supper. And then, if we were interested, he wanted us to stay for a meeting. Jerry belonged to an organization called the New Age Fellowship, which was a religious group.

When you're as hungry and tired as we were, you'll hang out anywhere for a while. But we weren't too comfortable in the atmosphere where everyone called each other brother and sister in soft voices. They were all as nice as could be, but it just wasn't our scene. We had to take our shoes off outside the door before entering the house. We also had to tie Schnapps and leave her on the front porch, which of course she fussed loudly about. Inside, there was a long table on the floor in the living room. The age range was probably between seventeen and fifty, and everyone sat around the table on the blue floor. We were the only new guests. After rice, vegetables, and a few other items from the staples of life, everyone sat around and sang a bunch of Peter, Paul, and Mary-type songs. We'd been uncomfortable from the moment we walked in, but it wasn't that bad. After the songs, the leader of the group—a tall, thin red-haired man in his mid-twenties—got up and started lecturing on Jesus Christ and his second coming. The lecture ended at ten thirty and was followed by a discussion that we got very involved in.

Little Schnapps had been barking on and off the entire time. Once we broke into groups for discussions, no one saw any harm in letting her crash the party. Once inside, she quickly became the center of attraction as she scampered around, sniffing and introducing herself to everyone.

But we *still* needed a place to sleep, so Steve asked Jerry if we could have the floor that night. In a voice filled with regret, Jerry said there was a strict policy of "no overnight sleepers." There was no point in asking why; it wasn't going to change anything. Then he suggested that we sleep in the city park and told us how to get there. The park wasn't very far from the house, but when we got there, it wasn't ideal: police were patrolling the place regularly.

We drove up into a shadowy area and got off the bikes to check out the area.

"What did you think of that group?" I asked when we were in a quiet, secluded spot.

"They were okay, but I didn't agree with a lot of what that guy said. Good people, but not my type, either. I was talking with a couple of them and I mentioned that I had high goals of being successful and well-off. A few of them really put that down, like I was aspiring to something worthless. Whatever, though."

It was too early to sleep and we were hungry, so we got on our bikes and drove to the center of the city. We cruised down a few streets until we ended up on a street loaded with XXX movies and massage parlors. There was a naval base nearby, and it was obviously the only thing keeping those places in business.

We were almost to the end of the strip when we noticed three so-called masseuses standing on the sidewalk in front of their place of employment. They looked enticing, standing around, posed in their low-slung knitted tops and hot pants. We made a U-turn on the wide, not-so-busy street, and parked our bikes by the curb a couple of stores down from them. By now our male instincts were getting the best of us, so we began scheming about how to make friends with the girls and see where the night could lead, although we sure as hell didn't plan on paying for anything.

Schnapps barked, which gave Steve an idea. "Hey, let's let her out and walk her by those girls. I bet they'll love her and then we're in." He was right about them paying attention to Schnapps. They petted her and showered her with compliments. One of them fed her part of a hamburger and most of her French fries. But we couldn't let Schnapps steal the entire show, so after about fifteen minutes, we finally got their attention off of the dog and onto us. We hoped to end up with a nice, comfortable place to stay for the night and whatever else could be arranged. But our efforts were shattered when the owner of the place came out. "Girls, get over here. You are out here to solicit customers, not play with a dog!"

The dream ended as quickly as it had begun. The girls said goodbye and hustled back to their spot in front of the massage parlor.

"Oh well, we tried," I said, putting Schnapps back in her box. "Let's go get something to eat."

Inside a nearby crowded restaurant, we sat at a booth near the front window. As we were looking over the menu, police were breaking up a brawl across the busy street, but no one seemed to be paying it much attention. After our meal, we jotted down the day's events in our journals. After, I was talking with the cashier about our trip when the owner overheard us. His name was Mr. Petrocelli, a nice Italian guy in his late forties or early fifties. He said that we were welcome to stay at his place if we didn't mind waiting around until two, so he could total up the cash register and get ready for the next day. That was fine by us, since it would give me more time to write. He offered us coffee and tea and took great care of us. We'd made another new friend, as easily as could be.

After he closed up, we followed Mr. Petrocelli to his beautiful house in the suburbs, where he told us to roll out our bags on the parlor floor. We decided that bringing Schnapps in might be asking too much, so we explained to her that she'd be on her own outside for the night, and then went inside after making sure she had what she needed. We were just about to crawl into our bags when the name Petrocelli rang a bell.

"Hey," said Steve, "are you any relation to Rico Petrocelli who used to play third base for the Boston Red Sox?"

"Yes, I'm his uncle," said Mr. Petrocelli.

"How do you like that!" I said. "We came all the way out here and then bump into a relative of a ball player from back home."

Mr. Petrocelli was too tired to ruminate on the wonders of this coincidence. "I'm headed to bed, boys. Good night." We thanked him again for letting us sleep in his house, and then we also rolled out our bags and went to sleep. It was just amazing all the different people we had met on this trip so far.

Morning came quickly. We woke up early, rolled up our bags, and since Mr. Petrocelli was still sleeping,left a thank-you note, and got our bikes ready to go. While Steve brought out the bags, I went out to let Schnapps run around a little, stretch, and water the lawn. Then we headed straight for the beach, which was about twenty minutes away. The sun was high in the sky when we finally parked our bikes next to a grassy area opposite the beach.

I decided to wash and wax my bike, which meant taking everything off the luggage rack. Once my gear was spread out all over creation, Steve decided to do the same thing. Within a couple of minutes, it looked like we were getting ready for a yard sale.

While we talked, a little brown dog came over, sniffed around, lifted his short little leg, and saluted my pack. Steve yelled at him to stop, but not in time. I cleaned my pack the best I could with a wet rag, muttering uncharitable things about the little beast.

On the way down I had seen a car wash. I told Steve I was going to go wash my bike, and then come back and watch Schnapps while he did the same. While Steve was gone, I finally began the tedious job of waxing my bike. While I was bending over the front wheel, I sensed someone standing behind me. When I turned around and looked up, there was a tall lady with a rouge-covered white face, red cheeks, frizzy hair, and round, wire-rimmed glasses. She wore an old-fashioned gray skirt-suit and stood there with her hands on her hips, looking mean. Before I could say anything, she barked, "Okay, Paul, I want my ring that you stole from me!"

Puzzled, shocked, bemused, and confused, I answered from my kneeling position. "Excuse me, ma'am, are you talking to me?"

"Yes, I followed you to this spot, Paul, and now I want my ring or the money to replace it." She obviously meant business, but I didn't even know where to start. So I started with the only thing I knew for sure—my own name.

"I'm sorry, ma'am, but my name is not Paul and I don't have the slightest idea of what you are talking about."

She repeated herself in a louder, more demanding voice. We were beginning to make a scene, and I didn't like that. With the way she was ramping up, I worried that she'd be shrieking at the top of her lungs in a few seconds. I stood up. "My name is not Paul and I don't have your ring. Now, if you don't mind, I'd like to finish waxing my bike without you making a scene." Surely that would help. Or, surely not.

"Okay," she said, "I'll wait here for a cop. He'll make you give me my ring or the money." She crossed her arms.

Now I was starting to get angry. "Are you kidding? *I'll* go get a cop if you don't get out of here and leave me be!"

Just then, a big man got out of a van that was parked nearby and walked over to stand by the woman's side. Thank goodness, maybe help had arrived. "Sir, can you please get her out of here before she gets in trouble for falsely accusing someone of theft?" I said.

"Hey buddy! Just do what the lady says!" The guy was bellowing like a gorilla.

My tolerance for the bullshit evaporated. "Look, lady, I'm sick of you and the crazy story. Now take your friend and get out of here before you gets hurt."

That's when Steve drove up with his clean and shiny bike, a Burger King bag hanging from his mouth. He shut off his bike, got off, and walked up next to me. "Hey, Mark," he said, with one eye on the weird couple, "here's a burger and some fries."

"Thanks," I said, also watching the couple. "I was hungry. And is that beer I see? That's going to hit the spot."

Finally Steve said, "Any trouble here, Mark?"

"Oh no, this lady just had me confused with someone else, right, ma'am?"

With that, the lady and her friend turned, walked back to their van, and drove away.

"What was that all about?" asked Steve as he took the beer off his bike and carried it to a nearby picnic table.

"I think I was being rolled by a couple of pros," I said. I told him the story, and he laughed and laughed. People can be endlessly surprising, and endlessly crazy. After we ate, we started waxing our bikes. "You know," I said, "it seems so ironic that as soon as we get to the West Coast, we run into trouble. Remember before we left home everyone said to be careful, especially down south?"

"Yeah, I know," he said. "And we ran into nothing but good people who helped us out all the way until we got here!"

As we talked, a little black dog approached and started sniffing around my gear. "Hey, Mark, watch it!" yelled Steve, but it was too late. The little devil had already lifted his leg and sprayed down the front of my pack.

"Man, that's the second time my stuff got pissed on!" My shouting scared the dog off as I ran to the bath house for paper towels.

An hour later we were finishing up. Steve was messing with his sissy bar when a huge tan-colored dog walked up. It was like being caught in the middle of a conspiracy, and all the dogs had told each other that they had a great new spot to pee. But this time I was ready, prepared to defend my pack against all urine-related threats. But the dog just glanced at my pack, stopping for only a second, and then mosied on by, tending to his own business.

We were getting ready to start strapping everything to my bike when Steve noticed a big wet spot on my pack.

"You've got to be kidding me!" The tan dog must have sneaked back by when we weren't looking. I decided to laugh, rather than lose my mind. But what was so special about my pack? I was never going to trust a dog again.

We finished with our bikes, took a quick dip in the ocean, and then got ready to leave. We drove down the street to the small business district where we stopped to run into a small grocery store for a snack. We weren't inside for more than five minutes. When we got back to our bikes, which were parked in a bank lot, two ladies and a little girl were standing behind our bikes and had Schnapps out on a rope. As we walked up, I was more curious than anything. Then one of them barked, "Is this your dog?"

"Yes," I said.

"Well, you should be ashamed of yourselves, having a poor little puppy cooped up in that box on a hot day!"

We tried to explain that we were only gone for a few minutes, but they weren't having it. They just kept rattling on, reprimanding us. "Look at the dog; it's thirsty," the one holding the child said. They went on for so long, so aggressively, that finally I said, "Okay, okay, okay, we'll take better care of her," just to get them to shut up, even though I knew we hadn't done anything to make Schnapps uncomfortable. This seemed to satisfy them, and they walked away, noses in the air, their righteous deed done for the day. So far, our experience with people on the West Coast had been a bust. That night, after an Italian dinner, we called our mothers from a pay phone on the sidewalk outside of the restaurant. They were thrilled to hear us both. When we told them we were calling from San Diego, they both sighed with relief. Hundred days, over nine thousand miles, and we finally made it to the dream state everyone talks about: California. After we said our goodbyes, I had an idea. I looked up the address of the Armenian church in San Diego.

"Why don't we give them a visit? Since I'm Armenian, they might give us a place to stay tonight."

"All right, but if we're going, let's go now. It's getting late."

We asked the attendant in the gas station next to the restaurant for directions to the church, and then mounted up and left at about eight thirty. We drove east on Route 8 for about ten minutes, and then found an exit that took us to the Mission Hill area. We were slowly driving up the main boulevard, looking for the street the church was on, when a loud motorcycle thundered by me on my right side, between me and a parked car. The long-haired, dirty-looking driver—who was wearing a black leather jacket and sunglasses even though it was dark—continued up the busy boulevard and passed Steve on the right and almost knocked him down.

I caught up to Steve quickly. "Hey, that nut almost knocked you over. Let's get him!"

We took off after the weirdo who was way up ahead, weaving his chopper in and out of the traffic, although as we chased him, we weren't driving safely either. Maybe the West Coast was rubbing off on us. We finally caught up to him at a red light and pulled up, one on each side of him.

"Hey, you idiot!" I yelled. "What the hell do you think you're doing? You almost knocked over my friend back there!"

The weirdo snapped back, "Who are you calling an idiot?"

"You, you moron. Pull over into that empty lot," I yelled over the loud rumble of his bike. The three of us pulled into the empty lot. Steve and the dude were off their bikes quickly, staring each other down while I struggled to find my kickstand, of all things, of all times. Finally, I got off and ran over, ready to take the dude on, but the mood had changed a little by the time I got over to them. Neither he nor Steve actually seemed to want to fight. After a few harsh statements on both sides, we decided to let the dude go unmolested even though he thought he could take us both on. That would have been a major mistake. We stood by and watched him drive away into the night. Maybe it's because we'd been heading to a church before the interruption, but we just weren't as aggressive that night. "Forget about it," said Steve. "Let's go find that church before it gets any later."

It didn't take us long to find the address, but when we got there, it was just a house. We wondered if we had the right place. After rechecking the address again in a nearby public phone booth, we went and knocked on the front door of the small white house. An elderly lady finally came to the door and asked us in Armenian what she could do for us. I was able to explain our situation in Armenian as she listened. Then she told us to walk down the long, narrow driveway on the side of the house, to the printing shop out back. We thanked her and went to check it out. At the end of the driveway was a small white wooden building that looked like a garage that had been converted into a printing shop. We knocked on the door.

"Come in! Come in!" yelled a hearty voice.

With a quick glance at one another, we walked in through the small office and into a back room filled with printing machines. There was a dark, curly-haired man with a full beard bending over one of them.

"Hello," I called.

The man was in his mid-thirties and wore dark green clothes. He gave us a big smile. "Hello, hello," he said with an accent. "What can I do for you boys?"

We explained our story and told him that this was the first time since leaving home that I had dropped into an Armenian church. The man never stopped smiling. He said, in Armenian, that they didn't have a church yet, but that they were raising the money to build one. I translated for Steve. "Oh, and by the way, my name is Vahi," he said. "Can I get you boys something?" he asked as he walked over to a refrigerator. "I'm here so much, I have a little kitchen and I sleep in the back room of the house."

He gave us each a beer and some crackers and cheese. "Help yourselves, boys. You are welcome to whatever I have. It was my mother who answered the door for you earlier. I bought the house for her and another Armenian family. I just stay in the back room."

We talked for a while, and then Vahi said we were welcome to stay as long as we wanted. He offered to show us around San Diego and help us find jobs if we planned to live there. We told him we weren't sure of what we would be doing in the future, but thanked him profusely. He showed us his room and said he would be staying with a friend tonight, so there would be no problem. He also left us the key to his shop in case we got hungry during the night.

We closed up the shop at eleven thirty, took what we needed off our bikes, and let Schnapps do her thing. Vahi couldn't believe that we had carried her on our bikes all the way from Corpus Christi, Texas. "She will be good company for Charlie," he said. Charlie was his black-and-white shepherd.

We were in bed by midnight. We had finally managed to meet a helpful, friendly person on the West Coast. We thanked God for everything we had, and turned out the lights.

# CHAPTER 16

# Homeward Bound - The final chapter

S teve and I stayed in California until April 26, 1977, heading up and down the coast, visiting with both Steve's and my distant cousins, also making many new friends. We drove on the famous Pacific Coast Highway (State Route 1) from Seal Beach up to Oakland and back. The highway actually runs from a little north of San Diego to Leggett, Mendocino County, which is north of San Francisco. What a drive it was; so many points of interests, beautiful scenery, sharp turns, hills, and valleys. After a short stay in Oakland with Steve's cousins, we headed south back to Seal Beach to stay with my distant cousin Everett, who was a retired engineer. Everett was a bachelor and was thrilled to meet us; he let us live with him through the winter months.

While we stayed with Everett he took us to meet my other cousins, Mr. and Mrs. Lindquist and their son Gary who was close to our age. It was great spending time with relatives I never knew before. We got jobs as a substitute teacher and taught physical education at a Huntington Beach elementary school to earn spending money. At first, the education department required us to take an exam to teach in California, but once they found out we were from Massachusetts and went to the University of Massachusetts, the red carpet was rolled out. We were not required to take their exam and could teach at any school in Orange County. Wow, we felt like celebrities - *Again.*

Here we were, two young guys with beards when beards were not in vogue, driving up to the school each day on our Hondas. Once, we showed up all the kids would flock over to talk to us. They wanted to hear about our adventures; it was great! We met many nice people during our three month stay in California. Our Honda's took us everywhere we needed to go even grocery shopping.

The adventures never stopped coming our way all during our stay in California.

One day, in February, I learned how God is in control of our lives, especially mine. On the morning of February 20, it was a nice warm sunny day with clear skies and light wind. Steve went off early to see a friend, and I decided to work out with weights in the room. We had moved out of my cousin, Everett's apartment and lived in a one room motel/apartment complex with mostly illegal immigrants living there. After a two-hour hard work-out, I went down to Seal Beach, which was only three blocks away. I ran hard for two miles in the sand; it was exhausting. Once I got back to where I started, I wanted to cool down but knew I couldn't go in for a swim since I was very tired from my workout. There were only a few people on the beach because locals generally don't go to the beach in February.

The waves were huge, but I thought to myself, *it should be okay to just stand knee deep and cool down.* A few minutes after entering the water and facing the ocean, I heard a girl yell behind me, "Could you get our ball?" I turned around, faced the beach and saw a guy and girl. The ball they were playing with was in the water near me so I reached down, picked it up and threw it back to them.

Everything happened very quickly from that point. I found myself knocked down in the water but didn't think anything was wrong. I tried to touch bottom and stand but couldn't reach the bottom so I started to swim toward shore but wasn't getting any closer. In Southern California, most of the coastline has long stone jetties running out from shore, a couple of hundred yards. As I tried to swim, I looked to my right at the jetty and saw that I was moving rapidly backward out to sea. Right then, I knew I was in a rip tide. Now, since I was a Red Cross Water Safety Instructor who used to teach lifeguard classes, I knew I was in trouble because I was too tired from working out to swim. Plus, I broke the cardinal rule—*never turn your back to the ocean*. When the rip tide finally let me go, I was so far out that when I was in between swells, I couldn't see land. For some reason, I wouldn't yell for help; maybe I thought no one would hear me or I was just too proud. I was never in a position of hopelessness before and always felt I could out run, out swim or out fight just about anyone or anything. I was strong and agile, and felt I could handle anything that came my way. Of course, that's how most macho guys think when they are 25 years old. Wether it's true or not doesn't matter. The Lord must have wanted to teach me a lesson in humility. My situation seemed hopeless. While I was struggling to stay afloat, I heard the devil's voice telling me to let myself slip under the water and open my mouth, letting the water in to drown. There was almost a peaceful feeling about the idea. So I began to go under the water. When I was about three feet down, I started to open my mouth and take in the ocean. Just then I heard the Lord's voice telling me to close my mouth and swim to the surface; that it was not my time to die. Looking up through the light green water, I could see rays of the light coming down to me so I obeyed and swam up to the surface. Once I reached the surface, a certain calm came over me. I remembered my lifeguard training. I started swimming parallel to shore using every stroke I knew. Once I was out of the rip tide, the long slow swim back to the beach was before me. It was a struggle because I was already so tired. As I was heading in, the girl that was on the beach ran to the water to get her ball, and all of a sudden, she got pulled out in the rip tide but not close to me. My first instinct was to go rescue her, but I knew I was too tired. I looked up and said, "Lord, forgive me, but I can't help her." As I looked back at the beach, her boyfriend was jumping in the water, and I yelled to him in a weak voice not to go in the water without something that floats, but he couldn't hear me and dove in, and he too was also pulled out to sea but not near either of us. Now they were both singing a duet for help. All of a sudden, a rescue boat came for them. Two rescue swimmers brought them back onto the beach, but no one came back to help me, so I kept swimming in. As I neared the beach, the huge seven-foot waves were breaking and driving me down into the sea bed. With bruises and scrapes, I finally dragged myself out of the water and laid at the water's edge too tired to move. The lifeguards were tending to the two that were rescued. After a while, I was able to get up and walk up the beach, and as I walked by the two lifeguards, I asked why they didn't come out for me. They said they saw me out there, but it appeared I knew what I was doing and was okay. At that moment, I realized that God could take me out anytime he wanted and that I was not in control, HE was. I learned a valuable lesson that day. God clearly saved my life, and to this day, I thank the Lord for all his blessings.

While we lived in Seal Beach, California, every day and each place we went was something new for us. But by April 1977, we had to start thinking whether we would permanently live in California or start our trip home. We both liked it in California but decided we should be home with our families. We said our good- bys to all and now that home was actually on the horizon, the adventures started to feel a little different, since we now we had an end point in sight. We did have many great stops along our route home like Death Valley, the big hike down and up The Grand Canyon, carrying all our gear(60lbs), hiking and camping in the big woods and mountains of Colorado up and over the Eisenhower Pass in the Rockies. We spent almost a week in Denver having a grand time. We met Mary, this beautiful blond girl, when we stopped at the YMCA in Denver to clean up. She saw our Massachusetts plates and came over to speak with us as we got ready to go in for showers. When we told her we were from Bostonher eyes lit up and she said me too, and invited us to stay at her apartment while we were in Denver. So off we went again. At least we didn't have to sleep on the ground. One night we all went to a country western bar where Mary won the wet T-shirt contest, I almost won an arm wrestling contest even against all odds. The reigning champ that beat me looked like the giant Goliath and I felt like David, but I didn't have a slingshot. When I sat down at the table across from this giant of a man, after making it past rounds one and two, I was thinking what now? But Mary was cheering me on throughout the contest and was now whispering in my left ear and giving me a double shot of whisky. Her promises and whisky gave me a false sense of confidence, so I stacked four books under my right elbow and stretched to reach the giant's hand. I could see the look in his eyes, his not-so-nice-looking teeth grinding, showing he was jealous that Mary was on my side. The crowd of onlookers was cheering for me, the smaller guy from Boston. But how I almost won is a story for another time. After four days and nights we said by to Mary and thanked her for her hospitality. She said she was sad we were leaving because we were a lot of fun to be with and we told her that maybe someday our paths wouild cross again.

Once we left Denver, the clock was ticking and real life was on its way back to us, or we were on our way back to it. Little by little, reality was setting in, and for me, it was depressing to think our adventure and wandering throughout this great country was coming to a close. However, we had many more exciting adventures along our ride home throughout the northern states.

We finally got back to Massachusetts on May 17, after driving up throughout the rust belt and suddenly, all the license plates were from our home state and all the signs were familiar again; it was like we'd never left. Life had carried on here while we had been out and about.

I wanted to see my dad before he went to work on the night shift, so we kept a steady clip around seventy miles per hour until we reached central Mass.

"I'll see you later," I said to Steve as we split up. It seemed like such a small, ridiculous way to part after so much time together on the road. But that was that. Steve went to Milford to see his parents, and I headed for Hudson.

Once I pulled into the driveway, which I left over nine months ago, I tooted my horn and my mom and dad came to the front door. My Mom, who was only 4 rushed out to give me a big hug, practically trying to lift me off the ground. One would have thought I was returning from World War II. "Glad you're back safely," said my dad, shaking my hand. My younger brother Gary hugged me as well. You could see it in their eyes when they said, "We missed you."

I had missed them, and of course, I was happy to see they were all doing well. I'd always felt it was my duty to watch over these three people that I loved so much, and I was happy to be back to do just that.

The Big Trip was over. I'd seen one of my dreams through from start to finish, and although it was sad to see my dream trip come to an end, it was good to be home. Our little family reunion was only a few seconds old before I heard someone shouting "Mark! Is that you?" I turned to see my good friend Danny running up the street toward me. He wrapped me up in a hug then tore off down the street, telling everyone I had come back, like he'd heard the greatest news in creation and wanted everyone else to hear about it.

I spent a lot of that next day telling stories and visiting people I had missed. The next week, Steve and I were interviewed by several different newspapers who then published articles about our great adventure. But during all the conversations, in my heart, I just kept thanking God for the opportunity of a lifetime and for bringing me home safely, after nine months and 22,300 miles on my 1975 Honda CB360T.

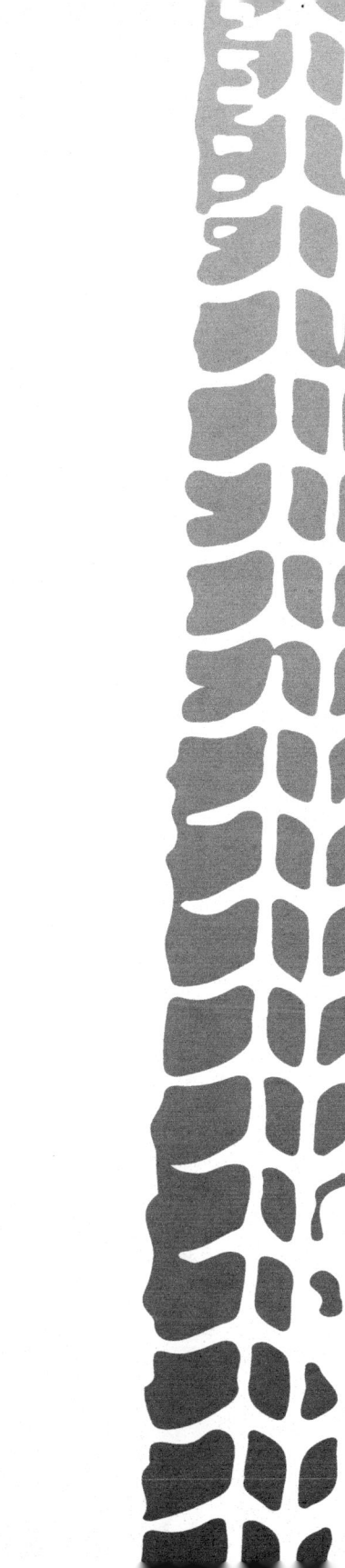